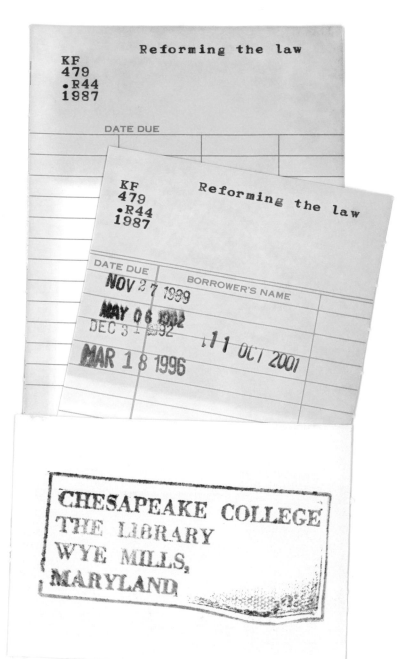

REFORMING THE LAW

REFORMING THE LAW

Impact of Child Development Research

Edited by

GARY B. MELTON
University of Nebraska—Lincoln

THE GUILFORD PRESS
New York   *London*

© 1987 The Guilford Press
A Division of Guilford Publications, Inc.
72 Spring Street, New York, N.Y. 10012

Printed in the United States of America

Library of Congress Cataloging in Publication Data

Reforming the law.

(The Guilford law and behavior series)
"Developed from a study group sponsored by the Society for Research in Child Development"—Pref.
Includes bibliographies and index.
1. Children—Legal status, laws, etc.—United States. 2. Child development—Law and legislation—United States. 3. Child development—Research—United States. I. Melton, Gary B. II. Society for Research in Child Development. III. Series.
KF479.R44   1987   344.73′0088054   87–31
ISBN 0–89862–278–6   347.3040088054

Contributors

GORDON BERMANT, PHD, Division of Research, Federal Judicial Center, Washington, D.C.

THOMAS GRISSO, PHD, Department of Psychology, St. Louis University, St. Louis, Missouri

THOMAS L. HAFEMEISTER, JD, Office of Mental Health, State of New York, Albany, New York

GERALD P. KOOCHER, PHD, Department of Psychiatry, Harvard Medical School, Boston, Massachusetts

GARY B. MELTON, PHD, Department of Psychology and College of Law, University of Nebraska–Lincoln, Lincoln, Nebraska

MICHAEL J. SAKS, PHD, MSL, College of Law, University of Iowa, Iowa City, Iowa

RUBY TAKANISHI, PHD, Carnegie Council on Adolescent Development, Washington, D.C.

CHARLES R. TREMPER, JD, PHD, College of Law and Department of Psychology, University of Nebraska–Lincoln, Lincoln, Nebraska

CAROL H. WEISS, PHD, Graduate School of Education, Harvard University, Cambridge, Massachusetts

LOIS A. WEITHORN, PHD, School of Law, Stanford University, Stanford, California

RUSSELL R. WHEELER, PHD, Division of Special Educational Services, Federal Judicial Center, Washington, D.C.

Preface

This volume developed from a study group sponsored by the Society for Research in Child Development (SRCD) with funds provided by the Foundation for Child Development. The Foundation for Child Development is a private foundation that makes grants to educational and charitable institutions. Its main interests are in research, social and economic indicators of children's lives, advocacy and public information projects, and service experiments that help translate theoretical knowledge about children into policies and practices that affect their daily lives. The contributors to this volume have donated their royalties to SRCD to be used for future study groups on topics in child development research.

The study group that prepared this volume developed from an earlier SRCD-sponsored study group, "Developmental Factors in Competence to Consent." Several of the members of the earlier study group met about 5 years later to determine their effectiveness in influencing legal policymakers' judgments about children's competence. They were joined by several other individuals who are expert in knowledge diffusion or whose job includes the task of disseminating social science research to the legal system. Some of the social scientists in the latter category are not involved with children's issues, but their experience in working with practicing lawyers and judges has been very helpful.

This volume has special significance for child development researchers who wish to reach legal policymakers and practitioners, and vice versa. It should also be useful for readers who are interested in the development of child legal policy. The book should have broader interest, however, for scholars who wish to understand the interaction between law and social science, and for social scientists (other than specialists in child development) who seek to inform the law.

In addition to the authors of the chapters in this volume, several other social scientists and lawyers contributed to the study group's discussions. Among them were the following: Donald N. Bersoff, a psychologist–lawyer in Ennis, Friedman, & Bersoff, the law firm that serves the American Psychological Association (APA); Patricia Falk, an advanced JD–PhD student who at the time was a clerk in the magistrate's office of the U.S. District Court for the District of Columbia and is now is a lawyer in the Department of Justice; and Ellen Greenberg Garrison, a psychologist who formerly was a staff member for the U.S. Senate Committee on Juvenile Justice and now is a staff member in APA's Office of Legislative Affairs.

A number of other staff of federal agencies, scientific organizations, congressional support agencies, and congressional offices joined the group for a luncheon discussion of Carol H. Weiss's chapter. The luncheon was sponsored by the APA Office of Scientific Affairs, which also provided space for the meeting. Acknowledgment is due Virginia Holt and Ruby Takanishi for their assistance with the arrangements.

Gary B. Melton

Contents

PART III. PROCEDURES FOR INTRODUCING CHILD
DEVELOPMENT RESEARCH INTO THE LEGAL PROCESS

PART IV. CONCLUSIONS

Child Development Research and the Law: Potential Contributions and Actual Effects

I

1

Children under Law: The Paradigm of Consent

GERALD P. KOOCHER

RATIONALE FOR THIS VOLUME

In 1980 a study group was convened in Charlottesville, Virginia, under the auspices of the Society for Research in Child Development (SRCD) with funding from the Foundation for Child Development, to assess the existing psychological and legal views of children's competence. The volume that grew out of that meeting, *Children's Competence to Consent* (Melton, Koocher, & Saks, 1983), summarizes and discusses the literature in law, psychology, and medicine regarding children's abilities to make major decisions on their own behalf. The prime thesis of the book is that children are indeed more capable of expressing preferences and participating in making major life decisions than is generally recognized under the law. Specific topics addressed include the following: general competencies as a function of development (Melton, 1983a); psychological risks and benefits of children's decisionmaking (Melton, 1983b); social-psychological perspectives on consent problems (Saks, 1983); health, medical, and pediatric contexts (Grodin & Alpert, 1983; Lewis, 1983; Wadlington, 1983); psychotherapy (Koocher, 1983); psychoeducational assessment (Bersoff, 1983); research participation by children (Keith-Spiegel, 1983); legal socialization research (Tapp & Melton, 1983); and involving children in de-

Gerald P. Koocher. Department of Psychiatry, Harvard Medical School, Boston, Massachusetts.

cisions (Weithorn, 1983). *Children's Competence to Consent* represents a first effort by an interdisciplinary group interested in both child development and the law to synthesize what is known and potentially useful to policymakers and the courts.

It was evident to the participants in the 1980 study group that a significant body of psychological knowledge with direct relevance to juvenile and family law exists (see Melton, 1984b). As behavioral scientists show increasing interest in the legal arena, this body of literature continues to expand. At the same time, an ever-increasing number of legal cases involving children are turning up in the courts. These are often cases where psychological concerns are overriding issues. The range of issues includes abortion (e.g., *Bellotti v. Baird,* 1979; *City of Akron v. Akron Center for Reproductive Health,* 1983; *H.L. v. Matheson,* 1981; *Thornburgh v. American College of Obstetricians and Gynecologists,* 1986), school prayer (e.g., *Wallace v. Jaffree,* 1985), search and seizure issues in the school locker or classroom (e.g., *Dow v. Renfrow,* 1981; *New Jersey v. T.L.O.,* 1985), interracial custody and adoption (e.g., *In re R.M.G.,* 1982, *Palmore v. Sidoti,* 1984), due process rights (e.g., *In re Gault,* 1967), and even access to video games (*Aladdin's Castle v. City of Mesquite,* 1982; *Shorez v. City of Dacono,* 1983; *Walker v. City of Warren,* 1984). Terms such as "the child's best interests" abound in both statutes and court opinions. At the same time, however, the behavioral scientists and those charged with carrying out public policy or administering the law seldom cross paths. When their paths do cross, it is likely that they are not speaking the same language.

A second study group sponsored by SRCD convened in Washington, D.C., in May 1985. This time the group's mission was an impact assessment. Given the continued emphasis on psychological concepts in child and family law cases and the rapidly growing body of relevant psychological literature, the task in 1985 was to explore the impact of child development research on the law. The central questions in 1985 were whether child development research ought to be a consideration in legal decisions, and, if so, how such information could be most usefully disseminated. Our goals were fivefold:

1. To identify the impact of the work of the 1980 study group over the intervening 5 years.
2. To discuss means of assessing the impact of social science (particularly child development) research on the law.
3. To review what is known about factors affecting the use of social and behavioral science research in the law, including the impact of such factors in executive, legislative, and judicial policy.
4. To suggest guidelines to child development researchers seeking to disseminate their work to policymakers (insofar as an adequate data base is available).
5. To suggest questions for future research on the impact of developmental research on the law.

The present volume is the product of the 1985 study group and discusses several questions based on the five goals cited above. First, how does one determine when scientific findings constitute the "truth"? How do we know when we have something worthwhile to say? Second, ought such findings to be delivered to policymakers (i.e., members of legislatures, senior executive branch officials, and appellate courts) and to "grassroots users" (i.e., judges, attorneys, and probation officers)? Third, what is likely to make the most difference, and will such changes have a positive impact on child and family welfare? Does it really matter (in terms of outcomes) whether findings that are ostensibly policy-related are disseminated to policymakers? Finally, does the legal process so distort research findings that society is sometimes better served by not disseminating the work?

The focus of this chapter is on consent as a paradigmatic example of how the law and principles of child development cross paths. The whole notion of consent and related competence often involves capacities and functions that psychologists have long studied. One might presume that developmental psychologists would have much to say to the courts about children's abilities to reason and make decisions. Unfortunately, the data we have available often do not translate well to the issues of central concern in the courts. Even if the meaning of all related child development research were unambiguous and easily applicable, it is not at all clear that the legal system would want to make use of it.

THE CONCEPT OF CONSENT AS APPLIED
TO CHILDREN

The degree to which children ought to be permitted to make binding decisions on matters involving their own welfare is a matter of much controversy (Wadlington, 1983). The point of this chapter is not to argue a position so much as to clarify the issues with respect to the psychological capacities of children to make such decisions. Although the law has seldom been guided by psychological principles, increasing numbers of psychological studies are shedding new light on how children's decision-making capacities, as a function of development, interact with legal concepts.

Use of the term "competence" as a legal concept in this chapter is no accident. In many ways, the concept of competence provides a paradigm for the manner in which the legal system deals with children. Adults are presumed competent and children (i.e., minors) are presumed incompetent under the law in virtually all contexts. While there are a variety of circumstances under which children may be "heard" on behalf of themselves or may be treated as adults, these situations are generally preceded by a qualifying process (some specific statutory and common-law exemptions are discussed below). At times the basic elements of the process may be quite specific under statute, as in the matter of whether or not a juvenile offender is to be tried as an adult. On most occasions, however, the process by which a minor is deemed competent for any given purpose is open to determination by the broadest judgment of the court. The process of determination of competence and the reasoning applied vary widely as a function of both the case context and the willingness of the court to consider psychological input. In at least one context (i.e., decisions about admitting a minor to a psychiatric facility for inpatient treatment), the U.S. Supreme

Court gave approval to the concept of an administrative or "neutral fact finder" instead of a judicial one (*Parham v. J.R.*, 1979).

Competence to consent as a legal notion is generally categorized as *de facto* or *de jure* in nature. "*De jure* competence" refers to competence under law as dictated by statute, while "*de facto* competence" refers to the actual or practical capacities of the individual to render a competent decision (or to cooperate competently in some ongoing process such as a trial). In most jurisdictions, people over the age of 18 are presumed to be competent unless proved otherwise before a court. When a determination of incompetence is made for adults, it is quite specific. That is to say, under law a person's competence is conceptualized as a specific functional ability. The noun "competence" is usually followed by the phrase "to . . ." rather than presented as a general attribute of the person. An adult who is deemed incompetent to stand trial for a specific offense is still presumed competent to function as a custodial parent or to manage his or her financial affairs. For the adult, specific incompetence must be proven on a case-by-case basis.

Conversely, minor children are presumed incompetent for most purposes without any concern for whether or not the children have the capacity to make the requisite decision(s) in a practical sense. Children who are deemed legally competent for one purpose are likewise still considered generally incompetent in other decision making contexts. For example, a juvenile offender who has been found competent to stand trial and competent to waive rights, and who has even been bound over for trial as an adult, would still be considered generally incompetent to consent to medical treatment or make contracts.

One class of exceptions to the presumption of incompetence is children who have been specially designated by the courts as "emancipated" or "mature" minors under specific state statutes. Although specific criteria vary widely across jurisdictions, this category would generally include minors who have married or enlisted in the military (presumably with valid parental consent), or who are financially independent and living apart from their parents. If the minor in question is not legally married or in the military, the status of "emancipation" or "maturity" must generally be conferred by a court hearing. Because financial or residential independence is at issue, the cognitive or reasoning abilities of the minors need not routinely be addressed in such hearings. Indeed, emancipation statutes may yield the anomaly of a 16-year-old runaway working in a gas station being accorded the right to self-determination, but a 16-year-old "responsible" member of the National Honor Society being legally defined as incompetent.

Another specific context in which minors may be deemed competent to consent involves certain types of medical treatments. These generally include specific medical conditions where the individual right to privacy of the minor and/or the public interest is best served by permitting the person to consent directly. These situations are discussed later in this chapter under the specific context headings, but they generally include contraception, venereal disease, abortion, drug and alcohol problems, and, in at least one jurisdiction, mental health treatment.

ELEMENTS OF COMPETENCY AND CONSENT

Assessment of specific competency (in the case of children) or incompetency (in the case of adults) revolves around four basic elements (Leikin, 1983; Weithorn & Campbell, 1982):

1. The person's ability to understand information that is offered regarding the consequences of the decision to be made.
2. The ability to manifest a decision.
3. The manner in which the decision is made.
4. The nature of the resulting decision.

These elements involve psychological aspects of comprehension, assertiveness and autonomy, rational reasoning, anticipation of future events, and judgments in the face of uncertainty or contingencies. In the following pages, relevant developmental trends are discussed in relationship to these basic elements of competency. The points discussed here represent an overview of the various approaches to determining competence to consent. The matter of whether or not any single circumstance represents a valid consent situation is obviously linked closely to context and subjective interpretation.

With respect to giving one's fully informed consent regarding any specific decision, there are five key elements (Lidz *et al.*, 1984): information, understanding, competency, voluntariness, and decisionmaking ability (i.e., reasoning). In this context, "information" refers to access to all data that might reasonably be expected to influence a person's willingness to participate. In this respect, it represents what is offered or made available to the person. "Competency" includes the *capacity* to understand (as opposed to actual understanding), the ability to weigh potential outcomes, and also the foresight to anticipate the future consequences of the decision. "Voluntariness" is the freedom to choose to participate or to refuse. "Decisionmaking ability" refers to the ability to render a reasoned choice and express it clearly.

While the concepts of competency and informed consent are different, it is clear that there are many overlapping elements. Competency is a prerequisite for informed consent. An offer to provide a person with informed consent is simply not meaningful unless the individual in question is fully competent to make use of it. Many aspects of human development act to inhibit or enhance competency and the ability to give consent across the developmental trajectory between infancy and adulthood.

APPLICABLE PRINCIPLES
OF CHILD DEVELOPMENT

SOCIALIZATION

It is no secret that we begin life as egocentric beings, unaware of our own capabilities and without verbally based interpersonal relationships. We then progress through developmental stages that involve a focus on interactions in the family, in the peer group, and ultimately in society as a whole. Along the way we are "socialized" or taught about various interpersonal and societal roles by our parents and social institutions (chiefly our schools). In general, we are taught to do what older and bigger (i.e., more powerful) people tell us.

There is a substantial body of data to suggest that even after children become capable of understanding that they have certain rights or societal entitlements, their exercise or assertion of those rights is often a function of their social ecology (Melton *et al.*, 1983). Many children quite literally regard their rights as those entitlements that adults permit them to exercise (Melton, 1980). Although a parent may say to a child, "Please pick up your toys," children as young as 3 are well aware that adverse consequences will follow a failure to respond. Although adults' interactions with children are often framed as requests, children are seldom fooled into thinking that they have a real option to decline. Even young children, though, find freedom meaningful and are motivated to act to restore the choices that have been available when they are removed (Brehm, 1977; Brehm & Weintraub, 1972).

The "terrible twos" and "rebellious adolescent years" are well-known societal concepts presenting the adult perspective that it is difficult to deal with children who challenge or question authority. The point to be made here is that the process of socialization presents considerable pressure to conform or acquiesce to adults. As a result of these pressures, it is quite likely that offers to exercise various rights will not be recognized or acted on by many children. Likewise, oppositional responses may sometimes occur more as a function of developmental stage than of reasoned choice.

TIME PERSPECTIVE

"Do you want a little candy bar today, or a big one next week?" To the young child for whom next week may seem a decade away, immediate gratification is the obvious choice. Psychologists have conducted a considerable amount of research investigating children's time perspective, including the classic body of social learning theory (Mischel, 1971). The ability to go beyond the present and conceptualize the future, including hypothetical or potential outcomes, is closely linked to stages of cognitive development and continues to develop throughout adolescence (Lewis, 1981). We must keep this in mind when asking children to participate in decisions or give consent involving long-term consequences of future outcomes.

Time perspective becomes critically important whenever a decision involves being able to weigh short- versus long-term consequences of a decision. It is also an important issue when developmental level predisposes a child to choose immediate gratification while ignoring or failing to weigh his or her longer-term best interests. The impact of development has been especially well documented as an issue in health-related decision-making (Jessor, 1984; Lewis, 1981; Roberts, Maddux, & Wright, 1984). The classic paradigm, of course, is the adult patient facing major surgery who says, "Well, Doc, what are the odds?" The ability to weigh probabilities and to make some kind of long-term cost–benefit analysis is crucial to an informed decision. The significance of developmental trends in time perspective must be tempered, however, by the fact that adults too have difficulty in applying base rates to their own decision-making (see generally Kahneman & Tversky, 1973; Saks & Kidd, 1980–1981; Tversky & Kahneman, 1974).

Concept Manipulation

The ability to manipulate concepts using a developmental model of consent has been well described in the 1980 study group's volume (Melton et al., 1983), as well as in many subsequent studies (e.g., Belter & Grisso, 1984). The Piagetian model in simplified form, for example, proposes that basic reasoning shifts occur between the preoperational, the concrete-operational, and the formal-operational stages (Phillips, 1975).

In the preoperational stage, the child is limited to his or her own experiences as a primary data base for decisionmaking. Fantasy and magical thinking are also very powerful at this stage and may carry equal weight with more valid or reality-based data in a child's reasoning. While such children are very interested in their environment and interpersonal relations, their perspective is self-centered. Others' behavior and their own experiences are interpreted chiefly in terms of how these happenings affect them personally. When they ask questions or observe events happening to others, such children interpret the events chiefly via projection and identification.

During the concrete-operational stage, the child for the first time becomes capable of truly taking the perspective of another person and using that data in decisionmaking. While observational learning and asking questions are obvious in much younger children, the concrete-operational child is able to integrate and reason with these data in a more logical and effective manner than is possible earlier. In addition, this is the stage at which children first become able to explore their motivation from the standpoint of another person (Phillips, 1975).

With the arrival of formal operations, the child becomes able to use hypothetical reasoning. For the first time, the way things *are* now is recognized as a subset of the way things *could be*. Cause-and-effect reasoning becomes generalized in a manner that permits the child to extrapolate and theorize about future events and outcomes. Likewise, the ability to understand contingencies and consider probabilities (e.g., "There is a 50% chance that you will get well without treatment") will generally require cognitive talents that are not developed prior to formal-operational thought. Such thinking is obviously critical if a child is to make a decision regarding his or her long-term best interests.

Critics of Piagetian theory (see generally Siegel & Brainerd, 1978) have argued that children can be trained in some reasoning skills earlier than Piaget's theory of cognitive structures and development would predict to be possible. Although this line of research has considerable theoretical significance in understanding child development, it does not rebut the basic point that young children have difficulty in conceptualizing complex events outside the realm of their personal experience (cf. Melton, 1980). Such research does indicate, however, that current views for children's capacities may be underestimates. When children are "liberated" and actively involved in decisionmaking, greater competence may be demonstrated (see Bersoff, 1983; Tapp & Melton, 1983). In the meantime, Piagetian ideas about cognitive development give some guidance as to the quality of reasoning expectable among children faced with making decisions (e.g., Grisso & Vierling, 1978).

CONSENT VERSUS ASSENT

Among those writing on the interaction of developmental stages with competence to consent, a clear distinction is often made between the terms "consent" and "assent" (Leikin, 1983). "Consent" is generally taken to be a reasoned and voluntary acquiescence. We usually like to see the adjective "informed" precede "consent," implying that the relevant data needed to make a reasoned decision have been offered and understood. In recognition of the fact that children may not, as a function of their developmental level, be capable of giving such consent, many commentators prefer the term "assent." This recognizes the involvement of the child in the decisionmaking process, while also indicating that the child's level of participation is less than fully competent.

Granting assent power, however, is essentially the same as providing a veto power. What can be done to respect the rights of a child or another "incompetent" when the consequences of a poorly exercised veto could be disastrous to the individual in question? This is often the case when some high-risk medical procedure offers the only hope of long-term survival or when the person in question is preverbal, mute on the matter, or comatose. In such situations, a substitute or proxy is needed. At the same time, though, it should be noted that in the case of "routine" medical decisions, children tend to make adult-like decisions, even if their reasoning is poor (see, e.g., Lewis, 1983; Weithorn & Campbell, 1982). In such instances, little risk is accrued by permitting minors to make decisions on their own, while there may be substantial benefit (Melton, 1983b; Tapp & Melton, 1983).

SUBSTITUTED JUDGMENT

As discussed earlier, the law generally regards children as incompetents per se. When a decision is to be made on their behalf, it is usually exercised by a parent, guardian, or other responsible party acting *in loco parentis*. The general assumption is that the adult is providing a kind of proxy consent, exercising "substituted judgment." In this model, the adult is supposed to stand in the shoes of the child and make the decision that the child would be expected to make were he or she competent.

The concept of substituted judgment presumes a great deal. Most notably, it assumes that the person making the decision is willing and able to act in this capacity on the child's best interests (i.e., without a conflict of interests). Even within the loving, intact, two-parent family, not all parental decisions regarding children are without conflicts of interest (Melton, 1982, 1983a; Koocher, 1983). Parents often subordinate their needs and preferences to the best interests of their children (or to what they believe to be their children's best interests), but this is not always the case.

The courts have traditionally respected the sanctity of the family unit, and are quite reluctant to become involved without clear evidence of abuse, neglect, or similar dramatic turns of events. In the vast majority of situations, this is a very appropriate stance. Unfortunately, however, the threshold for intervention is often set beyond the level at which psychological problems are precipitated. That is to say, errors or decisions that are not in the child's best interests often do not come to the attention of the law or reach a level where legal intervention is possible, despite the fact that psychological harm may be occurring.

In some cases, courts have ruled that the children's rights are to be held paramount when parents' and children's rights conflict (see *Doe v. Doe*, 1979; *In re Male R.*, 1979; *In re Pernishek*, 1979). In other cases involving substantive conflicts, courts have been willing to terminate parental rights (see *In re C.M.S.*, 1979; *Jewish Child Care Association v. Elaine S.Y.*, 1979; *Nebraska v. Wedige*, 1980); such cases, however, are generally extreme exceptions. Recent U.S. Supreme Court decisions have belied a rather naive "parents know best" attitude (Rothman & Rothman, 1980).

SPECIFIC CONTEXTS

CONSENT TO TREATMENT

Many jurisdictions grant minors the right to seek treatment on their own authority, despite their presumed general incompetence. These authorizations are usually granted in cases where it is deemed to be in the public interest for the minor to be treated, and where the necessity of disclosure to parents might deter treatment-seeking behavior. For example, many states permit minors to seek medical treatment without parental consent if the minors believe that they have drug (or alcohol) addiction or a venereal disease. Abortion rights also fall into this category, although the emotional nature of the abortion issue often leads to a great deal of statutory gymnastics in some jurisdictions (aimed at encouraging parental involvement in the decision). Laws of the Commonwealth of Virginia authorize minors to consent to psychotherapeutic treatment without their parents' involvement, but this is an exception rather than the rule.

Other medical conditions or circumstances may dictate the child's involvement in decisionmaking, although practices vary widely. Katz (1984) presents an interesting historical analysis, which concludes that a patient's involvement in decisionmaking regarding health is a concept alien to the practice of medicine. Katz also notes that the law of informed consent as currently articulated by the courts fails to insure for the patient a proper role in such decisionmaking. The law mandates only the disclosure of information, but does not require the give-and-take conversation that is needed for shared decisionmaking or the detail and reframing of information that may be needed to help a child grasp the issues (Weithorn, 1983).

Unanswered questions remain: Where will the time to involve the child patient in decisionmaking come from? How will it be done in crisis? Who will teach the physician principles of child development and ethics related to the issues? Physicians may well involve young patients in decisionmaking when major surgery or complex treatment protocols are at issue, but how about with more mundane procedures? How about the role of other (nonphysician) health professionals in this process?

One type of situation that draws dramatic attention is the request to terminate life support equipment, as in the case of Karen Ann Quinlan. A recent case similar to that of Quinlan was *In re Guardianship of Barry* (1984). Barry was an infant whose parents sought to terminate life support equipment when it was clear that he was "in a permanent vegetative state with more than 90 percent of his brain function gone and without cognitive brain function." The parents' petition was supported by the child's attending physician and a court-appointed guardian *ad litem*. The state objected, arguing that its interest in preserving life outweighed parental assertions of Barry's right to privacy. Although Barry had minimal brain stem function and therefore did not meet the state's definition of "brain death," the court authorized termination of life support equipment, basing its order on the doctrine of substituted judgment. In Barry's case, the court determined that the parents and their medical advisors should make the decisions. The level of proof required was clear and convincing evidence.

Other problematic situations involve so-called "no code" or "DNR" (i.e., "Do Not Resuscitate") orders entered in patients' medical records. These are medical decisions or orders to withhold care that could extend a patient's life. Such orders require a balancing of any given patient's right to treatment and right to refuse treatment. Sometimes DNR orders are upheld by courts on the grounds that it is not in the patient's best interest to be resuscitated (Robertson, 1983). The Massachusetts courts upheld such an order in the case of a 5-month-old infant who was abandoned at birth and also suffered from profound congenital heart and lung malformations (*Custody of a Minor*, 1982). The child had no medical hope of survival beyond a year and was admitted to a hospital with a severe bacterial infection. The child was placed on a respirator, and his physician recommended that the Massachusetts Department of Social Services, which was his legal guardian, authorize a DNR order in the event that the child suffered a respiratory arrest. When the Department refused to consent, the hospital sought authorization from the juvenile court. The juvenile court authorized the DNR order; this was subsequently upheld by the Massachusetts Supreme Judicial Court, which found that a "full code" order would involve a substantial degree of bodily invasion, discomfort, and pain, and would only prolong the infant's agony and suffering. In substituting its judgment, the court ruled that it would therefore not serve the child's interests to be resuscitated, and that the child would reject resuscitation were he competent to decide.

CHILDREN IN THE COURTS

Cases covered in the context of children in the courts involve criminal or delinquency actions, child custody decisionmaking, or other civil litigation (e.g., civil commitment vs. parental commitment of minors to psychiatric hospitals). This is one interface of behavioral science and the law in which the evolution of psychological concepts and legal decisions has been very rapid.

Criminal Law

In the criminal area, there is an increasing tendency to treat juveniles charged with major crimes (especially homicides) as adults. This is often referred to as a "transfer" or "waiver" from juvenile to adult jurisdiction. This is not an issue of "competency to stand trial," which involves the ability to comprehend the roles of court officers, to cooperate in one's own defense, and to appreciate the potential consequences of the proceedings. Rather, it represents a growing public sentiment that dangerous children (i.e., violent juvenile offenders) ought not to be "let off the hook" simply by virtue of their age.

In *Morris v. Florida* (1984), a state appeals court upheld a ruling that a 13-year-old murder defendant must undergo an evaluation to determine her competence to stand trial before her presumed incapacity could be overcome. Previously, juveniles under 14 were presumed incapable of criminal acts under Florida law, but now youthful offenders are examined in order to assess their ability to be tried as adults.

The burglary conviction of a mentally handicapped 17-

year-old with an IQ of about 80 was overturned when his
confession was deemed involuntary (*Illinois v. Berry*, 1984). The
judicial panel cited the defendant's age, education, mental capacity, emotional characteristics, and relative inexperience in
criminal matters in determining the voluntariness of the confession. The panel noted that the youth was below average in
intelligence, had little education, was dependent on his parents,
lacked a history of criminal experience, and respected the police. At police headquarters he was isolated from his mother,
did not have an attorney, and was subjected to some deceptive
questioning. In addition, his *Miranda* warnings were not given
because Berry was told that he was not in custody.

A considerable body of work has focused on juveniles' exercise of their "*Miranda* rights" (Grisso, 1981, 1983). In *Miranda
v. Arizona* (1966), the U.S. Supreme Court established the constitutional requirement that persons accused of a crime both
have a right to counsel and have the right to avoid self-incrimination. The Supreme Court subsequently rendered the *In re
Gault* (1967) decision, which extended these rights of the accused to minors (see also *Fare v. Michael C.*, 1979).

In a series of empirical studies, Grisso (1981, 1983) found
that the vast majority of juveniles aged 14 and under did not
grasp the meaning of the *Miranda* warnings they were given
upon arrest. Likewise, 15- and 16-year-olds with IQ scores of
80 and below were similarly unable to comprehend the presentation of these rights. When considering juveniles of 15 and
16 who had low-average or better intelligence, Grisso discovered that their comprehension of *Miranda* warnings did not
differ significantly from that of adults. (This does not necessarily mean that adults fully understood their rights; Grisso also
found that 25% of adults lacked an adequate understanding of
the warnings and their implications.) Interestingly, "prior experience" with the courts and police, race, and socioeconomic
status were unrelated to comprehension of these rights by juveniles.

Using specific examples, Grisso (1983) has summarized the
problem of integrating developmental knowledge with such cases
very well. The message is simple: No matter what the technical
minimum requirements of a law may be, there are always some

jurisdictions that will be sensitive to these issues, and some that will not have the time or inclination. It is not clear whether knowledge of relevant psychosocial data would necessarily change the situation.

Are Psychological Data Used?

Courts' views of children's competence have been determined more often by context than by psychological data. This is best illustrated by the juxtaposition of two U.S. Supreme Court decisions handed down on the same day in 1979.

One case (*Parham v. J.R.*) involved the question of whether or not a hearing is necessary prior to involuntarily committing a minor to an inpatient psychiatric facility. Presenting a rather romanticized view of the American family, the Burger Court asserted essentially that "parents know best" and that they (in concert with the facility's admitting officer) are adequate proxies for a child. In *Parham*, the adolescent patients were deemed incompetent to request a hearing or otherwise assert their own competence to make a decision regarding hospitalization.

The second case (*Fare v. Michael C.*) involved an adolescent suspect in a murder case who was the same age as some of the patients in the *Parham* case. Michael C. was apprehended by the police and read his *Miranda* warnings. Recordings of the interview and his subsequent confession made it clear that Michael was in great emotional distress and feared that the police were trying to "trick" him. The context strongly suggested that he did not understand his rights fully. Nonetheless, the Court's decision indicated a belief that Michael, as an experienced juvenile offender, was competent to waive his rights and confess without consulting an attorney.

A comparison of the decisions makes it clear that, without benefit of psychological data, the Court ruled that teenagers are not competent to object to involuntary hospitalization but *are* competent to confess to murder without first consulting a lawyer. Furthermore, it is not at all clear that the Court would have attended to psychological research (e.g., Grisso's work) had it been available. The "common knowledge" available to the Justices seems their most relied-upon source in such situations.

The Child as Witness

So much for the child as defendant. What about the child as a witness in court? Here, too, competence is a central issue. While children have been offering testimony in courts of law for centuries, questions are often raised regarding the value of their statements (Goodman, 1984a). A superb review of the historical background and current research dealing with the child witness is presented in a special issue of the *Journal of Social Issues* (Goodman, 1984b). Topics include the reliability of children's memories, children as eyewitnesses, children's ability to differentiate fact from fantasy, testimony by child victims of sexual assault, and jurors' reactions to child witnesses.

The data suggest that children can indeed be competent and credible witnesses, but also that special factors must be considered in questioning them. A complex interaction of factors related to suggestibility, semantics, social demand characteristics, developmental phenomena, and other situational factors may influence the accuracy of their testimony (Goodman, 1984b). This has become an area of intense interest among both clinical and developmental investigators. The resulting progress is likely to be beneficial both to the children who testify (i.e., by making it possible to reduce stresses on them) and to those who are seeking justice (i.e., by establishing optimal circumstances and methods for eliciting the most accurate testimony).

Aside from procedural changes that might grow out of the research noted above, it does not necessarily follow that empirical data are well used by judges in making their decisions. In addition, there may be times when constitutional issues demand that a child's "best interests" be ignored. A series of rulings on a case involving the *Boston Globe* between 1980 and 1982 (Melton, 1984a) may be used to illustrate the point. The rulings involved a test of the constitutionality of a Massachusetts law barring persons "not having a direct interest in the case" from courtrooms during the testimony of minors who were the victims of sex offenses (Mass. Gen. Laws, 1923/1972). The *Boston*

Globe objected to having its reporters excluded from the trial of an adult defendant who was charged with the forcible and "unnatural" rape of three girls (aged 16–17 at the time of the trial). The early decisions at the state level upheld the exclusion, noting that the statute was intended to encourage young victims to come forward and to protect them from undue psychological harm at trial. The U.S. Supreme Court (*Globe Newspaper Co. vs. Superior Court*, 1982) ultimately overruled the early decisions upholding the law (although this did not happen until long after the actual trial had ended). Part of the Court's reasoning was that the statute was overly broad in providing for *mandatory closure* in such cases.

More interesting, however, was the Court's statement that there was "no empirical support" for the notion that such a statute facilitates the reporting of such crimes. In a dissenting opinion, Chief Justice Burger argued that the reality of severe psychological damage to child witnesses in this context was "not disputed," and that states ought to be encouraged to experiment in order to generate empirical data of this sort. It was not clear that real searches for meaningful data had been undertaken. Melton (1984a) notes that study of this case "does little to promote faith that the Supreme Court will make good use of social science data" (p. 118) in its opinions.

Custody Decisions

The special context of divorce raises other interesting questions. Decisions to be made in the "best interests" of children are highly subjective in such situations and require complex reasoning skills to conceptualize, let alone resolve. In an as-yet-unpublished manuscript based on her doctoral dissertation, Greenberg (Greenberg & Rappaport, 1984) reports on a study that evaluated the degree to which children of different ages were able to employ a rational decisionmaking process to arrive upon a custodial preference between divorcing parents.

The study involved the judgments of 144 children between the ages of 9 and 14. A group of 18-year-olds was included to provide the perspective of legal adults, and 44 domestic relations judges evaluated the decisions reached by the children.

The major finding of the study was that age, IQ, sex, and socioeconomic factors were not very useful in predicting competent decisionmaking. Rather, process-oriented problem-solving skills and knowledge about divorce were better predictors of children's competence to participate in making decisions on custody. Children who were able to isolate relevant aspects of the problem and to generate alternative solutions, and those who were familiar with what a divorce involves (i.e., those with the capacity to reason and experience), exercised the soundest judgment. The data suggest that judges who seriously wish to attend to statutory guidelines for taking a child's wishes into account ought to consider these factors. What Greenberg does not make clear, and what the present volume is basically about, is how one communicates this information to judges in a way that is both comprehensible and useful.

DEVELOPMENTAL ASSUMPTIONS AND PUBLIC POLICY

Psychological research continues to answer many questions about children's competencies. The study of social institutions and systems (e.g., the family, the court, and the hospital) also increasingly assists us in understanding the interaction of children's capacities with enabling, restricting, or permission-granting forces. The resulting work is at once exhilarating and frustrating.

The exhilaration grows out of informed solutions that we see evolving as well as the new sense of understanding and confidence that the available body of behavioral science data is helping to bring about. The frustration grows out of the fact that many of the available data go unnoticed by the various policymakers in the best position to provide meaningful implementation. In addition, when our findings are noticed, they are occasionally interpreted in ways that fail to recognize the limits of validity inherent in such research.

It is also important to recognize that there are times when policy implications of certain research findings will of necessity preclude their application. The absence of human service resources, political realities, and fiscal austerity are all examples of inhibiting factors that are not prominent in the minds of researchers. This does not mean that we should not attempt to answer important questions. Rather, it requires that we address ourselves to the most important issues in as rigorous a manner as possible. We must then attempt to translate our findings into useful information and to communicate it in the media most often read, seen, or heard by the policymakers we hope to influence. Only in this way can we retain any hope of ultimately exerting effective influence.

REFERENCES

Aladdin's Castle v. City of Mesquite, 630 F.2d 1029 (5th Cir. 1980), *reversed in part and remanded*, 455 U.S. 283 (1982).

Bellotti v. Baird, 443 U.S. 622 (1979).

Belter, R.W., & Grisso, T. (1984). Children's recognition of rights violations in counseling. *Professional Psychology: Research and Practice, 15*, 899–910.

Bersoff, D.N. (1983). Children as participants in psychoeducational assessment. In G.B. Melton, G.P., Koocher, & M.J. Saks (Eds.), *Children's competence to consent* (pp. 149–178). New York: Plenum.

Brehm, S.S. (1977). The effect of adult influence on children's preferences: Compliance versus opposition. *Journal of Abnormal Child Psychology, 5*, 31–41.

Brehm, S.S., & Weintraub, M. (1972). Physical barriers and psychological reactance: 2-year-olds' responses to threats to freedom. *Journal of Personality and Social Psychology, 35*, 830–836.

City of Akron v. Akron Center for Reproductive Health, 462 U.S. 416 (1983).

Custody of a Minor, 385 Mass. 697 (1982).

Doe v. Doe, 119 N.H. 773, 408 A.2d 785 (1979).

Dow v. Renfrow, 475 F. Supp. 1012 (N.D. Ind. 1979), *aff'd in part, remanded in part*, 631 F.2d 91 (7th Cir. 1980), *reh'g and reh'g en banc denied*, 635 F.2d 582 (7th Cir. 1980), *cert. denied*, 451 U.S. 1022 (1981).

Fare v. Michael C., 442 U.S. 707 (1979).

Globe Newspaper Co. v. Superior Court, 457 U.S. 596 (1982).

Goodman, G.S. (1984a). Children's testimony in historical perspective. *Journal of Social Issues, 40*(2), 9–31.

Goodman, G.S. (Ed.). (1984b). The child victim witness [Special issue]. *Journal of Social Issues, 40*(2).

Greenberg, E.F., & Rappaport, J. (1984). *Predictors of children's competence to participate in child-custody decision making.* Unpublished manuscript.

Grisso, T. (1981). *Juveniles' waiver of rights: Legal and psychological competence.* New York: Plenum.

Grisso, T. (1983). Juveniles' consent in delinquency proceedings. In G.B. Melton, G.P. Koocher, & M.J. Saks (Eds.), *Children's competence to consent* (pp. 131–148). New York: Plenum.

Grisso, T., & Vierling, L. (1978). Minors' consent to treatment: A developmental perspective. *Professional Psychology: Research and Practice, 9,* 412–427.

Grodin, M.A., & Alpert, J.J. (1983). Informed consent and pediatric care. In G.B. Melton, G.P. Koocher, & M.J. Saks (Eds.), *Children's competence to consent* (pp. 93–110). New York: Plenum.

H.L. v. Matheson, 450 U.S. 398 (1981).

Illinois v. Berry, 463 N.E.2d 1044 (Ill. App. 1984).

In re C.M.S., 609 P.2d 240 (Mont. 1979).

In re Gault, 387 U.S. 1 (1967)

In re Guardianship of Barry, 445 So.2d 365 (Fla. App. 1984).

In re Male R., 102 Misc. 2d 1, 422 N.Y.S. 819 (Kings Co. Fam. Ct. 1979).

In re Pernishek, 268 Pa. Super. 447, 408 A.2d 872 (1979).

In re R.M.G., 454 A.2d 776 (1982).

Jessor, R. (1984). Adolescent development and behavioral health. In J.D. Matarazzo, S.M. Weiss, A.J. Herd, N.E. Miller, & S.M. Weiss (Eds.) *Behavioral health: A handbook of health enhancement and disease prevention* (pp. 69–90). New York: Wiley.

Jewish Child Care Association v. Elaine S.Y., 73 A.D.2d 154, 425 N.Y.S.2d 336 (1979).

Kahneman, D., & Tversky, A. (1973). On the psychology of prediction. *Psychological Review, 81,* 237–251.

Katz, J. (1984). *The silent world of doctor and patient.* New York: Free Press.

Keith-Spiegel, P.C. (1983). Children and consent to participate in research. In G.B. Melton, G.P. Koocher, & M.J. Saks (Eds.), *Children's competence to consent* (pp. 179–214). New York: Plenum.

Koocher, G.P. (1983). Competence to consent: Psychotherapy. In G.B. Melton. G.P. Koocher, & M.J. Saks (Eds.), *Children's competence to consent* (pp. 111–127). New York: Plenum.

Leikin, S.L. (1983). Minors' assent or dissent to medical treatment. *Journal of Pediatrics, 102,* 169–176.

Lewis, C.C. (1981). How adolescents approach decisions: Changes over grades seven to twelve and policy implications. *Child Development, 52,* 538–544.

Lewis, C.E. (1983). Decision making related to health: When could/should children act responsibly? In G.B. Melton, G.P. Koocher, & M.J. Saks (Eds.), *Children's competence to consent* (pp. 75–92). New York: Plenum.

Lidz, C.W., Meisel, A., Zerubavel, E., Carter, E., Sestak, R.M., & Roth, L. (1984). *Informed consent: A study of decisionmaking in psychiatry.* New York: Guilford Press.

Mass. Gen. Laws Ann. ch. 278, §16A (West 1972) (enacted 1923).

Melton, G.B. (1980). Children's concepts of their rights. *Journal of Clinical Child Psychology, 9,* 186–190.

Melton, G.B. (1982). Children's rights: Where are the children? *American Journal of Orthopsychiatry, 52,* 530–538.

Melton, G.B. (1983a) Children's competence to consent: A problem in law and social science. In G.B. Melton, G.P. Koocher, & M.J. Saks (Eds.), *Children's competence to consent* (pp. 1–20). New York: Plenum.

Melton, G.B. (1983b). Decision making by children: Psychological risks and benefits. In G.B. Melton, G.P. Koocher, & M.J. Saks (Eds.), *Children's competence to consent* (pp. 21–40). New York: Plenum.

Melton, G.B. (1984a). Child witnesses and the First Amendment: A psycho-legal dilemma. *Journal of Social Issues, 40*(2), 109–123.

Melton, G.B. (1984b). Developmental psychology and the law: The state of the art. *Journal of Family Law, 22,* 445–482.

Melton, G.B., Koocher, G.P., & Saks, M.J. (Eds.). (1983). *Children's competence to consent.* New York: Plenum.

Miranda v. Arizona, 348 U.S. 436 (1966).

Mischel, W. (1971). *Introduction to personality.* New York: Holt, Rinehart & Winston.

Morris v. Florida, 456 So.2d 925 (Fla. Dist. Ct. App. 1984).

Nebraska v. Wedige, 205 Neb. 687, 289 N.W.2d 538 (1980).

New Jersey v. T.L.O., 105 S. Ct. 733 (1985).

Palmore v. Sidoti, 104 S. Ct. 1879 (1984).

Parham v. J.R., 442 U.S. 584 (1979).

Phillips, J.L. (1975). *The origins of intellect: Piaget's theory.* San Francisco: W.H. Freeman.

Roberts, M.C., Maddux, J.E., & Wright, L. (1984). Developmental perspectives in behavioral health. In J.D. Matarazzo, S.M. Weiss, A.J. Herd, N.E. Miller, & S.M. Weiss (Eds.), *Behavioral health: A handbook of health enhancement and disease prevention* (pp. 56–68). New York: Wiley.

Robertson, J.A. (1983). *The rights of the critically ill.* Cambridge, MA: Ballinger.

Rothman, D.J., & Rothman, S.M. (1980). The conflict over children's rights. *Hastings Center Reports, 10,* 7–10.

Rozovsky, F.A. (1984). *Consent to treatment: A practical guide.* Boston: Little, Brown.

Saks, M.J. (1983). Social psychological perspectives on the problem of consent. In G.B. Melton, G.P. Koocher, & M.J. Saks (Eds.), *Children's competence to consent* (pp. 41–56). New York: Plenum.

Saks, M.J., & Kidd, R. (1980–1981). Human information processing and adjudication: Trial by heuristics. *Law and Society Review, 15,* 123–160.

Shorez v. City of Dacono, 574 F. Supp. 130 (D. Colo. 1983).

Siegel, L.S., & Brainerd, C.J. (Eds.). (1978). *Alternatives to Piaget: Critical essays on the theory.* New York: Academic Press.

Tapp, J.L., & Melton, G.B. (1983). Preparing children for decisionmaking: Implications of legal socialization research. In G.B. Melton, G.P. Koocher, & M.J. Saks (Eds.), *Children's competence to consent* (pp. 215–234). New York: Plenum.

Thornburg v. American College of Obstetricians and Gynecologists, 54 U.S.L.W. 4618 (U.S. June 11, 1986).

Tversky, A., & Kahneman, D. (1974). Judgment under uncertainty: Heuristics and biases. *Science, 185,* 1124–1131.

Wadlington, W.J. (1983). Consent to medical care for minors: The legal framework. In G.B. Melton, G.P. Koocher, & M.J. Saks (Eds.), *Children's competence to consent* (pp. 57–73). New York: Plenum.

Walker v. City of Warren, 135 Mich. App. 267, 354 N.W.2d 312 (1984).

Wallace v. Jaffree, 105 S. Ct. 2479 (1985).

Weithorn, L.A. (1983). Involving children in decisions affecting their own welfare: Guidelines for professionals. In G.B. Melton, G.P. Koocher, & M.J. Saks (Eds.), *Children's competence to consent* (pp. 235–260). New York: Plenum.

Weithorn, L.A., & Campbell, S.B. (1982). The competency of children and adolescents to make informed treatment decisions. *Child Development, 53,* 1589–1598.

The Impact of Social Science Research on the Judiciary

THOMAS L. HAFEMEISTER
GARY B. MELTON

This book reflects one of the overriding concerns of scholars conducting social science research and analysis—the impact of their work. After investing great care, time, and effort in a project, nearly all scholars have both a professional and a personal interest in the influence of their scholarship. Indeed, influence on a particular audience may have been the motive for the work.

Perhaps one of the most prestigious targets for diffusion of research is the judiciary. Judicial rulings have an enormous potential impact. Their influence is felt directly in the specific case that is decided. However, they have a larger indirect impact as the propagator of guiding principles affecting both subsequent judicial decisions and the behavior of future litigants and people in general (see Melton, 1985; Perry & Melton, 1984).

Given the significance of the problem of insuring that legal decisionmakers have thorough, up-to-date information available to them, it is important to know how to increase legal authorities' awareness of social science research. With that goal in mind, this chapter reports three studies designed to assess the frequency of use of child development research by the judiciary and to determine the means of dissemination that are

Thomas L. Hafemeister. Office of Mental Health, State of New York, Albany, New York.

Gary B. Melton. Department of Psychology and College of Law, University of Nebraska—Lincoln, Lincoln, Nebraska.

most likely to result in use of research in judicial decision-making.

HISTORICAL FOUNDATIONS

Consideration of questions about the actual and proper role of social science research in judicial decisionmaking is a relatively recent jurisprudential phenomenon. This development reflects changes in both social science and the law. As true of most social science, the serious study of human development has been almost exclusively a 20th-century phenomenon. Similarly, a scholarly, "scientific" approach to law has been largely a product of this century. The first law review did not appear until 1887 (at Harvard), with only two others (at Yale and the University of Pennsylvania) in place by the turn of the century (Stevens, 1983). As we shall see, substantial judicial use of social science is much more recent—limited largely to the past three decades.

The integration of social science into the legal process began late in the 19th century. Oliver Wendell Holmes (1897), later to be appointed to the U.S. Supreme Court, argued that an appreciation of social reality—not just knowledge of legal rules—is necessary for rational legal decisionmaking. "For the rational study of law," he wrote, "the black-letter man may be the man of the present, but the man of the future is the man of statistics and the master of economics" (p. 469). With Louis Brandeis and Roscoe Pound, Holmes influenced legal scholars to think of law as "social engineering" (Pound's phrase) that could be best informed by consideration of scientific evidence. The law, they argued, consisted of variant principles shaped by social needs and not of hard rules applicable through purely formal logic. As we shall see, such ideas became predominant in legal scholarship with the realist movement of the 1920s and 1930s (Stevens, 1983; Woodard, 1968).

The beginnings of actual application of social science to the law paralleled these developments in jurisprudential theory, although substantial application came much later. The first appearance of social science evidence in a judicial opinion occurred in 1908 in *Muller v. Oregon.* Future U.S. Supreme Court

Justice Brandeis submitted a lengthy brief (excerpted in Monahan & Walker, 1985) filled with extralegal authorities to support the rationality of Oregon's statute limiting women's work
day to 10 hours. *Muller* was noteworthy in that the Supreme
Court expressly recognized and accepted the "Brandeis brief"
(now the term used to describe briefs including extralegal authority) and the "expressions of opinion from other than judicial sources" it contained.

Muller did not mark the beginning of a general influx of
social science research into the judiciary. Reviewing the Supreme Court's opinions from 1917 (when Brandeis was appointed to the Court) to 1926, Newland (1961) found that only
Brandeis cited extralegal sources. Citation of extralegal authorities, and then primarily from economics and the physical
sciences, did not become common until the New Deal Court
beginning in the late 1930s (Konopka, 1980; Newland, 1961;
Rosen, 1972).

The first case in which social science formed an integral
part of the Court's analysis did not occur until 1954 (*Brown v.
Board of Education*). The degree to which the Court's analysis
actually turned on the psychological and sociological studies
presented was controversial and remains a matter of scholarly
debate. Whatever the actual reliance, though, *Brown* marked at
least two important developments in the relationship between
law and social science. First, the Court accepted a brief that
included nothing but social science (Allport *et al.*, 1953), unlike
the Brandeis briefs, which involved at least nominal integration
of the social science evidence with legal arguments. Second,
Brown marked the first application of social science to attack,
rather than support, the rationality of state action.

The furor over the legitimacy of the Court's apparent reliance on social science in *Brown* may actually have chilled such
applications for the next decade (Loh, 1981). However, attention to social science greatly expanded in the 1960s and 1970s
with the social activism of the time. The growth of "law and
. . ." courses in law schools reflected renewed calls for social
relevance of the law. As the courts were called upon to protect
the civil rights of racial minorities, women, students, mental
patients, and prisoners, the nature of the institutions dominat-

ing such groups became a matter for formal evidence and judicial speculation.

Increasing acceptance of social science in the legal process also may reflect simply the rationalization and secularization of a bureaucratized, technologically sophisticated society (Rosen, 1972; Woodard, 1968). Exclusion of scientific evidence from the process of legal policymaking now may seem stranger than its inclusion. For example, in certain areas the courts appear increasingly to be, in effect, relinquishing their decisionmaking authority to experts by relying on professional judgment as a legal standard (see, e.g., *Benitez ex rel. Catala v. Collazo*, 1984; *Harding v. Kulhmann*, 1984; *Rennie v. Klein*, 1981; *Siu v. Johnson*, 1984; *Youngberg v. Romeo*, 1982; see also Perry & Melton, 1984, analyzing the impact of *Parham v. J.R.*, 1979). This standard invites empirical evidence about prevailing professional practices and deference to "scientific" judgments.

HOW JUDGES MAKE DECISIONS

THEORETICAL PERSPECTIVES

Questions about the actual and proper role of social science in the legal process have been shaped by jurisprudential debates about how judges reach their decisions. Historically, legal decisions were believed to be dictated by the formal properties of the law. In this classical or "slot-machine" concept of judicial decisionmaking, judges were believed to "find" the proper rule in the black-letter law (the U.S. Constitution, a statute, or a common-law principle) and then simply to apply the rule logically to the facts in the immediate case. From this perspective, the law operated mechanically and autonomously, without any need for the insights of other disciplines.

However, with the rise of legal realism in the 1920s and 1930s came the view that judges rely on more than the black-letter law and logic, even if judges do not admit their consideration of other factors. As an empirical matter, the realists asserted that "the law in action" often differs from "the law on the books" (Pound, 1910) and that judges' opinions emanated from their social background and intuition (see, e.g., Cardozo,

1921). Decisions were presumed by the realists to be mere post hoc rationalizations of judicial biases (Llewellyn, 1962). The realists also noted the logical impossibility of a purely formalist approach to law, because competing precedents may be applied. Rules of law alone cannot explain what leads the judge to a specific result in a particular case (Burrus, 1962; C. Kaufman, 1980; Paul, 1957–1958).

The maintenance of the illusion that the law functions autonomously was thought by the realists to result in arbitrary uninformed policymaking. Contrasting existing "mechanical jurisprudence" with his own "sociological jurisprudence," Pound (1909), for example, described the courts' decisionmaking as "the rigorous logical deduction from predetermined conceptions in disregard of and often in the teeth of the actual facts" (p. 462), with the result that decisions were made because of mere "technicalities." Similarly, Brandeis (1916) wrote, "No law, written or unwritten, can be understood without a full knowledge of the facts out of which it arises, and to which it applies" (p. 467).

Legal realism eventually fell out of favor, because of its lack of an organizing theory about how decisions should be made and its complete rejection of the special formal analytic properties of law. Nonetheless, its basic ideas are now well ingrained in legal scholarship and judicial action. By the 1930s, judges had begun to attend to the socioeconomic impact of legal doctrines. The notion that political, economic, and social factors shape judicial reasoning is now commonplace. Indeed, prevailing "postrealist" jurisprudential movements have been shaped by the realists' observations and their challenges to examine the empirical foundations of the law (Monahan & Walker, 1985, pp. 27–29). Perhaps the most obvious extension of realist theory is presented by the critical legal studies movement, which perceives law as a tool of particular class interests (see, e.g., Unger, 1983).

JUDICIAL SELF-PERCEPTIONS

Judges themselves have recognized that they cannot rely solely on legal precedent for guidance. Although the judges who have

written publicly about their perceptions of how they make decisions have happened to be "liberal" judges who may not be
representative of the bench, their observations are still useful.
They also clearly reflect the influence of the realist movement.

For example, Judge I.R. Kaufman (1984) of the Second
Circuit Court of Appeals has asserted that learning "to resist
the seduction of pure logic . . . may be among the most important lessons for those embarking on careers in law" (p. 2).
Acknowledging that the law "bears the indelible imprint of the
[judge's] values and beliefs" (p. 12), he has concluded that
"[w]hether judicial pronouncements are perceived as oppres-
sive commands or as just solutions depends to a great extent
on a judge's capacity to discern and sound the common note
of an era" (p. 14). To do so, he argues, the judge should "refer
to the contributions of the great figures in philosophy, literature, history, psychology and other studies as well as law" (p. 14).

Similarly echoing realist dogma, Judge J.M. Wisdom (1975)
of the Fifth Circuit has noted the role of social factors in judicial
decisionmaking:

> Sociology has always played a part in the decision-making process, al-
> though frequently it comes in wearing a mask. . . . In these instances the
> judge, perhaps unwittingly[,] may be functioning as a sociologist without
> benefit of witnesses and solid empirical data and perhaps is treating the
> litigants unfairly. (p. 137)

The answer, Judge Wisdom maintains, is to seek the assistance of social scientists:

> Judges should profit from other disciplines. In a sense, a judicial decision
> represents social science in action. Judges should acquire more knowledge
> of the social sciences to enable them to fulfil[l] their policy-making func-
> tion of using law as a means to the ends of serving society wisely and to
> its good. (p. 148)

Other federal judges, especially those who have heard large
class action suits, have reached similar conclusions (see, e.g.,
Craven, 1975; Johnson, 1976; McMillan, 1975; Wald, 1984).

JUDICIAL OPINIONS AS ARCHIVAL DATA

Although introspection by a few judges is interesting and useful,
it gives few clues about how judges in general make decisions.

With rare exceptions (e.g., Kalven & Zeisel, 1966; Sanders, Rankin-Widgeon, Kalmuss, & Chesler, 1981–1982), researchers interested in judicial decisionmaking have been forced to rely on indirect measures, because judges typically are reluctant or unavailable to discuss the bases for their decisions.

The most readily available avenue for exploring the impact of social science research on the judiciary is that of their written opinions. Judges typically will cite various sources to justify their opinions. Among these citations may be references to studies by social scientists. However, commentators differ about how much these citations reflect the court's reliance on the materials referenced. For example, in attempting to measure the impact of legal periodicals, Maru (1976) noted that "it is very nearly impossible to weigh the impact or influence of a particular article on a writer unless the writer provides a simple declaration to the effect that he had no idea what he was about until he came upon that particular article. I would be very surprised indeed ever to come upon such a declaration" (p. 231, note 14). Citations may be mere makeweight or post hoc rationalizations for views originating from other, unexpressed sources.

Other scholars, however, share the opinion of Friedman, Kagan, Cartwright, and Wheeler (1981) that "opinions [are] as good an indicator as we have of what counts as sound legal reasoning" (p. 773). Indeed, while sounding his caveat, Maru (1976) proceeded to use a citation count to assess the impact of legal periodicals on the judiciary. He did caution that concluding that the court placed a specific degree of reliance on any particular referenced material would be mistaken and misleading. Nonetheless, he asserted:

> When an author cites something, it is a reasonable assumption that he has nearly always read, analyzed, and thought about it and that he finds it significant enough to refer to in his own work. I do not think that we can describe use in more significant terms than these or that we can find a better way to measure it. (Maru, 1976, p. 230)

Friedman *et al.* (1981) used a similar rationale for their study of judicial citations:

> Judges, generally speaking, have derivative, rather than primary, authority. Even though they have great power, they are *not* supposed to

act free and unfettered. . . . Judges are expected to *justify* their decisions. . . . Everybody knows—at least since the realists hammered home
the point—that a judicial opinion does *not* tell us what went on in judges'
minds. It may be a mere rationalization. But we can say, with some
certainty, that the opinion and its reasoning show what judges *think* is
legitimate argument and legitimate authority, justifying their behavior.
(pp. 793–794)

Thus, although it is recognized that citations in judicial
opinions are far less than perfect measures of the actual bases
of judges' decisions, they still represent useful information. At
a minimum, as Friedman *et al.* (1981) have argued, they tell us
what the judge thinks *does* justify his or her decision, even if it
is not the actual justification. As such, citations of social science
materials give a rough indication of judges' awareness and consideration of social science and their view of its legitimacy as a
basis for legal decisionmaking.

TRENDS IN COURTS' RELIANCE ON
SECONDARY AUTHORITY

Several studies have shown a marked trend toward increasing
use of *secondary sources* in judicial opinions. As the term is used
in the law, a "secondary source" is an authority other than the
law itself. Thus, as used throughout the rest of this chapter,
the term *"primary sources"* refers to cases, statutes, and regulations. Secondary sources are broken into two categories. "Legal
secondary sources" include legal commentaries published in law
reviews, legal treatises (books), or legal reference books. "Nonlegal sources" include all other secondary sources including
social science journals, treatises, and reference books. Any nonlegal source is a secondary source for purposes of law, regardless of whether it contains original data or ideas.

U.S. SUPREME COURT

Daniels (1983) has documented the increase in citation of secondary sources by the U.S. Supreme Court during this century.

In 1978, 41.7% of all opinions (59.7% of majority opinions) cited a legal secondary source, nearly double the proportion of opinions citing such authorities in 1900 and 1940. The number of citations of legal secondary sources per opinion rose dramatically, from 0.485 in 1900 to 0.589 in 1940 to 2.072 in 1978.

Much of the growth in citation of legal secondary sources was attributable to the Court's increasing reliance upon law reviews. Only one case cited a legal periodical in 1900. The number of citations of legal periodicals increased to 35 in 1940 and mushroomed to 343 in 1978 (37.2% of all citations of secondary sources in that year). Although the number of law reviews cited also rose dramatically (from 13 in 1940 to 97 in 1978), 12 reviews still accounted for the majority of citations in 1978. The Court's new reliance on law reviews for authority might be more properly termed the Court's reliance on the journals of a few distinguished "national" law schools from which, perhaps not coincidentally, Justices often select their clerks, who in turn do much of their research and sometimes draft their opinions.

At the same time, the Court became increasingly unlikely to rely on legal treatises and reference books (i.e., restatements, annotations, and legal encyclopedias) that merely state the law without analyzing the nature or wisdom of the underlying analyses or the directions that legal reform should take. Although the absolute number of such citations rose, their relative contribution to the total number of secondary citations dropped from 85.7% in 1900 to 40.4% in 1940 and 34.4% in 1978.

About one-fifth of opinions published in 1978 (34.1% of majority opinions) cited a nonlegal source, double the percentage of 1940 and a 1,000-fold increase since 1900. Nonlegal citations per opinion rose even more markedly proportionally than the rate of citation of legal secondary sources, from 0.075 to 0.463 to 0.815. The absolute growth also was striking: from 17 citations of nonlegal sources in 1900 to 99 in 1940 and 260 in 1978. The sources cited were quite diverse. In 1978, 26 different journals accounted for the 49 citations of nonlegal periodicals. They were drawn from accounting, anthropology, business, foreign affairs, history, insurance, optometry, political science, psychiatry, psychology, and sociology.

However, the Court's reliance on law reviews and nonlegal authorities should not be overemphasized. Examination of the summary data in Daniels's study can be somewhat misleading. Much of the citation of secondary sources was done in a few cases by a few of the Justices. Of the 129 cases decided during the 1978 term, 20 cases, mostly on constitutional issues, contributed over half of the citations of secondary sources. Although citation of law reviews was relatively constant across Justices, Justice Blackmun and Chief Justice Burger accounted for almost three-fourths of the citations of nonlegal periodicals.

Total citation of secondary sources was correlated with judicial philosophy. Justices Brennan and Marshall, usually regarded as the liberals on the Court, ranked first and second, respectively, in the frequency of such citations per page, with Justices commonly regarded as moderates (i.e., Blackmun, Stevens, and Powell) in the middle rankings. Brennan also ranked first in total citations of nonlegal sources, with Blackmun second. The anomaly in the rank ordering of reliance on secondary sources was Chief Justice Burger, who ranked third in citations per page of secondary sources, but who was usually considered second only to Justice Rehnquist in conservatism.

STATE APPELLATE COURTS

The trend toward increasing reliance on secondary sources, especially law reviews, has also been observed in studies of citations by state appellate courts. In the largest such study, Friedman et al. (1981) examined 5,900 randomly selected cases from 16 state supreme courts over the period 1870–1970. Law review citations were essentially nonexistent before 1940, but 12% of state supreme court opinions in 1960–1970 included such references. State supreme courts recognized as innovative, "liberal" courts and widely cited by appellate courts in other states were especially likely to rely upon law reviews. Thus, the supreme courts of New Jersey and California cited legal periodicals in 34.9% and 26.2% of their opinions, respectively, during 1960–1970.

On the other hand, state supreme courts rarely cited social

science authorities. In Friedman *et al.*'s (1981) sample, only 0.6% of opinions between 1940 and 1970 included such citations. The degree to which this lack of attention is ubiquitous among state courts is starkly demonstrated by close examination of citations by the California Supreme Court, probably the state court that has the greatest influence and is the most willing to depart from established doctrine. Merryman's (1977) study of citations by the California court shows the court's increasing reliance on law reviews and decreasing attention to legal reference books, such as encyclopedias (see Table 2-1). It also shows, though, how little the court considered nonlegal sources. Through 1960, such references were nonexistent. Even in 1970, only one nonlegal source was cited three or more times, and that was *Webster's Dictionary*. Social science authorities were essentially absent. Although it is a court that, as lawyers say, "makes a lot of law," even the California Supreme Court apparently is reluctant to consider social science evidence.

CONCLUSIONS

The notion that the judiciary may look outside the law itself for answers to legal problems appears well established, at least

TABLE 2-1. Citations by the California Supreme Court

Type of authority	Citations per opinion		
	1950	1960	1970
Primary legal sources	14.997	15.147	15.088
Law reviews	0.292	0.429	0.603
Restatements	0.107	0.041	0.051
Legal encyclopedias	0.450	0.271	0.092
Annotations	0.198	0.124	0.070
Other secondary sources	0.456	0.424	0.423
Legal treatises	—	0.394	0.332
Reference (dictionaries)	—	0.029	0.037
Nonlegal authorities	—	0.000	0.055
Total secondary sources	1.503	1.288	1.239
Total	16.500	16.435	16.327

Note. The data are from Merryman (1977).

for certain kinds of cases. Although state courts are less likely than their federal counterparts to consider secondary authorities, a substantial proportion of opinions in appellate state cases include such citations, especially in those courts that are known for carving new doctrines.

The increasing reliance on secondary sources coincided with postrealist expansion in legal doctrines. Notably, the use of law reviews in U.S. Supreme Court opinions mushroomed in the years of the Warren Court. With the expansion of constitutional interpretation in such areas as equal protection and due process, attention to novel legal theories (usually disseminated through law reviews) increased, and proportionately less attention was given by judges in justifying their decisions to more traditional secondary statements of the law.

Citation of nonlegal sources by the Court also increased substantially during the years of the Warren Court. Nonetheless, reliance on nonlegal authorities remains a rare phenomenon still not well entrenched on the legal landscape. As of 1970, even the most innovative state courts almost never cited social science authorities. Consideration of such evidence by state appellate courts may have increased somewhat since then because of its increased development in trial records (see, e.g., *Arizona v. Chapple*, 1983; *Hovey v. Superior Court*, 1980). However, notice of social science authorities by state courts is probably still rare.

On the U.S. Supreme Court, Justices who have relied on extralegal authority generally have been the most liberal members of the Court—that is, those most receptive to change and most strongly committed to political, economic, and social reform (Rosen, 1972). Rosen contended that liberal Justices are more likely to make use of social science citations because they are less hesitant to issue decisions that cannot be explained solely by reference to established precedents. In a later publication, he elaborated this view: "Social science engenders conservative suspicion simply because liberal courts and counsel are likely to be the proponents of social science findings as justification of substantive legal change, whereas conservatives with precedent ready at hand have less need for additional ammunition to fight change" (Rosen, 1980, p. 11).

Rosen's conclusion was supported by the findings of Newland (1961), who studied U.S. Supreme Court opinions from 1907 to 1957. Newland noted 13 Justices who cited a learned journal two or fewer times during that period. At least 12 of them were not considered liberals (Rosen, 1972). For example, of these 13 Justices, all who sat on the bench from 1932 to 1937 opposed the New Deal. Of the eight Justices who cited learned journals most frequently, two were leading legal realists (Brandeis and Cardozo), and the other six were Roosevelt appointees who usually are regarded as having been liberals.

The high correlation between judicial ideology and frequency of citation of secondary sources by individual Justices suggests that Rosen's hypothesis is still largely valid. However, reliance on social science is sufficiently acceptable now that factors other than ideology may affect the frequency of citation. For example, although he usually was considered a swing vote on the Burger Court, Justice Blackmun has been especially likely to find, cite, and clearly rely on extralegal authorities in cases involving medical or scientific expertise (Schlesinger & Nesse, 1980). Blackmun's comfort with such evidence is probably related to his scientific background, first as a mathematics major and later as counsel for the Mayo Clinic.

Although certainly on the right wing of the Court, Chief Justice Burger also commonly cited nonlegal sources. Nonetheless, Melton (Chapter 9, this volume) argues he did so in fundamentally conservative ways, tending to use extralegal authorities to corroborate the rationality of state action without assessing their validity or sometimes even their applicability.

THE U.S. SUPREME COURT'S USE OF SOCIAL SCIENCE IN CHILDREN'S CASES

The still-shaky status of social science in judicial decisionmaking may be less tenuous in children's cases. As Koocher has noted in Chapter 1, psychological issues, particularly as related to competency, are ubiquitous in children's cases. Use of social science evidence at trial also seems to be common in children's litigation, at least major test cases (Mnookin, 1985), and juvenile and family courts have had a realist flavor since their inception at the turn of the century. Also, judges may find children's cases an irresistible opportunity to expound on their views about primary social institutions, such as the family (Melton, 1984; Perry & Melton, 1984).

The case in Daniels's (1983) study of U.S. Supreme Court opinions that produced the longest opinion, the most secondary citations generally, and the most nonlegal citations specifically was in fact a children's case, *Parham v. J.R.* (1979), which concerned whether parents may "volunteer" their children for admission to psychiatric facilities without a hearing. Although the Court has been described as careless, unscholarly, and often simply mistaken in its approach to the social facts related to the issue (Perry & Melton, 1984), *Parham* may nonetheless be illustrative of a greater willingness to seek and consider child development research than other social science sources.

To test this hypothesis, we conducted a study of citations by the U.S. Supreme Court in children's cases. We focused on the Supreme Court for two reasons. First, previous citation studies indicated that the Supreme Court is the most likely to consider social science materials. Second, the Supreme Court's citations tend to have a life of their own and to affect other courts' vision of social reality (Marvell, 1978; Perry & Melton, 1984).

METHOD

Cases were chosen for the study by referring to *West's Federal Practice Digest*. Using more than 400 headings, this widely used indexing service generates summaries of the issues discussed in all federal decisions. Three of the *West's* headings concern children and families: "Infants," "Parent and Child," and "Children Out-of-Wedlock." All cases listed under these headings and decided by the U.S. Supreme Court during 1975–1984 were selected for the study. The search in *Federal Practice Digest* uncovered 24 such cases, in which 54 opinions (8 unanimous, 16 majority, 15 concurring, and 15 dissenting) were published in 538 pages of text.

For purposes of comparison, Daniels's (1983) categories of citation were generally used to tabulate the frequency of citation of various types of secondary sources. Unlike Daniels, however, we counted primary legal citations in order to have a baseline against which to compare use of secondary sources. In that regard, only citations to prior judicial decisions were counted. Statutes, regulations, administrative orders, attorney generals' opinions, and legislative materials were omitted from the study. The use of these materials appeared to vary widely with the type of case before the court, the framing of the issues, and the Justice writing the opinion. References to prior court decisions seemed to be used more consistently and therefore to reflect better the incidence of citation to traditional legal authority. However, as a result of the omission, the figures we report about citation of primary authorities are conservative.

Multiple references to the same source in the same paragraph or footnote were counted as only one citation. References to sources without a page or section number were not tabulated as citations. For example, allusion to the "*Gault* line of cases" was considered a reference to a general concept rather than to the source itself. When a cited source included a reference to another source (e.g., a quotation includes allusion to other sources), only the cited source was counted, because the judicial author probably examined only the first source.

The distinction between legal and nonlegal periodicals, and legal and nonlegal treatises, was made by a process of elimination. A source was identified as a legal periodical if it was indexed within the *Index to Legal Periodicals*. All other periodicals were classified as nonlegal. In distinguishing between legal and nonlegal treatises (books), a three-step decision rule was used. First, the title of the treatise was reviewed to determine whether it made any reference to law or a topic peculiar to the legal system, such as *habeas corpus*, with no indication of an accompanying empirical basis. Then the title was examined to determine whether it indicated an attempt to provide standards or goals for areas such as criminal or juvenile justice, with no indication of an accompanying empirical basis. Finally, we consulted the reference series *Law Books 1876–1981: Books and Serials on Law and Its Related Subjects* to determine whether the treatise was listed. If the treatise did not meet any of the three criteria, it was counted as nonlegal.

Results

Type of Citation

A summary of the Court's citations per opinion is presented in Table 2-2. Overall, the Court displayed a pronounced tendency to rely on prior judicial opinions, especially its own, to substantiate the positions taken in children's cases. During the decade studied, the Court cited cases 1,335 times, but it cited secondary sources only 197 times. About two-thirds (68.2%) of the citations to prior cases were to the Court's own decisions. The remainder were divided about equally between state courts (16.8%) and lower federal courts (15.1%). Most of the opinions (92.6%) contained a primary citation, but only about half (51.9%) referred to a secondary source.

TABLE 2-2.   Citations by the U.S. Supreme Court

	Citations per opinion	
Type of authority	All cases, 1978[a] (319 opinions)	Children's cases, 1975–1984 (54 opinions)
Primary legal sources	—	24.722
Legal periodicals	1.075	1.463
Legal treatises	0.903	0.852
Restatements	0.066	0.037
Annotations, encyclopedias	0.028	0.000
Total secondary legal sources	2.072	2.352
Nonlegal periodicals	0.154	0.222
Nonlegal treatises	0.376	0.444
Reference	0.038	0.000
Government reports	0.176	0.630
Statistics	0.072	0.000
Total nonlegal sources	0.815	1.296
Total secondary sources	2.887	3.648
Total citations	—	28.370

[a] The data in this column are from Daniels (1983).

Although the more limited time span covered by Daniels (1983) does not permit direct statistical comparison with our data, the frequencies of citation in the children's cases in this sample did not differ markedly in absolute terms from those found in Daniels's general survey of the 1978 term (see Table 2-2). Just as for general cases, opinions in children's cases cited case law as their principal authority. However, the children's cases appeared to rely somewhat more heavily on law reviews and nonlegal sources. Of particular note, children's cases were especially apt to cite official reports. Government reports were cited almost three times more frequently than nonlegal periodicals in children's cases. Government reports were 3½ times more commonly cited in children's cases than general cases. These statistics in fact underestimate the reliance on official reports. Several of the nonlegal treatises cited in children's cases were reports published by professional organizations or privately published reports of government commissions (e.g., Hobbs, 1975; Joint Commission on Mental Health of Children, 1969).

The legal secondary sources cited were much more diverse than in Daniels's (1983) general sample. A total of 40 journals were represented among the 79 citations of legal periodicals; no law review published more than 6 of the articles cited. The most commonly cited journals were the *Harvard Law Review* (ranked 1st in Daniels's study of opinions in the 1978 term), the *Stanford Law Review* (13th), and the *Journal of Family Law* (uncited). Only five articles were cited in more than one opinion, and no author contributed more than one article cited by the Court. Among the 46 citations of legal treatises, there were 31 titles, only 4 of which were cited in more than one opinion.

As in Daniels's study, the nonlegal sources cited were also diverse. Six different journals and 19 different authors were represented among the 12 citations of nonlegal periodicals, with only one journal referenced in two different opinions. Among the 24 citations of nonlegal treatises, 22 titles were present, with none cited in more than one opinion.

Latency of Citation

Legal periodicals were cited in children's cases a mean of 11.0 years after publication, and nonlegal periodicals appeared in judicial opinions an average of 8.3 years later. However, the median for these two categories was an identical 6 years. Cited legal periodicals tended to be very recent or quite old. Almost 40% of the legal articles, compared with 20% of the nonlegal articles, had been published within 5 years of citation by the Court. On the other hand, almost one-fourth of the legal articles but none of the nonlegal articles had been published more than 15 years prior to citation.

Legal treatises showed a distribution similar to legal periodicals, although older volumes were relied upon even more. Cited legal treatises had been published a mean of 28.4 years and a median of 10.5 years prior to the opinion date. One-fourth had been published within 5 years of citation, and about 40% had been available for more than 15 years. Nonlegal treatises, like nonlegal periodicals, did not show such extremes (mean latency = 8.9 years; median latency = 8 years). Only 14.3% had been published within 5 years of citation, and even fewer (4.8%) more than 15 years prior to citation.

Government reports were cited in a manner similar to the citation of legal authorities. Almost one-half had been published within the previous 5 years, and 17.4% had appeared more than 15 years prior to citation. Mean length of latency was 8.9 years, with a median of 6 years.

Individual Jurists

Among the seven Justices on the Court during the entire study period, the number of opinions in children's cases was relatively evenly distributed. Except for Justice White, who wrote only two opinions, each of the Justices wrote five to nine opinions. The division of the Court was more complicated than its general ideological divisions. The liberal and conservative wings were equally represented in majority and dissenting opinions. Indeed, of the three majority opinions written by Justice Marshall, Justice Rehnquist joined in two of them. Justice Marshall joined in one of the two majority opinions written by Justice Rehnquist.

Similarly, no clear ideological bias was demonstrated in the Court's use of secondary sources in children's cases (see Table 2-3). The two Justices who cited secondary sources most fre-

TABLE 2-3. Citations by Individual Supreme Court Justices

Justice	Pages text issued	Primary cites per pages of text	Secondary cites per pages of text
Blackmun	75	3.03	0.28
Brennan	49	2.02	0.78
Burger	95	2.13	0.64
Douglas	1	5.00	0.00
Marshall	106	2.34	0.34
O'Connor	5	1.20	0.40
Powell	66	2.92	0.12
Rehnquist	83	2.55	0.19
Stevens	28	2.96	0.11
Stewart	21	2.19	0.57
White	3	0.33	0.00
Per curiam	6	1.33	0.00
Total	538	2.46	0.36

quently were Brennan, a liberal, and Burger, a conservative. However, a clear pattern did emerge that those Justices who were relatively likely to cite secondary sources were relatively unlikely to cite primary sources. Among the eight Justices who wrote more than 20 pages of text in the cases studied, frequency of citation of primary sources was strongly inversely correlated with frequency of citation of secondary sources ($r = -.88$, $p < .01$).

DISCUSSION

Children's law is a relatively unsettled area of law. Not only are traditional family structures in flux (Conger, 1981), but many of the critical policy questions about distribution of power among child, family, and state began to come before the courts only recently. Until its decisions in *In re Gault* (1967) and *Tinker v. Des Moines Independent School District* (1969), the U.S. Supreme Court had never announced that children are "persons" with constitutional rights. With this declaration, the door was open to consideration of a wide range of questions about the limits of children's autonomy and privacy. Therefore, most of the children's cases decided by the Supreme Court have arisen in the past two decades. Competing values are at stake even among child advocates—protection of children and promotion of their autonomy (Melton, 1983a; Mnookin, 1978)—and little precedent exists for resolving the resulting dilemmas. With such conflicts in values, the striking inconsistency of how the Court divides in children's cases is understandable. When family cases present "serious problems of policy disguised as questions of constitutional law" (*Parham v. J.R.*, 1979, opinion of Justice Stewart, pp. 624–625) in a virtual vacuum of law, judicial philosophy may provide little guidance for decisionmaking.

With such ambiguity, a disproportionate reliance on secondary sources might be expected. Some difference does appear to exist, although not strikingly so in the aggregate. Despite an absence of clear precedent, some Justices apparently choose to continue to look for guidance in the Court's previous holdings; others look to descriptions of social reality. Even for the latter group, however, these "hard cases" seem to require *authority* as well as facts (cf. Monahan & Walker, 1986). Although they seek an understanding of social reality that would inform their judgments, they look primarily for "official" statements of social fact. Such statements not only are more authoritative; they may be more easily assimilable to the Court.

In general, the study of children's cases in the Supreme Court leads to two conclusions for child development researchers who wish to reach the Court with their findings: First, publish in law reviews (however, for children's cases, the choice of law review may be less crucial than for most issues). Second, seek state-of-the-art declarations by professional organizations, and become involved in both organization- and government-sponsored task forces.

DOES CHILD DEVELOPMENT RESEARCH REACH THE JUDICIARY?

The study just described did not control, of course, for whether social science research was available to assist the Court. Therefore, in a second study, we examined whether the work of a selected group of child development researchers had affected judicial decisions. For this study, the universe of cases studied included all cases available on LEXIS, a computerized data base of judicial opinions and other legal materials, not just opinions of the Supreme Court for a particular time period.

METHOD

The search focused on citations to the publications of members of the initial 1980 study group, "Developmental Factors in Competence to Consent" (Melton, Koocher, & Saks, 1983). As Koocher (Chapter 1, this volume) explains, competency is a common question of legal policy and case adjudication that involves significant empirical questions. The members of the study group tended to focus their work on children and families, represented a diverse range of professional experience and interests, had generated sufficient publications so that their work was relatively easily accessible, and had published their work in varied journals and treatises. The members of the study group who were used in the search included Joel Alpert, Donald Bersoff, Norma Feshbach, Thomas Grisso, Michael Grodin, Patricia Keith-Spiegel, Gerald Koocher, Robert Mnookin, Michael Saks, June Tapp, Walter Wadlington, and Lois Weithorn. The data base searched included all reported opinions through May 1985.

Unlike the preceding study, in which individual citations were counted, the primary dependent variable in this study was the number of opinions in which a given publication was cited. The different measure was chosen in order to assess awareness of information rather than its impact and to provide some control for the vagaries of judicial writing style.

RESULTS

A total of 26 publications produced by this group of 13 authors were cited in 100 separate judicial opinions, 5 of which cited 2 of the publications. Seven of the authors were cited, in a range of 1 to 30 opinions (median = 10). The most journal or treatise titles by a single author cited was 11. The most citations generated by a single publication was 30. Publications on child and family issues accounted for 68 of the citations.

Citations appeared in 17 federal court opinions, including 7 U.S. Supreme Court opinions, 8 circuit court opinions, and 2 district court opinions. The remaining 83 opinions were issued by the appellate courts of 24 states. New York accounted for almost one-fourth of the state court citations (20), followed by California and Massachusetts (8 each). Cases originating within the 10 states in the First, Second, and Third Judicial Circuits (roughly the Northeastern region) accounted for 42.9% of the citations of publications of members of the study group. By contrast, a review of *West's Federal Practice Digest* and *West's General Digest* showed that from 1975 to 1984, only 21.0% of federal cases dealing with children's issues, and during a 6-month period of 1982, 24.3% of the state cases, originated in this region.

For a broader perspective, 838 cases on children's issues were reported by state courts for just *6 months* of 1982, and 557 federal cases on children's issues were decided for the *decade* of 1975–1984. Although the citations of the work of the study group were dwarfed by comparison, it appeared that citation by federal courts was disproportionately large, although children's issues were and remain matters largely reserved to the states (see Takanishi & Melton, Chapter 4, this volume).

Legal periodicals accounted for 82.9% of the citations in opinions and 73.1% of the titles cited. Overall, 88.6% of the citations in opinions and 84.6% of the titles cited were drawn from legal secondary sources, even though most members of the study group published most of their work in nonlegal sources. State and federal courts did not differ in that regard. The single article from a nonlegal periodical that was cited was Mnookin's (1973) article on foster care in the *Harvard Educational Review*, an article on a legal topic by a well-known law professor that was subsequently cited in law reviews.

As in the preceding study, the specific sources of the articles cited were diverse. The 19 law review articles came from 16 different journals; only the *Virginia Law Review*, which published 4 of these articles, was responsible for publishing more than 1 article. Of the 11 journals that were cited by the Supreme

Court in children's cases in the previous study, 7 were included in the citations of study group members' work.

An average of 4.7 years elapsed between year of publication and year of citation. The latency for federal courts ($M = 2.7$ years) was less than for state courts ($M = 5.2$ years), $t (102) = 2.75$, $p < .01$. About 60% of the citations were for articles published within the previous 5 years.

Discussion

The results of this study are consistent with the picture presented by the preceding study and other studies of court behavior: To reach the courts directly, research needs to be published in law reviews.

Also consistent with previous work, it appears that federal courts are the most responsive to extralegal sources even in children's cases, where most of the legal questions traditionally are regarded as state issues (e.g., matrimony and divorce law). Federal courts are disproportionately responsive to interdisciplinary work, and they apparently learn of it more quickly than state courts.

In terms of the specific question of the impact of the 1980 study group on children's competency, the frequency of citation has been less than overwhelming. Nonetheless, given the fact that just 2 years had elapsed since publication of the study group's report (Melton et al., 1983) and that most of the related research also was quite recent, the number of citations in absolute terms shows some promise. Related law review articles— the most likely to be cited—were even more recent (e.g., Melton, 1983b, 1984; Perry & Melton, 1984; see also King, 1985). In view of the average latency of citation, the preponderance of citations to publications of this study group would be expected in the next few years.

DOES CHILD DEVELOPMENT RESEARCH REACH LEGAL COMMENTATORS?

The preceding studies have demonstrated that the courts tend to rely on law reviews when they reach beyond case law to substantiate their opinions. Traditionally, law reviews have provided limited access for social science researchers wishing to publish their work. However, it may not be necessary for social scientists to publish their research in law reviews. Sufficient dissemination may result if those commentators publishing within law reviews refer to social science research appearing elsewhere.

To determine the frequency with which this alternative means of dissemination occurs, a study similar to the preceding one was conducted. Using LEXIS's law review data base, we counted the number of references to publications of the members of the study group listed previously.

METHOD

Only 26 of the 478 journals listed in the *Index of Legal Periodicals* were available on LEXIS at the time we conducted our search. However, these 26 journals included the 8 law reviews most frequently cited in the U.S. Supreme Court's 1978 opinions, and 16 of the top 21 (Daniels, 1983). Therefore, the citations made in the journals included on LEXIS were probably the most likely to have been noted by the courts.

In addition, only recent volumes were available; generally, they covered late 1982 to late 1985. However, because all of the members of this research group were (and continue to be) active authors and several were/are young scholars, such volumes were the most likely to contain citations to their work.

Essentially the same method was used as in the previous two studies. All references within these law reviews to the publications produced by the research group were noted. A citation was coded only once if the reference was repeated within the same paragraph or footnote. A citation was not recorded if the researcher's name was listed without accompanying bibliographic information. Because the goal of this study was to determine whether the publications produced by the research group might be having an indirect rather than a direct effect on the courts, a citation was not recorded when one of the members of the study group was listed as the article's author. Also omitted were references contained within lists of recent publications that simply named the reference without accompanying commentary about its content.

RESULTS

A total of 98 articles cited at least one of the publications of members of this research group. Of the 26 journals on LEXIS, 25 contained at least one such citation. Altogether, 309 citations appeared in the 98 articles.

Publications by 9 of the 13 study group members were cited in law review articles, including 2 members who had not been cited by the judiciary. The courts had cited 26 publications by members of the group, but the law reviews cited 52 such publications. Only 6 publications cited by the courts were not cited in a law review article, and 3 of those were published from 1966 to 1972, perhaps outside the range of interest of these contemporary law review articles. While the judiciary referred to 19 law review articles produced by this group of researchers but only 1 article appearing in a nonlegal periodical, the law reviews cited 20 law review articles and 11 articles in nonlegal periodicals.

For comparison, the 26 law reviews studied published 1,351 articles in 1984 alone.[1] For this study, an average of 3.2 volumes per journal were available. To extrapolate from these figures, about 2% of the law review articles appearing during the period studied contained a citation to the publications of this research group. Perhaps a more valid comparison is with law review articles focused on children's issues. Using the same categories as in the previous two studies (i.e., "Parent and Child," "Infants," and "Illegitimacy"), we conducted a search in the *Index to Legal Periodicals* for articles published during the period studied by the LEXIS law reviews. This search turned up 25 articles, 11 of which included citations to publications produced by the members of this study group.

Although more diversity was noted in the sources of cita-

1. We are indebted to Cindy Stark, librarian at Albany Law School, for compiling this figure.

tions by the law reviews than by the courts, most still relied primarily on publications in legal periodicals. Furthermore, the citations from law reviews were used more frequently. Only 38.5% of the titles cited were from law reviews; however, these citations appeared in 53.2% of the articles that included any such citations, and 68.3% of the total citations were to legal periodicals. The corresponding figures for legal treatises were 30.8%, 23.4%, and 15.5%, respectively. For nonlegal periodicals, the figures were 21.2%, 19.9%, and 14.6%. The remainder of the citations were to nonlegal treatises and unpublished manuscripts.

The two full-time law professors in the group at the time the study group was held (i.e., Mnookin and Wadlington) accounted for 71.8% of the total citations, a figure apparently due to their primary use of law reviews as publication outlets for their work. Although neither Mnookin nor Wadlington is a social scientist, their reliance on empirical research, integration of it with their legal writing, and occasional collaboration in original empirical research made their inclusion in the study appropriate.

Of the nonlegal periodical articles cited in the law reviews, all either appeared in journals that routinely address legal issues but are not included in *Index to Legal Periodicals* (e.g., *Victimology, Law and Human Behavior*), or included a legal catchphrase in their title (e.g., "First Amendment," "best interests").

The 20 law review articles cited were published in 16 different journals. Although 6 of these journals were among the 10 journals cited most frequently by the U.S. Supreme Court in its 1978 terms, 6 others were not cited at all (Daniels, 1983). Using Daniels's data, we made a median split of the 16 journals according to the frequency of their citation by the Court. The study group members' articles that appeared in the 8 journals favored by the Court were cited 183 times in the law reviews studied. The articles published in the remaining 8 journals provided only 28 citations. Even when weighting was done for the number of articles published in each group, a substantial gap in frequency of citation remained.

Discussion

The members of the 1980 study group, "Developmental Factors in Competence to Consent" (Melton *et al.*, 1983), have been more successful in reaching legal scholars than the courts. The citation rate in articles on children's law (44%) is impressive, given the facts that some of the articles were on topics outside the scholarship of the authors studied and (as noted in the preceding study) that much of their work has been quite recent.

It is noteworthy that under 2% of the articles in the frequently cited, high-prestige journals available on LEXIS concerned children's issues. This lack of attention to children's issues perhaps reflects the low prestige of family law, although the rise in scholarly attention to basic issues of children's status may be increasing the stature of the field. In terms of dissemination, this low frequency of publication of articles on children's issues is a double-edged sword. On the one hand, it is relatively easy to have an individual impact. There are few recognized scholars in children's law among both law professors and social scientists. Therefore, careful interdisciplinary scholarship with relatively little effort focused upon dissemination may reach a high proportion of the active scholars in the field and may be cited in a high proportion of relevant articles. On the other hand, it may be especially difficult for authors on children's issues, particularly scholars not affiliated with prestigious law schools, to succeed in publishing their work in the law reviews that are likely to be cited frequently.

The infrequency of major law reviews' publication of articles on children's law may explain the U.S. Supreme Court's reliance on a broader range of law reviews in children's cases than is common in other areas of law. At the same time, this study clearly indicates that publication in high-prestige journals does increase the probability of citation, at least in other high-prestige journals. Publication in a "national" law review is clearly the easiest way of reaching legal scholars and probably legal policymakers. As an alternative, social scientists should seek to publish their work in specialized law reviews (e.g., *Family Law Quarterly, Journal of Family Law*). Given the dispersion of legal scholarship on children's issues, such publication is most likely to result in works being found by lawyers searching for authorities on a particular topic. In fact, our study of U.S. Supreme Court citations found that the *Journal of Family Law* was as commonly cited as the highest-prestige journals in children's cases.

This study also showed the law reviews to be more diverse—but not much more so—than courts in their search for authority. Although law reviews did cite some nonlegal periodicals, they cited only articles that were explicitly interdisciplinary in content and often in publication outlet. The message is clear: If social scientists wish their work to reach legal commentators, they must learn to "think like lawyers" and write for a legal audience, or at least to collaborate with scholars who are skilled in legal analysis. Without an integration of the findings with legal questions, even very relevant research is unlikely to be noticed by its intended audience.

In that regard, it should be noted that the "social science" citation counts in all three studies are somewhat inflated, if they are taken to mean citations of empirical findings or social science theory. For example, in the second and third study, besides the inclusion of the sometimes "pure" legal writing of Mnookin and Wadlington, the law review articles included among the citations to other authors in the study group were cited at times for their legal reviews and analyses rather than their discussion of social science research.

CONCLUSIONS

In the past 40 years, the use of secondary authority has become commonplace on the U.S. Supreme Court and, to a lesser extent, the lower federal courts and the state appellate courts. This trend has been both a cause and an effect of the expansion of constitutional doctrines and the reshaping of judicial roles in response to realist and postrealist critics of the law. These shifts are especially noteworthy in children's law, where most of the major cases have been decided within the past two decades.

Nonetheless, the use of social science is still controversial and rather uncommon, especially in state courts. Courts appear unsure of whether and how to use social science to examine the policy questions that they have been asked to decide in recent decades. As a result, with the exception of a few judges who "specialize" in cases involving scientific expertise, reliance on social science is still largely a "liberal" practice of judges who have an expansive view of the judiciary's role in shaping legal doctrine and protecting disenfranchised groups.

This pattern is not well entrenched in children's law, where social science materials and other secondary sources are used somewhat more often and ideological lines are not rigid. Even in children's cases, however, the law reviews are by far the most commonly cited secondary authorities. When judges move beyond the law reviews, they still look for publications generated by recognized authorities. Therefore, official reports are favored nonlegal sources.

Whether one examines judicial opinions directly or tracks the dissemination of social science research to the judiciary through legal commentators, the message is the same: For social science to reach legal policymakers, social scientists must learn to use the law reviews, especially the most prestigious law reviews, to publish their work. "Pure" social science, even when it has significant application to legal policy, is unlikely to be found; if found, it is unlikely to be cited unless the findings are placed into legal context. If social science is to assist the legal system, the work must be consciously interdisciplinary—framed in terms of legal questions and, ideally, reported in legal periodicals.

Although the overall picture is one still of minimal use even of obviously relevant child development research, we are reasonably optimistic about the future influence of such research on children's law. The "hit rate" is high for citation of child development research in the law reviews, at least when directly reported at some point in other law reviews. The availability of legally sophisticated social scientists and empirically sophisticated lawyers in children's law is a recent and still infrequent phenomenon. However, a start has been made toward generation of legally relevant child development research, often produced by interdisciplinary teams, with attention given to optimizing the dissemination of the research (as reflected by the establishment of the study group that has compiled the present book). Therefore, although researchers must be prepared for some disappointments in diffusion of their work, we anticipate substantially greater use of child development research in the next few years.

This conclusion might be tempered by the changes currently taking place in the federal judiciary. Although the years of the Burger Court were, for the most part, not ones of great judicial innovation, a decidedly conservative swing is likely as a result of the "Reaganization" of the federal judiciary at both the circuit court and the district court levels (Goldman, 1985). Soon the majority of federal judges will be Reagan appointees, who generally have shared their benefactor's social and political values and his concept of a limited judicial role. It is possible that the federal judiciary's consideration of secondary sources will diminish accordingly. However, we suspect that changes in that direction may be less marked than many expect, at least in regard to children's cases. As we have shown, the clash of values in children's cases is not easily characterized conceptually or empirically as "liberal" versus "conservative." Moreover, several of President Reagan's most heralded judicial appointments have been of conservative law professors (e.g., Richard Posner) who unquestionably have an analytic, conservative approach to the law but who also have been active in interdisciplinary scholarship, usually in the context of economic studies of law. They may look farther afield than their predecessors for theories of law, and they may be especially open to empirical analysis of questions of social fact. Finally, the social sciences may be "coming of age" in that this culture and the courts which reflect it may be becoming more accepting of its research use in general.

The opportunities for influence are and probably will continue to be present in the legal system. However, for such opportunities to be fulfilled, methods of diffusing research and perhaps of formulating research questions must change. Perhaps this book will serve as a landmark in movement toward such reform of the enterprise of child development research as a prelude to guiding the law.

REFERENCES

Allport, F.H., Allport, G.H., Babcock, C., Bernard, V.W., Bruner, J.S., Cantril, H., Chein, I., Clark, K.B., Clark, M.P., Cook, S.W., Dai, B., Davis, A., Frenkel-Brunswik, E., Gist, N.P., Katz, D., Klineberg, O., Krech, D., Lee, A.M., MacIver, R.M., Merton, R.K., Murphy, G., Newcomb, T.M., Redfield, R., Reid, I.D., Rose, A.M., Saenger, G., Sanford, R.N., Sargent, S.S., Smith, S.B., Stouffer, S.A., Warner, W., & Williams, R.M. (1953). The effects of segregation and the consequences of desegregation: A social science statement. *Minnesota Law Review, 37,* 429–440.

Arizona v. Chapple, 135 Ariz. 281, 660 P.2d 1208 (1983).

Benitez *ex rel.* Catala v. Collazo, 584 F. Supp. 267 (D.P.R. 1984).

Brandeis, L.D. (1916). Living law. *Illinois Law Review, 10,* 461–471.

Brown v. Board of Education, 347 U.S. 483 (1954).

Burrus, B.R. (1962). American legal realism. *Howard Law Journal, 8,* 36–51.

Cardozo, B.N. (1921). *The nature of the judicial process.* New Haven, CT: Yale University Press.

Conger, J.J. (1981). Freedom and commitment: Families, youth, and social change. *American Psychologist, 36,* 1475–1484.

Craven, J.B. (1975). The impact of social science evidence on the judge: A personal comment. *Law and Contemporary Problems, 59,* 150–156.

Daniels, W. (1983). "Far beyond the law reports": Secondary source citations in United States Supreme Court opinions October terms 1900, 1940, and 1978. *Law Library Journal, 76,* 1–47.

Friedman, L.M., Kagan, R.A., Cartwright, B., & Wheeler, S. (1981). State supreme courts: A century of style and citation. *Stanford Law Review, 33,* 773–818.

Goldman, S. (1985). Reaganizing the judiciary: The first term appointments. *Judicature, 68,* 313–329.

Harding v. Kuhlmann, 588 F. Supp. 1315 (S.D.N.Y. 1984).

Hobbs, N. (1975). *The futures of children: Categories, labels, and their consequences.* San Francisco: Jossey-Bass.

Holmes, O.W. (1897). The path of the law. *Harvard Law Review, 10,* 457–478.

Hovey v. Superior Court, 28 Cal. 3d 1, 168 Cal. Rptr. 128, 616 P.2d 1301 (1980).

In re Gault, 387 U.S. 1 (1967).

Johnson, F.M. (1976). The Constitution and the federal district judge. *Texas Law Review, 54,* 903–916.

Joint Commission on Mental Health of Children. (1969). *Crisis in child mental health: Challenge for the 1970's.* New York: Harper & Row.

Kalven, H., Jr., & Zeisel, H. (1966). *The American jury.* Boston: Little, Brown.

Kaufman, C. (1980). The scientific method in legal thought: Legal realism and the fourteen principles of justice. *St. Mary's Law Journal, 12,* 77–112.

Kaufman, I.R. (1984). The anatomy of decision making. *Fordham Law Review, 53,* 1–22.

King, P.A. (1985). Treatment and minors: Issues not involving lifesaving treatment. *Journal of Family Law, 23*, 241–265.

Konopka, A.F. (1980). Applied social research as evidence in litigation. In M.J. Saks & C.H. Baron (Eds.), *The use/nonuse/misuse of applied social research in the courts* (pp. 129–135). Cambridge, MA: Abt.

Llewellyn, K.N. (1962). *Jurisprudence: Realism in theory and practice.* Chicago: University of Chicago Press.

Loh, W.D. (1981). Psycholegal research: Past and present. *Michigan Law Review, 79*, 659–707.

Maru, O. (1976). Measuring the impact of legal periodicals. *American Bar Foundation Journal,* 227–249.

Marvell, T.B. (1978). *Appellate courts and lawyers: Information gathering in the adversary system.* Westport, CT: Greenwood Press.

McMillan, J.B. (1975). Social science and the district court: The observations of a journeyman trial judge. *Law and Contemporary Problems, 39*, 157–163.

Melton, G.B. (1983a). *Child advocacy: Psychological issues and interventions.* New York: Plenum.

Melton, G.B. (1983b). Minors and privacy: Are legal and psychological concepts compatible? *Nebraska Law Review, 62*, 455–493.

Melton, G.B. (1984). Developmental psychology and the law: The state of the art. *Journal of Family Law, 22*, 445–482.

Melton, G.B. (Ed.). (1985). *Nebraska Symposium on Motivation: Vol. 33. The law as a behavioral instrument.* Lincoln: University of Nebraska Press.

Melton, G.B., Koocher, G.P., & Saks, M.J. (Eds.). (1983). *Children's competence to consent.* New York: Plenum.

Merryman, J.H. (1977). Toward a theory of citations: An empirical study of the citation practice of the California Supreme Court in 1950, 1960 and 1970. *Southern California Law Review, 50*, 381–428.

Mnookin, R.H. (1973). Foster care: In whose best interest? *Harvard Educational Review, 43*, 599–638.

Mnookin, R.H. (1978). Children's rights: Beyond kiddie libbers and child savers. *Journal of Clinical Child Psychology, 7*, 163–167.

Mnookin, R.H. (Ed.). (1985). *In the interest of children: Advocacy, law reform, and public policy.* New York: W.H. Freeman.

Monahan, J., & Walker, L. (1985). *Social science in law.* Mineola, NY: Foundation Press.

Monahan, J., & Walker, L. (1986). Social authority: Obtaining, evaluating, and establishing social science in law. *University of Pennsylvania Law Review, 134*, 477–517.

Muller v. Oregon, 208 U.S. 412 (1908).

Newland, C.A. (1961). Innovation in judicial technique: The Brandeis opinion. *Southwestern Social Science Quarterly, 42*, 22–31.

Parham v. J.R., 442 U.S. 584 (1979).

Paul, J. (1957–1958). Foundations of American realism. *West Virginia Law Review, 60*, 37–54.

Perry, G.S., & Melton, G.B. (1984). Precedential value of judicial notice of social facts: *Parham* as an example. *Journal of Family Law, 22,* 633–676.

Pound, R. (1909). Liberty of contract. *Yale Law Journal, 18,* 454–487.

Pound, R. (1910). Law in books and law in action. *American Law Review, 44,* 30–41.

Rennie v. Klein, 653 F.2d 836 (3rd Cir. 1981).

Rosen, P.L. (1972). *The Supreme Court and social science.* Urbana: University of Illinois Press.

Rosen, P.L. (1980). History and state of the art of applied social research in the courts. In M.J. Saks & C.H. Baron (Eds.), *The use/misuse/nonuse of applied social research in the courts* (pp. 9–15). Cambridge, MA: Abt.

Sanders, J., Rankin-Widgeon, B., Kalmuss, D., & Chesler, M. (1981–1982). The relevance of "irrelevant" testimony: Why lawyers use social science experts in school desegregation cases. *Law and Society Review, 16,* 403–428.

Schlesinger, S.R., & Nesse, J. (1980). Justice Harry Blackmun and empirical jurisprudence. *American University Law Review, 29,* 405–437.

Siu v. Johnson, 748 F.2d 238 (4th Cir. 1984).

Stevens, R. (1983). *Law school: Legal education in America from the 1850s to the 1980s.* Chapel Hill: University of North Carolina Press.

Tinker v. Des Moines Independent School District, 393 U.S. 503 (1969).

Unger, R.M. (1983). The critical legal studies movement. *Harvard Law Review, 96,* 561–676.

Wald, P.M. (1984). Thoughts on decisionmaking. *West Virginia Law Review, 87,* 1–12.

Wisdom, J.M. (1975). Random remarks on the role of social sciences in the judicial decision-making process in school desegregation cases. *Law and Contemporary Problems, 39,* 134–149.

Woodard, C. (1968). The limits of legal realism: An historical perspective. *Virginia Law Review, 54,* 689–739.

Youngberg v. Romeo, 457 U.S. 307 (1982).

II

Diffusion of Child Development Research to Legal Audiences

The Diffusion of Social Science Research to Policymakers: An Overview

CAROL H. WEISS

SOCIAL SCIENCE AND PUBLIC POLICY: THE "UNEASY PARTNERSHIP"

Social scientists often believe that they have learned something in their work that should contribute to public policy. Whether or not they have undertaken research with policy interests explicitly in mind, there often comes a point at which they say, "We have to get this message to the policymakers."

Many social scientists down through the decades have attempted to act upon that belief and make their voices heard (or their words read) in councils of action. They have usually expected that social science knowledge would have a direct influence on public policy, and all too often they have come away from the encounter disenchanted. With the occupational bent of social scientists, a fair number of them have proceeded to publish articles about their experience with policymakers and policymaking, and a large literature has accumulated over the years on the rocky road from social science to public policy. Gene Lyons's history (1969) of the relationship between social science and government from the beginning of the 20th century

Carol H. Weiss. Graduate School of Education, Harvard University, Cambridge, Massachusetts.

to the late 1960s is entitled *The Uneasy Partnership*, and the title is a splendidly fitting summary of experience.

Many thoughtful social scientists have gone beyond anecdotal accounts of policymakers' neglect of social science to analyze the reasons for the prevailing neglect. They have found that a host of obstacles litter the path from research to application. Some obstacles have to do with the limitations of social science—its shortcomings in producing valid knowledge (e.g., shortcomings in theory and in method, entanglement with values, emphasis on the past), and its lack of responsiveness to issues that policymakers care about. Some obstacles to policy use have to do with limitations at the policy end (e.g., fragmented responsibility, policymakers' short time horizon, their overwhelming concern with reconciling differences among interests rather than reaching "ideal" solutions). Some obstacles arise from ineffective communication: Most policymakers never hear about relevant research or hear only about sensational results, which are not necessarily the most valid. (For further discussion, see Weiss with Bucuvalas, 1980a, pp. 16–26.) Excellent analyses of the relationship between social science and policy appear in Lazarsfeld, Sewell, and Wilensky (1967), Frankel (1976), Rein (1976), Horowitz (1975), Rule (1978), Kallen, Kosse, Wagenaar, Klopregge, and Vorbeck (1982), Husen and Kogan (1984), and Holzner, Knorr, and Strasser (1983).

There is a historical literature as well, which describes the manner in which the social sciences gained professional status in the United States and their contributions to social thought and public policy (Furner, 1975; Haskell, 1977; Lyons, 1969; Ross, 1979). In addition, committees and commissions have deliberated on what the appropriate linkage should be between social science and government. A number of reports of this ilk have appeared (e.g., National Academy of Sciences, 1968; National Research Council, 1982; National Science Board, 1969). Because the commissions have been dominated by social scientists, it is not surprising that they have tended to recommend government support for the social sciences and more attention to social science conclusions.

In the past decade, something new has appeared—empirical research on the influence of social science on policy. More than mere descriptions of experience, these studies have set out, purposely and systematically, to examine the influence that the social sciences have had on policymaking. At least two dozen studies have now addressed the question of the uses of social science research, using a variety of policy areas, sites, and research methods. Notable examples are Caplan, Morrison, and Stanbaugh (1975), Berg *et al.* (1978), Rich (1981), Aaron (1978), Hayes (1982), Banting (1979), Weiss with Bucuvalas (1980a), and Kogan and Henkel (1983). Several important generalizations have begun to emerge that go beyond the insights of the speculative and anecdotal literature.

The lessons we have learned can be summarized as follows:

1. Direct efforts to alter specific policy provisions through social science are rarely successful.
2. Nevertheless, social science knowledge often comes into currency and affects the issues that policymakers think about and the ways they think about them.
3. This "enlightenment" function takes place through diverse channels, ranging from advisors and consultants to the mass media and interest groups.
4. As social science knowledge helps to reshape the policy agenda and the types of policy alternatives under debate, it can have far-reaching consequences—but usually on the main lines of policy rather than specific provisions, and sometimes after the lapse of considerable time.

THE INFLUENCE OF SOCIAL SCIENCE ON THE COURTS

Most of the recent empirical work has been done in administrative and legislative settings. Relatively little of it has examined the influence of social science on the courts. Although there have been informed analyses of social science and the judicial process (e.g., Mnookin, 1985; Rosen, 1972, 1977), the major themes of use-of-research literature are derived from research on executive and legislative bodies. I think that they apply to

some extent to courts as well. But courts have special characteristics that may make them more difficult to influence in some
ways and perhaps more responsive to social science in others.

In traditional litigation, courts are not particularly hospitable to the findings of social science research. By "traditional
litigation," I mean cases in which the parties initiate the case;
two individual parties are in contention; inquiry centers on
establishing right and remedy; litigants control the introduction
of evidence; and the trial judge assumes a largely passive and
reactive role (Chayes, 1976). In such cases, the trial court does
not choose which cases it will hear (although appellate courts
have considerable latitude). It has to deal with cases that come
up. Inasmuch as cases cover a diversity of issues, few judges
can specialize narrowly enough to become familiar with all the
relevant social science literature, even if they wish to. Each case
may present unique issues. Even juvenile/family court judges,
who do specialize to a degree, cannot master the range of social
science that applies to children.

Furthermore, in traditional litigation, judges rely on opposing attorneys to put the facts in evidence. Rarely do they
initiate the gathering of facts or theories on their own. Therefore, they tend to be captives of the social science proclivities
of counsel. If the attorneys in the case do not make use of social
science or social scientists, it is a rare judge who will go out to
seek social science on his or her own.

Traditional litigation focuses on individuals. Lawyers and
judges deal with specific people and organizations possessing
particular characteristics. Social scientists come to conclusions
about groups or classes ("employed mothers," "developmentally
disabled children"). Courts may be skeptical about applying
social science conclusions about categories of people to the specific individuals before them. A social science study may show
that most handicapped children profit from attending regular
school classes, but does that conclusion apply to little Lisa sitting
there on her mothers' lap? After all, social science conclusions
are probabilistic. At best, they tell us that 60% of a certain
category do such-and-such, or that these kinds of people under
this set of conditions are "significantly" more likely than other
kinds of people to have these outcomes. There is never cer-

tainty; no relationships reach 1.00. Judges are reluctant to assume that all individuals fit the generalization, particularly if they have Lisa or Mr. Greely in front of them and can seek a more specific, fine-grained determination of the facts.

In recent years, with the growth of "public law litigation," some of these traditional limits on the application of social science have diminished. Class actions have reduced the courts' concentration on a few individuals, and they have made the types of generalizations that social science produces much more relevant. It is now useful to know what the effects of transitional bilingual programs are for categories of students, at what age children generally understand the difference between "stories" and "facts," and what percentage of students classified as "educable mentally retarded" in school systems across the country turn out to be black.

Public law litigation also has a prospective orientation. It is not so much concerned with awarding monetary judgments to redress past wrongs as it is with enjoining future action or modifying the way that public agencies behave. The court, therefore, is less tied to events in the past. It has to consider whether threatened actions will in fact occur and with what consequences. In devising remedies, the court has to make estimates of the likely effects of a range of alternative programs. In this kind of predictive activity, the findings of social science are apt to be among the few sources of systematic information.

In public law cases, the judge often takes a more active role in factfinding. Judgments require complex information, have more far-reaching consequences, and involve the court on an ongoing basis over extended periods of time; these circumstances encourage a judge to help shape and organize the collection of information. In public law cases, judges have not infrequently turned to outsiders—masters, *amici*, panels, experts, advisory committees. Among the experts they have drawn upon are social scientists. They have asked social scientists to review existing research and indicate its applicability to the case in contention.

With all the increased hospitability of the judicial system to social science, obstacles remain. Social scientists are sometimes called upon for evidence on issues that the social sciences have not directly studied. They can say something about parallel situations, but only by a leap can they address the question at hand. For example, available studies may have looked at the "role model" effects of black teachers on the career choices of black students, but may not have inquired about Hispanics. What can a responsible social scientist say about Hispanics? Is there any reason for the court to assume that the same relationships occur?

The job of making social science relevant in the judicial process falls heavily on social scientists. Yet not many social scientists are regular actors in the judicial system. Because opportunities for social scientists' participation in legal proceedings have so far been limited, few have gained sufficient expertise and understanding of legal norms to make maximum use of the opportunities that do exist. For example, few would know about filing *amicus* briefs at the appellate level. Some social scientists are uncomfortable with the adversarial process and are unwilling to testify for one side in a case (see Weithorn, Chapter 10, this volume). For them to choose sides seems to require that they suppress any knowledge they have that fails to support "their" side. Only if they can come in as neutral third-party witnesses do they see the norms of social science as being compatible with the norms of the trial court. But, again, not many social scientists recognize that such opportunities exist.

Further examples can be given of the incompatibilities between social science and the law, but the trend seems to favor greater contact. As more lawyers come to the bar with training in the social sciences, and as the whole society seems to be undergoing a trend toward greater awareness of the social sciences, the barriers are dropping. An increasing number of court cases are drawing upon the social sciences in a wide range of fields. As more social scientists, like those represented in this volume, analyze ways in which social science can be made available to the courts, they are likely to increase their influence. A look at experience in administrative and legislative arenas should be grist for the mill.

DIRECT EFFORTS TO ALTER POLICY
THROUGH SOCIAL SCIENCE

Earlier commentaries that recounted the neglect of social science in policymaking were not wrong. Few efforts to use social science to change legislative or executive decisions actually work. Social scientists who try to provide "answers" to policymakers rarely find their recommendations heeded. Whether the issue is the location of an airport (Margolis, 1971) or the adoption of welfare reform (Lynn & Whitman, 1981), the attempt to alter a decision by brandishing social science analysis is unlikely to register much success.

Most policymakers are very busy people. More issues come at them each day than they have time to consider carefully. As former Vice President Walter Mondale (1981) wrote,

> The pressures of the executive branch of government require that every issue be summarized and categorized and filtered through intermediaries so that decisions can be made on a timely basis. The epitome of good staff work in Washington too often comes down to a three-page decision memo. Read it, choose an option, and on to the next subject. Often there's too little room or not enough time for subtlety or complexity. (p. 67)

That is an understatement. In legislatures, the pace is likely to be even more hectic than in administrative agencies, as legislators try to cope with bills on dozens of different subjects.

Even middle-level staff have too little time to seek out the best information. There is relatively little search for evidence or analysis. People tend to make do with what they already know. Since by and large, they deal with issues with which they have experience, they use that experience—their "ordinary knowledge" (Lindblom & Cohen, 1979)—in coping with situations that arise. If they know that some useful material exists, they may call a few people to locate it. But only under unusual circumstance are they likely to initiate a brand-new search for research or data or analyses.

The occasions that give rise to search for evidence are (1) new issues, something policymakers have not dealt with before and therefore need to be oriented to; (2) big questions with important or expensive consequences; (3) issues on which policymakers feel inadequately prepared; and (4) situations where their judgment may be challenged and they want authoritative support (Weiss, 1980). Even under these conditions, neither policymakers nor their aides are likely to embark on a library search, however computerized the system may be, unless they have prior awareness that a category of useful information on the topic actually exists. They are more likely to telephone people who they think have relevant information, or to go back to books and articles that they have already scanned, than to go through formal literature searches.

Another factor that limits policymakers' use of social science is the limited time they have available for reading. Members of the U.S. House of Representatives spend about 11 minutes a day reading, and their greatest complaint is that they do not have time to study and analyze (U.S. House of Representatives, Commission on Administrative Review, 1977). When they do read, it is usually staff memos, summaries of pending bills, crucial mail, and newspaper headlines. If there is time, they may quickly scan journals of their own profession—for lawyers, law journals. Almost nobody in high office reads social science journals.

When policymakers do come across social science evidence in the course of their daily work, they do not succumb to its truth and beauty on the spot. Intuitively, they subject it to a series of tests. They ask, Does it agree with what I know about how the world works? Is it credible? Policymakers have many sources of information other than social science, ranging from their own firsthand experience to systematic and unsystematic reports from the field. The extent to which they accept a research idea, or give it at least provisional hearing, depends on the degree to which it resonates with their prior knowledge. If it "makes sense," if it helps to organize and make sense of their earlier knowledge and impressions, they may incorporate it into their stock of knowledge (Weiss & Bucuvalas, 1980b).

They also tend to ask, Is the research relevant to the issue at hand? and, Does it give direction for action or offer new ways to think about the issue? Social science has to have a plausible relationship to the matters on the docket, and it has to yield guidance either for acting or, perhaps more commonly, for considering problems and strategies and solutions in new perspective. Policymakers say that they find social science useful even when it does not offer immediate solutions, in fact even when it challenges the traditional practice of the agency. They find it useful for helping them to rethink the definition of problems and to ponder alternative courses of action. Social science appears to affect the shape and content of policy discourse rather than concrete choices (Weiss with Bucuvalas, 1980b).

Legal institutions, with their traditions of continuity and precedent, are perhaps particularly conservative in accepting new formulations. At the least, it probably takes good-quality research, certified by trusted authorities and reinforced by bodies of experts, to receive serious attention in courts of law. Courts have a proclivity to turn to "professional standards" (e.g., American Psychological Association standards for test validation) to help them reach decisions. The stamp of authority that official bodies give transforms "findings" into consensually validated "knowledge."

ENLIGHTENMENT THROUGH "KNOWLEDGE CREEP"

Despite the limitations on its use, many policymakers in many fields believe that they are influenced by social science (Caplan, 1977; Rich, 1981; Weiss, 1980). They find it hard to identify specific studies that have influenced them or to specify how they have been influenced, but they have a strong and genuine sense that social science has helped to shape their views. They tend to be interested in what topics social scientists have studied and what results they have found, and they see social science as providing a general background of facts and ideas that are useful for keeping up with the world. It is a form of news, a kind of continuing education. It helps to update their map of the social world. They are likely to be more open to new information in the early phases of the policy cycle than in the later stages. Reformist governments with expansive programs may be more willing to listen to social science than conservative governments in times of retrenchment (Tarschys, 1983). But many policy actors have a basic hospitality to the kinds of knowledge that social science purveys.

Of course, social science is never policymakers' only source of information. They are barraged by information from many quarters. Claimants are frequently in the doorway, brandishing their own sets of arguments, their own sets of data. Nor does any one study, nor even any single body of research, encompass all the variables that decisionmakers have to attend to. They are inevitably interested in such factors as public reaction, financial costs, social costs, the risks of change and instability, and political advantage. Social scientists generally ignore factors like these—they are not built into the model. Social scientists deal in "rational analysis" of a problem, whereas policymakers have to take into account the likely consequences of their actions. So social science research is never a sufficient basis for decisions.

Moreover, social science does not provide certainties. It gives probabilistic conclusions that are time- and place-bound, provisional, and subject to revision. It tends not to simplify problems and converge on a single solution, but to provide a wide range of findings—some discrepant, some in outright conflict. As research continues over time, it tends to yield a complex and multifaceted view of reality. This may well be a realistic representation of a complex world, but it hardly simplifies the lot of decisionmakers looking for an "answer" (Cohen & Weiss, 1977). Moreover, social science evidence is based upon events in the past, and extrapolations to the future are always problematic. In all these senses, it fails to satisfy policymakers' yearning for easy solutions.

Nevertheless, social science is often the best source available for descriptive and explanatory knowledge. It is undertaken systematically, with care for methodological soundness and concern for objectivity. Social science tries to build a cumulative understanding of the ways in which the world works. Thus it provides both descriptive "facts" about a situation and understanding of cause–effect linkages (i.e., the theories underlying policy action). As its findings move into public view, they tend to reshape the images we all hold of the social world.

In our Western rationalist culture, reliance on systematic fact and tested theory is seen as a proper and rational mode of behavior. Even though many intellectuals and lawyers belittle the pretensions of social science, it maintains considerable prestige. Policymakers who consciously pay attention to social science view themselves, and are often viewed by others, as behaving rationally. It is often in their interest to commission studies, call in experts, and cite social science evidence. This shows their colleagues and the public that they are good decisionmakers (Feldman & March, 1981).

As social science evidence moves into currency and becomes accepted by informed publics, it tends to change the premises that are taken for granted and the issues that are seen as problematical. Thus, it can have two kinds of consequences for policy: (1) By clarifying the nature and extent of problems and their susceptibility to purposive action, it can reorder the policy agenda, demoting some items to insignificance and elevating others to a higher place. (2) By showing that some actions work well and others have little effect, social science can recast the types of alternatives that are considered as solutions. Needless to say, social science does not always have such profound effects. In certain periods and on certain topics, the influence of social science tends to fade. Yet, on a surprising range of issues, social science does seem to enlighten policy debates.

MICROPROCESSES BY WHICH SOCIAL SCIENCE GAINS ATTENTION

It is one thing to talk about "enlightenment" (and many students of the subject have come to accept this imagery as descriptive of the phenomena at work). It is another to describe how social science travels to policymaking arenas, which channels are activated, which personal links matter, what personal experiences or characteristics make policymakers more receptive, and what situations trigger attentiveness. Work on these issues is still in its early stages. There are quite a number of case studies but few generalizations that hold across time and place.

It does seem that there are certain policymakers who are

"users." The personal factor—a person's interest, commitment, enthusiasm—plays a part in determining how much influence a piece of research will have (Patton, 1978). We do not yet know why some people become committed enthusiasts; no identifiable background trait or experience has yet been shown to be consistently associated with frequent reliance on research. However, we do see a number of policymakers, and a larger number of staff aides, who give social science serious hearing in decisionmaking.

Most social science reports seem to have little effect on policymakers in and of themselves. A book, a journal article, or even a glossy, well-written, short, and spiffy summary document usually has little immediate effect. It often takes repeated messages, amplified by personal consultation and advocacy, before work gets through (Fairweather & Tornatzky, 1977). Even then, the work is unlikely to proceed very far unless and until it is "certified" by the certification authorities of the profession or field. Thus, controversial social science findings on alcoholism treatment make little headway if leaders in the alcoholism field dispute their validity; only when enough authorities and medical organizations line up behind the findings are treatment personnel willing to grant them at least provisional credibility.

Probably the most usual channels for transmitting social science to policymakers are expert consultants, blue-ribbon commissions, and in-house offices of research and planning. Consultants are widely called upon to provide knowledge and advice. In so doing, many of them draw upon their stock of social science knowledge. Expert commissions not only make use of the social science expertise of their members, but many of them also employ research staffs to pull together existing research data and undertake original studies (Bulmer, 1983; Komarovsky, 1975). Most federal agencies, and some state and city agencies, have set up offices of research and analysis to provide information to policymakers. The analysts in those offices are explicitly charged with linking the information needs of decisionmakers to existing data and new research (Meltsner, 1976; Orlans, 1973). The U.S. Congress has similar analytic resources available in the General Accounting Office (GAO), Congressional Research Service (CRS), Congressional Budget Office (CBO), and Office of Technology

Assessment (OTA). While there is considerable slippage in the process—the offices have difficulty in finding out about knowledge needs in sufficient time to allow them to do responsible analysis, and they have difficulties in finding (or acquiring) data sufficiently relevant to policymakers' questions—these offices remain an institutionalized testament to the perceived importance of the diffusion function.

The mass media seem to constitute an important channel for reaching policymakers. Even though many policymakers have their own specialized communications systems and their own analysis staffs, they are often not alerted to relevant social science findings until they hear about them in the public prints or on the airwaves. From the policymakers' perspective, media reporting of a study on a topic in their domain is a significant event. Policymakers prick up their ears, not only because *Time* or the *Washington Post* reaches them with a brief and simple version of social science, but also because they know that the same story reaches other players in the policy game. They will be asked about it. They had better know about it. They cannot sweep it under the rug.

In recent work, I have become aware of how much social science is relayed to congressional policymakers through the acitivity of interest groups. Each specialized lobby tries to advance its own case, and in so doing it makes use of whatever evidence supports its claims. If it finds supportive data in social science, it makes those data part of its case. Competing groups press different evidence on congressional staffs and criticize the data and analysis made available by opposition groups. Through these adversarial processes, lobbyists put a wide array of social science evidence on the table.

Congressional staff members appear to be more receptive to social science that arrives in this form, interlocked with argumentation and proposals for action, than they are to social science that arrives under the guise of pure and objective evidence. They tend to be suspicious of academics who come bearing objective research; they want to know, Why are the professors telling us this? What's in it for them? Their experience suggests that everyone has an axe to grind, and they don't know what axe the academics are grinding. They are more comfortable with lobbyists with whom they maintain ongoing long-term relationships. They can trust the lobbyists, because they know that they have to maintain credibility and are impelled to be trustworthy. If lobbyists lose the ear of congressional staff, they are out of a job. Furthermore, congressional staff members know where the lobbyist is coming from and what "spin" he or she is putting on the information. Thus, they know what kind of correction factor to apply. There is also the work that the lobbyists do—providing not only data but also interpretation, implications, and specific legislative proposals to capitalize on those interpretations. The information is digested and applied to the work at hand. For all these reasons, members of Congress and their staffs seem comfortable with social science that comes combined with political advocacy and legislative proposals. That is the context that they know and understand.

As congressional staff members try to resolve conflicting policy positions through negotiation, they often test the cases of the various groups and therefore also test the empirical evidence on which the different cases seem to rest. No research experts themselves, they may ask experts, especially those in the congressional support agencies, to review the data and see how adequately the data justify the claims being made. They may also ask each group what it has to say about the case made by others. They assume self-interest and an adversarial process, and they also tend to assume that the facts lie somewhere between the extremes posited by opposing groups. Political considerations probably prevail in the end, but they will be tempered by clearer understanding of what social science has to say. Thus, advocacy groups are major disseminators of social science data, generalizations, and ideas. They do not undertake the task in the interests of knowledge but rather of advocacy. Knowledge is a side effect—sometimes of significant scope.

Perhaps the most potent purveyor of social science to policy makers is what Heclo (1977) has called the "issue network." Around each of many major issues in contention, there has grown up a set of people who have knowledge and long-term interest in shaping policy. These people include members of Congress and their staffs, leaders of major executive-branch agencies charged with developing and implementing policy, some state and local leaders in the field, academics, consultants, interest-group representatives, and think-tank experts. They talk, argue, meet, discuss, telephone, debate, write. As policy on an issue develops and is modified over time, these people maintain contact, circulating material and exchanging ideas. According to Heclo (1977), they establish "a common language for discussing the issues, a shared grammar for identifying the major points of contention, a mutually familiar rhetoric of argumentation" (p.117). Because researchers and analysts are members of many of the most active issue networks, such as those concerned with welfare reform and energy policy, they become catalysts for the dissemination of social science research. Embedded in the common language that issue networks develop are often the relevant research findings and theoretical assumptions of the social sciences. The ongoing network conversation becomes the source of social science knowledge.

INFLUENCE ON ASSUMPTIONS, THEORIES, AGENDAS

For a long time, social scientists were discouraged by the seeming failure of social science to alter policy. They expected one study and its recommendations to have a direct and immediate effect on policy action—to switch policy from A to B by the strength of scientific findings. Once in a while, they found a "nugget"—an exemplary case where social science did in fact change policy outcomes. But usually social science appeared to be ignored.

We now know better. We have revised our expectations. We cannot expect social science to take the politics out of policymaking. Many factors matter in the development of policy, and each institution that makes policy (legislative, administrative, or judicial) has to take account not only of information but also of elements in its own organization and its own environment. Organizational maintenance and organizational advantage are legitimate concerns. But every policy also involves assumptions of fact and theory. It is at this cognitive level that social science has an opportunity to make a contribution.

Research on knowledge use in administrative and legislative arenas shows that social science does influence policy. Often the influence is indirect and slow. But over time social science can, and sometimes does, help to alter the manner in which each of us makes sense of the world. It can change both the facts that we assume and the models by which we put the facts together. It can alter the significance we attach to problems and the priorities we assign them. As changes in thinking occur, they change the premises on which policy is made. Such conceptual shifts, like tectonic plates in geology, may in time move mountains.

IMPLICATIONS FOR ACTION

Knowing that social science research may in time lead to long-term enlightenment of administrative, legislative, and perhaps judicial decisionmaking is a pleasant antidote to the disheartening pessimism about the effects of research that prevailed a few years ago. But the process of enlightenment by no means heralds a resounding victory. Much important social science research still goes by unnoticed. Many decisions rely on obsolete or flawed evidence. (For a discussion of the evidence used in the *Bakke* case, see Cole, 1978.) Are there ways in which social scientists can speed up the diffusion process so that better information gets to decisionmakers in a timely fashion? Can "quality control" mechanisms be instituted so as to screen out outdated, partial, sensationalized, poorly conceptualized, and poorly conducted studies?

Energetic efforts by social scientists, or by social science interpreters and popularizers, can perhaps accomplish something. Experience shows that nothing will guarantee the prompt and judicious dissemination of social science to appropriate officials, not even under seemingly ideal circumstances—as, for example, when the officials have themselves requested and funded the research (Weiss, 1978). But certain steps may hold promise. Certainly, taking an active part in channeling social science findings to policymakers is likely to be more productive than waiting for the world to beat a path to one's door. Testifying before legislative committees; writing articles in "practice" journals (law, social work, etc.) as well as academic journals; serving as a consultant to government bodies and private associations; cultivating personal contacts with influential officials and their aides—these kinds of activities are likely to improve the odds of getting the message through.

Given recent findings about the roles played by issue networks, advocacy groups, and the mass media, social scientists who wish to make their work known can also seek to exploit these channels. These attempts would go beyond efforts at direct intercession and would try to capitalize on existing linkage mechanisms. Thus we can try to identify key actors in the "issue networks" that deal with child development issues and be sure that they receive copies of relevant articles, or, better yet, first-hand accounts of research results and their policy implications. Similarly, we can try to locate sympathetic interest groups whose case is strengthened or amplified by the best child development research, and be sure that they are aware of the findings. We can then rely on their self-interest to make the research better known. More problematically, we can try to reach advocates of opposing positions and use research results to seek to convince them to alter their views. Experience suggests that they will not often oblige, but even an occasional victory will be noteworthy.

Getting stories about child development research into the mass media would certainly widen the effective audience. More people—even more policymakers—probably read a single story in the *New York Times* or *Newsweek* than would hear about social science research in any other way. They are likely to pay attention, too, because they know that other policymakers in their arena will also have seen the story. However, it is not easy to get the attention of reporters; they are besieged by publicity seekers and showered with blizzards of press releases. Nor is it usually obvious how a social scientist can turn a social science report into something interesting and newsworthy enough to grab a reporter's interest. Furthermore, stories in the media are inevitably short and simplified. Because of limitations of space and time, and because the media aim for a mass audience, news stories cannot include all the detail of substance and method or all the technical caveats that social scientists usually believe to be important (Weiss, 1985a, 1985b). Stories about child development research in the mass media, for all their attraction, carry costs as well as benefits.

Perhaps the most significant implication for social scientists who are interested in gaining policymakers' notice is this: While no single avenue is likely to be highly effective, and while each avenue runs risks (e.g., of distortion or biased promotion), use of multiple dissemination channels increases the likelihood that messages will come through. And when policymakers hear about similar research findings from many sources, they tend to give greater credence to the message. They receive a sense of convergence, of consensus, of "ideas in good currency" (Schon,1971). They come to believe that "this is what social science says." If the evidence is further "certified" through endorsements from leaders of professional associations and other representatives of the discipline, the evidence— and generalizations from it— gain in legitimacy.

This is encouraging , I think, but still there are dangers in the process. Because of the lack of critical review of social science findings in the policy system (few policymakers have the knowledge or the staff to analyze the conceptual sense or methodological validity of social science), shoddy research that is well and widely disseminated can come to appear authoritative. Some policymakers may dispute the conclusions, but they will usually make their case on ideological or value-related grounds rather than on the basis of the flaws in the research, and their opposition may appear short-sighted and self-serving. Few procedures exist to give decisionmakers the benefit of independent scientific review of the evidence. Only ready access to a qualified social scientist, either on staff or as a consultant, is likely to serve that purpose. Quite a number of federal agencies have offices of research, evaluation, and analysis that house social scientists who are qualified to undertake such critical reviews (although they are not regularly called upon to do so). The U.S. Congress support agencies—GAO, CBO, CRS, and OTA—have capabilities for reviewing social science research for the Congress, although, again, they are only occasionally charged with the task. But relatively few state legislatures or state agencies have in-house social science expertise available. Probably very few courts have institutionalized access to social science capabilities. Regular mechanisms for screening good social science from poor social science are generally in short supply, even within the disciplines themselves.

What about the special case of the legal system? How can child development research best reach the lawyers and judges who make significant decisions? Subsequent chapters in this volume consider an array of routes to judicial notice. Since my own research has not dealt with courts, I leave it to my colleagues to assess the relative efficacy of expert witnesses, *voir dire*, and other legal arcana.

Let me just note that the judicial system appears to have a number of special features relative to the application of social science knowledge. I focus here on three. One factor that works against application is the legal bent toward stability and precedent. Courts are charged with the mission of maintaining the social order, not with changing it. This is a conservative posture, and implicit in it is a sense of faith in the continuity of human knowledge. Over time judges adapt law to changing conditions, but they are not eager to overturn earlier decisions. They tend to be unwilling to bow to every new breeze emanating from the academy (or anywhere else). They are suspicious of radically new formulations. They have faith in the wisdom of the past as it is tested, winnowed, and strengthened over time. They have seen fads come into fashion, some of them supported by the social science of the day, and they have seen the same fads go out of favor, again with social science support. Their horizon is the long course of the law.

In recent years the judicial system seems to have become more receptive to social science, just as it has been more willing to provide equity to classes of citizens against government action. That courts have become more hospitable to social science—from the "Brandeis brief" to *Brown v. Board of Education* to the current shower of citations—is probably testimony to the rapid pace of change in American society. Whatever the judicial temperament may be, the courts are involved in a widening range of social issues, and they must call on every available resource to help them find wise and workable solutions to the problems before them. They need new approaches to understanding today's complex realities, and the social sciences (for all their limitations) are prime interpreters of the social system.

Another feature of the judicial system that can have appeal for social scientists is that the facts have to be determined for each specific case. Social scientists who help the court find the facts do not have to make the dangerously broad generalizations from their data that they are called upon to make in work with legislative and executive officials. A case is a delimited and unique situation, and social scientists can often make close-grained estimates that fit its particulars. For the same reasons, legal decisionmakers may be less reluctant to rely on social science evidence than policymakers dealing with sweeping policy decisions.

Still another feature of the judicial system that abets the call on social science is the system of legal documentation. Court decisions are published in orderly rows of volumes, and the indexing and retrieval system is second to none. One judge's footnote to one social science study goes into the system, and it becomes available from there on to attorneys who follow the chain of decision in preparing their cases. In few other fields—not even in the social sciences themselves—can the power of citation be so strong.

Social scientists who understand the special characteristics of the legal system are probably best able to make an impact. They will treat the law and its values with respect. They will have modest expectations for what the social sciences can contribute. They will work at generating understanding of social science among members of the legal profession, and they will shape their own advice and testimony to be maximally relevant to the issues as judicially defined.

ACKNOWLEDGMENT

I wish to thank Gary B. Melton and Jay Heubert for their helpful advice.

REFERENCES

Aaron, H.J. (1978). *Politics and the professors: The Great Society in perspective.* Washington, DC: Brookings Institute.

Banting, K. (1979). *Poverty, politics & policy: Britain in the 1960s.* London: Macmillan.

Berg, M.R., Brudney, J.L., Fuller, T.D., Michael, D.N., & Roth, B.K. (1978). *Factors affecting utilization of technology assessment studies in policy.* Ann Arbor: University of Michigan, Center for Research on Utilization of Scientific Knowledge.

Bulmer, M. (Ed.). (1983). Social science and policymaking: The use of research by government commissions (Special issue). *American Behavioral Scientist, 26* (5), 555–680.

Caplan, N. (1977). A minimal set of conditions necessary for the utilization of social science knowledge in policy formation at the national level. In C.H. Weiss (Ed.), *Using social research in public policy making* (pp.183–197). Lexington, MA: Lexington Books.

Caplan, N., Morrison, A., & Stanbaugh, R.J. (1975). *The use of social science knowledge in policy decisions at the national level.* Ann Arbor: University of Michigan, Institute for Social Research.

Chayes, A. (1976). The role of the judge in public law litigation. *Harvard Law Review, 89,* 1280–1318.

Cohen, D.K., & Weiss, J.A. (1977). Social science and social policy: Schools and race. In C.H. Weiss (Ed.), *Using social research in public policy making* (pp. 67–83). Lexington, MA: Lexington Books.

Cole, J. (1978, December). *Social facts and the Bakke case.* Paper presented to the Yale Law School Legal Theory Workshop, New Haven, CT.

Fairweather, G.W., & Tornatzky, L.G. (1977). *Experimental methods for social policy research.* New York: Pergamon Press.

Feldman, M.S., & March, J.G. (1981). Information in organizations as signal and symbol. *Administrative Science Quarterly, 26,* 171–186.

Frankel, C. (Ed.). (1976). *Controversies and decisions: The social sciences and public policy.* New York: Russell Sage Foundation.

Furner, M.O. (1975). *Advocacy and objectivity: A crisis in the professionalism of American social science, 1865–1905.* Lexington: University Press of Kentucky.

Haskell, T. (1977). *The emergence of professional social science: The American Social Science Association and the nineteenth century crisis of authority.* Urbana: University of Illinois Press.

Hayes, C.D. (1982). *Making policies for children: A study of the federal process.* Washington, DC: National Academy Press.

Heclo, H. (1977). *A government of strangers: Executive politics in Washington.* Washington, DC: Brookings Institute.

Holzner, B., Knorr, K.D., & Strassner, H. (Eds.). (1983). *Realizing social science knowledge.* Würzberg, West Germany: Physica Verlag.

Horowitz, I.L. (Ed.) (1975). *The use and abuse of social science* (2nd ed.). New Brunswick, NJ: Transaction.

Husen, T., & Kogan, M. (1984). *Educational research and policy: How do they relate?* Oxford: Pergamon Press.

Kallen, D.B.P., Kosse, G.B., Wagenaar, H.C., Kloprogge, J.J.J., & Vorbeck,

M. (1982). *Social science research and public policy-making.* Windsor, England: National Foundation for Educational Research–Nelson.
Kogan, M., & Henkel, M. (1983). *Government and research: The Rothschild experiment in a government department.* London: Heinemann.
Komarovsky, M. (1975). *Sociology and public policy: The case of presidential commissions.* New York: Elsevier.
Lazarsfeld, P.F., Sewell, W.H., & Wilensky, H.L. (Eds.). (1967). *The uses of sociology.* New York: Basic Books.
Lindblom, C.E., & Cohen, D.K. (1979). *Usable knowledge.* New Haven, CT: Yale University Press.
Lynn, L.E., Jr., & Whitman, D. deF. (1981). *The President as policymaker: Jimmy Carter and welfare reform.* Philadelphia: Temple University Press.
Lyons, G. (1969). *The uneasy partnership: Social science and the federal government in the twentieth century.* New York: Russell Sage Foundation.
Margolis, J. (1971). Evaluative criteria in social policy. In T.R. Dye (Ed.), *The measurement of policy impact* (pp. 25–31). Tallahassee: Florida State University.
Meltsner, A. (1976). *Policy analysts in the bureaucracy.* Berkeley: University of California Press.
Mnookin, R.H. (Ed.). (1985). *In the interest of children: Advocacy, law reform, and public policy.* New York: W.H. Freeman.
Mondale, W. (1981, November 8). The re-education of Walter Mondale. *New York Times Magazine,* p.67.
National Academy of Sciences. (1968). *The behavioral sciences and the federal government.* Washington, DC: Author.
National Research Council. (1982). *Behavioral and social science research: A national resource* (Part 1). Washington, DC: National Academy Press.
National Science Board. (1969). *Knowledge into action: Improving the nation's use of the social sciences.* Washington, DC: National Science Board, Special Commission on the Social Sciences.
Orlans, H. (1973). *Contracting for knowledge.* San Francisco: Jossey-Bass.
Patton, M.Q. (1978). *Utilization-focused evaluation.* Beverly Hills, CA: Sage.
Rein, M. (1976). *Social science and public policy.* New York: Penguin Books.
Rich, R. (1981). *Social science information and public policy making: The interaction between bureaucratic politics and the use of survey data.* San Francisco: Jossey-Bass.
Rosen, P.L. (1972). *The Supreme Court and social science.* Urbana: University of Illinois Press.
Rosen, P.L. (1977). Social science and judicial policy making. In C.H. Weiss (Ed.), *Using social research in public policy making* (pp.109–123). Lexington, MA: Lexington Books.
Ross, D. (1979). The development of the social sciences. In A. Oleson & J. Voss (Eds.), *The organization of knowledge in modern America, 1860–1920* (pp.107–138). Baltimore: Johns Hopkins University Press.
Rule, J.B. (1978). *Insight and social betterment: A preface to applied social science.* New York: Oxford University Press.

Schon, D. (1971). *Beyond the stable state*. New York: Random House.

Tarschys, D. (1983). Fluctuations in the political demand for policy analysis. In S.E. Spiro & E. Yuchtman-Yaar (Eds.), *Evaluating the welfare state* (pp. 375–385). New York: Academic Press.

U.S. House of Representatives, Commission on Administrative Review. (1977). *Final report, Ninety-Fifth Congress, First Session* (Vol. 2). Washington, DC: U.S. Government Printing Office.

Weiss, C.H. (1978). Improving the linkage between social research and public policy. In L.E. Lynn, Jr. (Ed.), *Knowledge and policy: The uncertain connection* (pp.23–81). Washington, DC: National Academy of Sciences.

Weiss, C.H. (1980). Knowledge creep and decision accretion. *Knowledge: Creation, Diffusion, Utilization, 1*(3), 381–404.

Weiss, C.H. (1985a). Media report card for social science. *Society, 22*(2), 39–47.

Weiss, C.H. (1985b). Social science in the media: Who reports it and who is reported. *Nieman Reports, 39*(3), 15–25.

Weiss, C.H., & Bucuvalas, M.J. (1980a). Truth tests and utility tests: Decision makers' frames of reference for social science research. *American Sociological Review, 45*(2), 302–313.

Weiss, C.H. with Bucuvalas, M.J. (1980b). *Social science research and decision-making*. New York: Columbia University Press.

Child Development Research and the Legislative Process

RUBY TAKANISHI
GARY B. MELTON

Although most of the chapters in this volume focus on the judicial system, the use of child development research by the legislative branch is also potentially important in stimulating legal reform. The standards and procedures upon which courts rely in making decisions about children and families are more typically creations of the legislature than of the judiciary. Except when constitutionally mandated, even judicially imposed standards may be overruled by the legislature. The legislature also may provide the executive branch with authority and funds to conduct research on legally relevant topics that may inform policymakers in all three branches. Therefore, this chapter examines the impact of child development research in the legislative process, with emphasis upon legislation related to children's involvement in the legal system.

Ten years ago, child development researchers bemoaned the lack of attention to research on children and families by policymaking bodies, including the U.S. Congress (Senn, 1977). Within a decade, progress has been made in bringing that knowledge to the attention of Congress and other policymaking

Ruby Takanishi. Carnegie Council on Adolescent Development, Washington, D.C.

Gary B. Melton. Department of Psychology and College of Law, University of Nebraska–Lincoln, Lincoln, Nebraska.

bodies. While that progress can be documented, the actual impact or influence of research on specific legislation is less clear. Indeed, questions about direct linkages between research and legislation are misdirected because of multiple players and the convoluted pathways of legislation.

There are specific examples in which a line of research has decisively affected the course of congressional action. Greenberger (1983) has provided an engaging case study of the impact of her testimony on the U.S. Department of Labor's proposal to revise time provisions of child labor laws. The meta-analysis of exemplary Head Start programs was influential in promoting the notion, particularly in Congress, that Project Head Start works and is particularly deserving of continued funding in the context of reduced social spending (Lazar & Darlington, 1982). Studies of the impact of low-level exposure to lead were cited in the decision of the Environmental Protection Agency to reduce the content of lead in gasoline. These specific examples, however, are exceptions to a general rule: Research may inform and illuminate issues; it only rarely settles them (Hayes, 1982). The complex interrelationships among research, chance, and policy are more typically described in the case studies of policymaking conducted by the Committee on Child Development and Social Policy of the National Academy of Sciences (Hayes, 1982). What has undoubtedly occurred is that researchers in child development have become part of the Washington policymaking scene. Whether their presence will continue, both in numbers and in influence, remains to be seen.

Several factors have stimulated tangible progress in bringing child development research to the attention of national policymakers. These factors include the participation of child development researchers in the Congressional Science and Engineering Fellowship Program, coordinated by the American Association for the Advancement of Science; the increased activity of professional associations in lobbying and public information; and the establishment of forums within the U.S. Congress that provide channels for presenting research to elected officials. Before we discuss each of these developments in detail, a very brief natural history of Congress is in order.

THE TARGET FOR INFLUENCE:
THE U.S. CONGRESS

In recent years, the U.S. Congress has become inundated by the sheer press of legislation and the budgetary crisis. In fact, the crisis has consumed much of Congress's energy, leaving the passage of substantive legislation in the background.

The sheer number of issues that face elected officials require them (except in special cases) to rely heavily on their staffs, sometimes described as "the unelected representatives." These individuals are themselves overworked and subjected to competing demands for their attention. The luxury of reading journal articles is nonexistent. The media and certain concise materials from trusted sources are relied upon heavily. Staff seek and rely upon a number of individuals whom they trust and consider to be knowledgeable about certain issues. As Weiss (Chapter 3, this volume) discusses, small "issue networks" of congressional staff, members of professional and lobbying associations, and researchers come over time both to frame and to supply the supporting information for selected issue areas.

Greenberger (1983) has justifiably criticized the restrictiveness of these issue networks. Among both associational and congressional staffs, certain individuals become consistently involved, to the exclusion of other researchers who might be equally or better qualified to present their work to policymakers. There is a natural tendency to select individuals whose views, credibility, and style of presentation are well known. Involvement of a broader spectrum of individuals who may be especially expert on a given issue remains a challenge.

Despite the lack of time for study, congressional staffs do not suffer from a dearth of information. Congress has also created its own support agencies, which are staffed by researchers in the behavioral and social sciences, and provide members and staffs with clearly written, policy-relevant briefs within short time constraints. In recent years, therefore, researchers have also identified these congressional support agencies as important targets for information dissemination as well. For example, the General Accounting Office occasionally examines the efficacy of children's policies, and the Office of Technology Assessment is called upon to determine the state of scientific knowledge on various issues (e.g., efficacy of child mental health services). The Congressional Budget Office, which prepares fiscal analyses for Congress, and the Congressional Research Service, which prepares issue briefings, are the other congressional support agencies.

The U.S. Congress is, in fact, an information-saturated environment. Research, as produced by child development researchers, is but one source of information that must compete with other sources to find its way to policymakers through a number of highly personal channels, as well as through congressional support agencies that both generate and consume research findings. The clear challenge for researchers who wish to have their work enter and inform the policymaking process is to identify the appropriate access points and to produce reports that are prepared to address policy issues directly (Takanishi, 1981).

FACTORS CONTRIBUTING TO INCREASED ACCESS

During the past decade, several new structures have been created to increase the visibility of child development research in the national corridors of legislation. In combination, they have resulted in the establishment of an informal association of individuals working in Congress, the professional and lobbying associations, and research institutions, to provide access to information for congressional representatives and staffs. Four factors have contributed to the greater penetration of child development research in Congress within the last decade: (1) the initiation of Congressional Science Fellowships in Child Development; (2) the development of lobbying by relevant scientific societies; (3) the development of the Bush Foundation's network of training programs; and (4) the establishment of congressional units focused on child development.

CONGRESSIONAL SCIENCE FELLOWSHIPS
IN CHILD DEVELOPMENT

In 1978, with support from the Foundation for Child Development and the William T. Grant Foundation, the Society for Research in Child Development (SRCD) initiated a Congressional Science Fellowship program for researchers within the child development field (Brim & Dustan, 1983). As of 1985, 38 fellows had completed a year working in Congress and continued in various roles to work at the intersection of Congress and the research community. Four fellows worked in Congress in 1985–1986. Fellows have been selected from researchers in anthropology, education, law, nursing, psychology, public health, social work, sociology, and urban planning.

Everett and Chase-Lansdale (1985) reported that 13 of the first 31 fellows went into academia or returned to academic positions. The other 18 fellows now work in the policy arena in professional associations and private sector organizations. Six of these former fellows work on the staff of Congress or professional and scientific associations that interface with the Congress. As in the Congressional Science Fellowship programs of other scientific societies, coordinated by the American Association for the Advancement of Science, these individuals have continued to bring research to the attention of Congress.

GOVERNMENTAL RELATIONS PROGRAMS
OF SCIENTIFIC SOCIETIES

The first Reagan administration produced significant reductions in research support for the behavioral and social sciences, and galvanized the scientific communities to increase their Washington presence. Although associations of scientific societies (e.g., the Federation of Behavioral, Psychological, and Cognitive Sciences and the Consortium of Social Science Associations) had been incorporated prior to 1980, the threats to research support led them for the first time to establish Washington offices to promote and protect research budgets. In so doing, they increased communication with Congress about the advances and potential of research in the behavioral and social sciences.

Several scientific societies with interests in children, youths, and families were among those involved in the new lobbying effort. Thus, research from these areas was included in science policy breakfasts and lunches for congressional staffers, and in public information and press releases for the broader public. Testimony before Congress, particularly related to budgets for research support, increased at a phenomenal rate.

It was also at this time that the Washington Liaison Office of SRCD increased its staff and presence in Washington, with support from the Foundation for Child Development and the William T. Grant Foundation. This office was instrumental in organizing Research Resources for Children, Youth, and Families—a group of staff members from behavioral and social science societies in Washington, which had the goal of facilitating the flow of information about child development between the research community and Congress.

Governmental relations offices within specific societies and consortia have increased the likelihood that staffers of these offices, typically from the research and academic community, will come to serve as information brokers between Congress and the respective research communities. For example, in the American Psychological Association (APA), the administrative officer for children, youths, and families plays such a role. Since the inception of the position several years ago, each of the three psychologists who has held it has been a former SRCD Congressional Science Fellow. This fact is illustrative of the way in which the new structures for bringing child development research to Capitol Hill have interacted to create a new issue network on child and family matters.

Bush Centers for Child Development and Social Policy

In 1977, the Bush Foundation of Minneapolis established four university-based centers for the pre- and postdoctoral training of individuals from various disciplinary and professional backgrounds to work at the intersection of child development and social policy. These centers have enabled university faculty and students to focus their research and teaching on such issues as child care, adoption, child abuse, early education, television, and health care. They have educated a group of individuals who have gone into the Congressional Science Fellowship programs, into staffs of the local, state, and national legislatures, and into professional associations. Other former Bush Fellows have become policy scholars in university training centers of their own. For example, the faculty of the proposed Center on Children, Families, and the Law at the University of Nebraska–Lincoln includes three former Bush Fellows. The Bush Centers have also served as a catalyst for the development of public information materials, internship programs, and conferences focusing on the intersections of research practice and policy-making.

ESTABLISHMENT OF CONGRESSIONAL UNITS FOCUSED ON CHILDREN

In 1983, both houses of Congress established units focused on issues related to children, youths, and families. The House Select Committee on Children, Youth, and Families (Miller, 1983), the Senate Caucus on Children, and the Senate Caucus on Families have no legislative authority. They were established primarily as conduits for gathering and disseminating information, in order to create a data base for informed decisions by congressional colleagues on issues related to families. The House Select Committee on Children, Youth, and Families has issued a series of valuable publications documenting the status of children, youth, and families. It also has held a series of hearings in which researchers in a variety of areas have testified and presented research findings for the record.

These congressional units can be viewed as policy forums to review and highlight issues that may have some impact on the course of legislation affecting children and families. As such, they are perfect channels for researchers to transmit research to Congress. These congressional units have actively sought advice from the research community about topics for hearings and appropriate witnesses. They have thus served to reinforce the working relationship between Congress and the scientific and professional societies. Three former Congressional Science Fellows in Child Development currently serve as senior professional staffers on the House Select Committee. This infusion of researchers into the committee staff has the effect of increasing opportunities for introduction of child development research into the legislative process.

FUTURE DIRECTIONS

The opportunity exists to study, both retrospectively and prospectively, the impact of research knowledge in a number of areas related to policy formation regarding children (Hayes, 1982). Such a systematic study of the ways in which research knowledge and professional practice influence the course of policy recommendations and directions awaits enterprising investigators. This chapter has documented increased levels of activity, but a systematic study of the *impact* of this activity remains to be done. How much progress—more importantly, what kind of progress—has been made since the activities described above were initiated in the middle and late 1970s? How do information networks regarding children, youths, and families operate? The existing literature that has addressed the (non) influence of the research community (e.g., Steiner, 1976, 1981) needs to be updated in the context of the developments described here.

There is a need to examine the information networks that exist to inform Congress and other policymakers about the knowledge base of child development. Greenberger (1983) was indeed perceptive when she noted a serious problem in the more equitable participation of researchers in policymaking. Granted, there will always be a large number of individuals who do not wish to enter this world, and a smaller number of individuals who wish to do so. However, it is also the case that only a small number of individuals are constantly called upon to testify on behalf of the research community. They are not only reliable, but adept at the necessary and crucial positioning and public image that are so central to effective communication in information-saturated settings. Yet the question can be raised as to whether all points of view and the broadest diversity of knowledge are presented before decisionmakers. Information technologies exist to provide up-to-date repositories of carefully evaluated articles and reviews in response to congressional inquiries. Similar systems are needed to bring researchers themselves into the legislative process.

Noteworthy progress has been made in bringing child development research to the U.S. Congress. Research is heard more regularly in hearing rooms and included in congressional hearing records more frequently. Despite this progress, however, we still lag behind some other collegial groups in engineering and the natural sciences. What is needed is the regularization of the process by which researchers communicate their best knowledge to policymakers on both national and state bases. The challenge is to create an ethos in which serious researchers, whose fundamental loyalties are to science, can appropriately contribute to the policy debates that can be informed by specialized knowledge. As already noted, a convergence of factors occurred in the late 1970s to create such an ethos in the child development field; whether it can be sustained will soon be at issue. As of this writing (early in 1987), funding for two of the programs that have stimulated researchers' activity in Congress—the Congressional Science Fellowships and the Bush Centers—will be terminated. Whether and in what form these programs will continue to be supported by host institutions remains to be seen.

If the new ethos of researcher involvement in the policy arena is to maintain itself and significantly affect the formulation of policy, it will also have to broaden. Not only should the issue network itself broaden, as we have noted, but its targets also should be more diverse. Because of the Reagan administration's redefinition of the federal role, policies that affect the well-being of children, youths, and families are increasingly being made at the state and local level. In an era of block grants and reduced federal spending on domestic programs, the critical questions about how resources are to be allocated to children, youths, and families are frequently being reserved to the states. This fundamental shift of the locus of policymaking requires researchers to develop the capacity for organized activity in the state legislatures and on municipal boards and councils.

An issue network of experts on child development was slow to form on Capitol Hill, and, as we have noted, its future is uncertain because of changes in the structures that led ultimately to the informal establishment of the network. Diligence will be required to insure that Congress continues to receive information based on research relevant to child, youth, and family issues. Although that task is not easy, substantially more difficulty will be encountered in establishing and maintaining issue networks in the state legislatures. Obviously, not every state has a major expert on any given issue to which child development research might contribute. An even more difficult structural problem is the fact that scientific societies rarely have state branches. When they do, the state affiliates are likely to be small, low-budget, and unstaffed.

Organized psychology is illustrative of this point. The state psychological associations are generally comprised primarily of professional (clinical) psychologists, with few representatives of scientific psychology. Although most state associations now are involved actively in the legislative process, their legislative activity is typically limited largely or exclusively to guild issues (Melton, 1985a). Smaller state associations lack the capacity for sustained effort even on these questions of importance to professional psychologists' pocketbooks. About 40% of the state associations do not have a paid executive officer or administrator. Some of the staffing and resource problems may be alleviated by the establishment of a well-funded Office of Professional Advocacy in the APA central office that, among other tasks, will assist state associations in lobbying on professional issues.

Even if the state associations are able to increase their visibility on these issues, they may not be motivated to extend their advocacy to social issues to which psychological research is relevant, including child, youth, and family issues. For example, the APA Division of Child, Youth, and Family Services (Division 37) has endeavored to establish a state legislative network to provide expertise on children's matters. However, a meeting held during the 1985 APA convention to establish such links drew a representative from only one state association (who in fact sent a student), despite invitations to the presidents of all the associations. Perhaps, though, the enhanced presence of state psychological associations in the capitals ultimately will increase the presence of psychology itself. It is important to remember that, on the national level, developmental researchers' increased lobbying on research support (in response to actual and threatened budget cuts) had the side effect of increasing their involvement in substantive matters not directly linked to financial support for child development research. By the same token, when state associations become more actively involved in lobbying on guild issues, their expertise may be sought on other issues. Also, state associations may find it advantageous to contribute knowledge about matters of clear public interest in order to enhance their credibility when they seek recognition of their professional interests (cf. Berry, 1977). Child development researchers may want to become visible in state associations so that the likelihood that their knowledge will be used will increase.

In the meantime, individual psychologists who believe that their findings are relevant to pending or possible legislation can seek out interested state legislators. Particularly in small states, access to legislators is often easy. They are apt to have one aide or no specially assigned aide at all. Therefore, they generally depend much more than their counterparts in Congress on formal testimony and direct contact with experts for information relevant to the myriad of issues before them (Ziegler & Baer, 1969). Although individual activity requires that psychologists invest the time required to monitor interesting issues as they arise (not always a realistic expectation), the probability of direct impact is substantial in many state legislatures.

When universities are located in or near state capitals, they may establish their own analogues to the Congressional Science Fellowship program. For example, the Law/Psychology Program at the University of Nebraska–Lincoln has placed graduate students in practica in state legislative offices and policymaking levels of the executive branch, including the Governor's office. Besides providing an additional source of student stipends, such a practicum program has several positive effects. It increases (1) the infusion of behavioral and social sciences, including child development research, into policymaking; (2) the sophistication of students in policy analysis and real-world applications of their knowledge; (3) the post-graduate marketability of students in high-level applied settings; and (4) the visibility of the university in state service (a point of some significance when state universities seek legislative support for graduate research training).

SPECIAL PROBLEMS IN LEGISLATION ON CHILDREN IN THE LEGAL SYSTEM

State-level legislative consultation is especially important on issues pertaining to children's involvement in the legal system. Although the Reagan administration's policies have exaggerated the distinctions among the various levels of government, most legal matters involving children, youths, and families have historically been primarily the province of the states. For example, domestic relations (including standards for child custody) is an area of law traditionally reserved to the states. Generally, so are the age of majority, juvenile justice (indeed, whether there is a juvenile court at all), the minimum drinking age, juvenile commitment laws, child labor laws, child care regulations, public education, child protective services, and so forth. The federal government sometimes has attempted to engineer state policies in these areas by attaching "strings" to federal dollars. Thus, among other reforms of children's law, deinstitutionalization of status offenders (Juvenile Justice and Delinquency Prevention Act of 1974) and mandated reporting of child maltreatment (Child Abuse Prevention and Treatment Act of 1974) were given impetus by fiscal incentives established by Congress for state legislation. However, federal activity in these areas *followed* statutory changes in many states. Even among the states that were induced by federal dollars, the specific statutory provisions and administrative procedures for implementation were left to state legislatures and agencies.

Even this limited federal involvement in issues related to children and the law is waning. The Reagan administration has taken the position that such matters should be left *exclusively* to the states. Thus, for example, the administration has sought repeatedly to delete funding altogether for the Office of Juvenile Justice and Delinquency Prevention (OJJDP), despite bipartisan support for continued federal involvement in study of issues in juvenile justice (see, e.g., Specter, 1986). The work that has occurred at OJJDP in the Reagan administration or has been funded by it has often been motivated more by ideology than by careful consideration of needs for information. At the same time, the U.S. Supreme Court under Chief Justice Burger proved reluctant to enforce expansive federal entitlements to state services (see, e.g., *Board of Education v. Rowley*, 1982; *Pennhurst State School & Hospital v. Halderman*, 1981), and it probably will continue to do so under Chief Justice Rehnquist.

In this political context, attention to what the federal role should be is of particular importance for psychologists and others with interest in children's involvement in the legal system. One function that almost everyone agrees is legitimate for the federal government is the development of information that may guide the formulation of policies by the states. In that regard, a persistent problem has been the lack of clear responsibility for such efforts among federal agencies. For example, a topic of wide public concern—children's testimony—has been without a home, despite the clear interest in the development of knowledge that states might use and programs that they might imitate. Because children often are witnesses in matters other than delinquency cases, OJJDP has lacked clear jurisdiction. The topic also extends beyond abuse cases and the child welfare system. Therefore, it does not fall clearly within the mission of the National Center for Abuse and Neglect, which, regardless, has been generally unreceptive to proposals for basic research. Similarly, the mental health aspects of the topic are sufficiently tangential that it is not obviously under the aegis of any of the centers of the National Institute of Mental Health. Analogously, the topic falls between the congressional committees dealing with human services and those concerned with the judiciary.

In such a context, researchers on children and the law may

focus their efforts on Capitol Hill upon the needs for author-ization of, and appropriations for, research itself. The infor-mation that researchers will bring to Congress may focus on what is *not* known: the knowledge that state policymakers need to make rational decisions about legislation and programs on children's involvement in the legal system. What *is* known is relevant to this argument only to show specific directions for future research and to demonstrate the usefulness of research in understanding the implications of various policy alternatives. Testimony of this sort by Melton (1985b) before the U.S. Senate Subcommittee on Juvenile Justice (1984) led to an amendment of the Missing Children's Assistance Act of 1984 to provide OJJDP with express authority to support research on mal-treated children's involvement in the legal system. Such changes in statutory language, although sometimes in the form of "tech-nical amendments" that attract no debate and carry no special appropriation, give messages to granting agencies about congressional intent and thus shape funding priorities and re-search initiatives. A mere mention of congressional findings about needs for research can have the same effect when it is included in the report that accompanies a bill released from committee to the full house, although such report language technically has no legal force.

By contrast, testimony and consultation on children and the law in the state legislatures are more likely to focus on substantive knowledge than on needs for research. What, for example, might be the effects of adopting a presumption in favor of joint custody in divorce cases (see Clingempeel & Rep-pucci, 1982; Scott & Derdeyn, 1984)? What procedures should be required for interrogation of juvenile suspects in delin-quency cases (see Grisso, 1981)? What might be the effects of laws permitting minors to consent to treatment (see Melton, 1981; Melton, Koocher, & Saks, 1983)? Should a presumption be established in favor of termination of mentally disordered persons' parental rights (see Melton, Petrila, Poythress, & Slo-bogin, 1987, § 12.05)? For many specific topics related to chil-dren and the law, research is still scanty (Melton, 1984). How-ever, by acting to inform state legislators about what *is* known, experts on child development can insure that legislators are aware of the level of uncertainty attached to proposed policies, and of the possible effects (actual and hypothesized) that existing research suggests.

Such clarification of the limits of expertise and the nature of the questions posed by a policy decision would be no small accomplishment. The confluence of several developments has made such clarification possible on child, youth, and family issues in Congress. Although the impending demise of the SRCD Congressional Science Fellowship program makes the continued existence of the children's issue network tenuous, advocacy by scientific societies on Capitol Hill is likely to continue. Therefore, at least for the short term, a small group of experts on child development will probably continue to work at the intersection of research and federal policy. On issues specifically related to children and the law, however, the principal action is in the state houses, not Congress. Although Congress remains an effective avenue for insuring that relevant research is conducted, the challenge to child and family policy researchers is to develop means of diffusing relevant knowledge to state-level policymakers.

REFERENCES

Berry, J.M. (1977). *Lobbying for the people: The political behavior of public interest groups*. Princeton, NJ: Princeton University Press.

Board of Education v. Rowley, 458 U.S. 176 (1982).

Brim, O.G., & Dustan, J. (1983). Translating research into policy for children: The private foundation experience. *American Psychologist, 38*, 85–90.

Child Abuse Prevention and Treatment Act of 1974, Pub. L. No. 93-247, 88 Stat. 4 (1974).

Clingempeel, W.G. & Reppucci, N.D. (1982). Joint custody after divorce: Major issues and goals for research. *Psychological Bulletin, 91*, 102–127

Everett, B.A., & Chase-Lansdale, L. (1985). The Congressional Science Fellowships in Child Development. In J.C. Masters (Ed.), *Models for training in child development and social policy* (pp. 45–50). Nashville, TN: Center for the Study of Families and Children, Vanderbilt University.

Greenberger, E. (1983). A researcher in the policy arena: The case of child labor. *American Psychologist, 38*, 104–111.

Grisso, T. (1981). *Juveniles' waiver of rights: Legal and psychological competence*. New York: Plenum.

Hayes, C.D. (1982). *Making policies for children: A study of the federal process.* Washington, DC: National Academy Press.

Juvenile Justice and Delinquency Prevention Act of 1974, Pub. L. No. 93-415, 88 Stat. 1109 (1974).

Lazar, I. & Darlington, R. (1982). Lasting effects of early education: A report from the Consortium of Longitudinal Studies. *Monographs of the Society for Research in Child Development, 47* (2–3, Serial No.195).

Melton, G.B. (1981). Effects of a state law permitting minors to consent to psychotherapy. *Professional Psychology, 12,* 647–654.

Melton, G.B. (1984). Developmental psychology and the law: The state of the art. *Journal of Family Law, 22,* 445–482.

Melton, G.B. (1985a). Organized psychology and legal policymaking: Involvement in the post-*Hinckley* debate. *Professional Psychology: Research and Practice, 16,* 810–822.

Melton, G.B. (1985b). Sexually abused children and the legal system: Some policy recommendations. *American Journal of Family Therapy, 13,* 61–67.

Melton, G.B., Koocher, G.P. & Saks, M.J. (Eds.). (1983). *Children's competence to consent.* New York: Plenum.

Melton, G.B., Petrila, J., Poythress, N.G., Jr., & Slobogin, C. (1987). *Psychological evaluations for the courts: A handbook for mental health professionals and lawyers.* New York: Guilford Press.

Miller, G. (1983). Children and the Congress: A time to speak out. *American Psychologist, 38,* 70–76.

Missing Children's Assistance Act of 1984, Pub. L. No. 98-473, 98 Stat. 2125 (1984).

Pennhurst State School & Hospital v. Halderman, 451 U.S. 1 (1981).

Scott, E., & Derdeyn, A. (1984) Rethinking joint custody. *Ohio State Law Journal, 45,* 455–498.

Senn, M.J.E. (Ed.). (1977). *Speaking out for America's children.* New Haven, CT: Yale University Press.

Specter, A. (1986, February 5). Senate Concurrent Resolution 106: Disapproving request for recission of juvenile justice funds appropriated for fiscal year 1986. *Congressional Record, 132,* S1068–S1070.

Steiner, G.Y. (1976). *The children's cause.* Washington, DC: Brookings Institute.

Steiner, G.Y. (1981). *The futility of family policy.* Washington, DC: Brookings Institute.

Takanishi, R. (1981). *Preparing a policy-relevant report: Guidelines for authors.* Los Alamitos, CA: National Center for Bilingual Research.

U.S. Senate, Subcommittee on Juvenile Justice. (1984, May). *Child sexual abuse victims in the courts* (Senate Hearing 98-1207, Serial No. J-98-119).

Ziegler, H., & Baer, M. (1969). *Lobbying: Interaction and influence in American state legislatures.* Belmont, CA: Wadsworth.

From Within the System: Educational and Research Programs at the Federal Judicial Center

GORDON BERMANT
RUSSELL R. WHEELER

This chapter shares with the others in this volume a concern with the relationship between social science information on the one hand, and the judicial process and its administration on the other. Most commentators on this relationship approach it from the perspective of social scientists, or perhaps social reformers or advocates, who desire to improve the amount and content of social science information that judges receive. In other words, the relationship is addressed from outside the judiciary as an institution, looking in and attempting to be, if not helpful, at least influential.

This chapter introduces a different perspective on that relationship—a view from inside the courts (specifically, the federal courts). But we emphasize immediately that we are not enunciating an official position on how third-branch administrative agencies should communicate social science information

The points of view expressed in this chapter are our own and should not be taken in any way as reflecting the positions of the Federal Judicial Center. On matters of policy, the Center speaks only through its Board. Information herein is accurate as of March 1987.

Gordon Bermant. Division of Research, Federal Judicial Center, Washington, D.C.

Russell R. Wheeler. Division of Special Educational Services, Federal Judicial Center, Washington, D.C.

to judges. For the most part, there is no official position; common sense and general concepts of professional responsibility provide implicit guidance. Rather, we are providing our perspectives as two social scientists and administrators whose daily responsibilities include collecting, organizing, and facilitating the distribution of one part of the voluminous stream of information on various topics that is received daily by the close to 1,500 judicial officers of the federal district courts and courts of appeals.

When viewed from the outside, the social scientist's problem, as it were, is to find how he or she can bring information and influence to bear on the judicial process. In a specific case, the social scientist may seek to educate a judge or jury as an expert trial witness or as a technical brief writer. Or the social scientist may wish to educate the judiciary by publishing articles that inform the judicial mind about general questions that will appear in various forms in different cases. In the first instance, the social scientist's behavior is shaped by the procedural rules that govern the adversary process. In the second instance, the social scientist is perceived for what he or she is: a scholar whose analysis judges may evaluate on its merit and its source, whereupon it may become part of a judge's frame of reference through judicial notice or more general absorption.

In both instances, however, there is usually some fact, generality, or body of coherent data that the scientist believes the court should know. This belief implicates basic questions, some of which are discussed elsewhere in this volume. For example, is social science information always in the category of "legislative facts," and never in that of "adjudicative facts"? Does social science information tend to invade the jury's factfinding province? Do legally appropriate standards exist for assessing the accuracy of social science information? To what degree may judges search beyond the boundaries of the adversary process for general information relevant in a specific case—that is, to what degree may they educate themselves about legislative facts?

Increasingly, some social scientists working outside the judiciary seek to bring another type of information to judges: information to aid them in their administrative duties: For example, does one jury selection procedure operate more efficiently and fairly than another? Social scientists who seek to impart information on judicial administration to judges are in much the same situation as those who hope to broaden the judicial perspective on matters likely to arise in litigation. The social scientist is perceived as a scholar whose analysis the judges may evaluate on its merit and source.

Our situation within the judiciary is quite different from that of the social scientist who is working outside the judiciary. We must approach the task of bringing information—some of which is social-scientific—to judges in ways and at times that thoroughly insulate us and the judges from the possibility, or even the appearance of the possibility, that the information is aimed at influencing any judge's decision in any specific case. The Federal Judicial Center is not any part of the legal research capacity judges draw upon in deciding individual cases. Moreover, members of the judiciary's own research and education agency have a special trust, even if the information they disseminate is in no way case-related: Judges must have confidence that the agency has no special axe to grind, that the information it provides to judges has no hidden biases.

Though it may come as no surprise that the federal judiciary as an institution has fostered its own research, development, and educational agency, we have discovered that the social science community is generally unaware of the Federal Judicial Center's history and scope. It is difficult to understand the potential and the limitations of internal judicial-branch research and education without first reviewing this material. We preface our discussion therefore with background material on the Center's history, purpose, and current operation—information that puts the important issues into accurate context.

THE FEDERAL JUDICIAL CENTER

Congress created the Federal Judicial Center in 1967 at the behest of the leadership of the federal judiciary (Wheeler, 1980). As we have indicated, it is decidedly an internal agency of the federal court system. Its lineage is not traceable in any direct sense to the "Ministry of Justice" that Cardozo (1921) proposed—two or three law or political science professors, a lawyer, and a judge who would recommend changes in the procedure, jurisdiction, and evidence rules to the legislature. That concept led to the state judicial councils, which flourished in the 1920s and 1930s but are now dead in all but a few states (Wheeler & Jackson, 1976).

The Federal Judicial Center, rather, is an extension of the concept of court administrative offices, born in the federal system when Congress created the Administrative Office of the United States Courts in 1939 to prepare the judicial budget, administer its personnel functions, and generally serve the courts' housekeeping needs. The Center is a companion agency to the Administrative Office. Until the Center was created, the Administrative Office had been trying to manage research and education projects in addition to its administrative tasks. Very important figures in the founding of the Center include Chief Justice Earl Warren, Warren Olney III (then Director of the Administrative Office), and Justice Tom Clark, who became the Center's first Director in 1968 upon his retirement from the U.S. Supreme Court. Justice Clark retired from the Center in 1970, and was followed as Director by Judge Alfred P. Murrah, a senior judge on the Tenth Circuit Court of Appeals. In 1974 Judge Murrah retired, and Judge Walter Hoffman from the Eastern District of Virginia became Director. Judge Hoffman served until 1977. The current Director of the Center is Professor A. Leo Levin, of the School of Law of the University of Pennsylvania.

The mandate of the Center is contained in the language of its statute codified at 28 U.S.C. §§ 620–629. The statute specifies that the Center is established "within the Judicial branch" of the federal government. That language reflects a decision not to make the Center a unit of the Administrative Office. Housing research and education offices in court administrative offices was the emerging pattern in state court systems. The organizational location of the Center apart from the Administrative Office reflected an awareness on the part of Congress, and especially Administrative Office Director Olney, that operational needs tend to drive out planning, research, and education.

The Center is moored to the Judicial Conference of the United States. The Judicial Conference, by statute the federal courts' administrative governing body, is chaired by the Chief Justice of the United States and includes 26 other judges serving *ex officio* or elected from regional circuits. The Conference, in turn, is served by an elaborate structure of almost 20 standing and ad hoc committees, with several hundred members, most of whom are judges. Congress has assigned a large number of tasks to the Administrative Office (e.g., preparing the courts' appropriations request and administering the budget, gathering descriptive caseload statistics, and maintaining personnel classification standards). The office, however, is to perform these tasks under the direction of the Judicial Conference; this arrangement vests considerable authority in the Conference.

The Center's relation to the Judicial Conference is somewhat different from that of the Administrative Office, for the Center's overall policy is set by its Board, an organizational entity separate from the Judicial Conference. The Center's statute calls for the Chief Justice to be the Chairman of the Board, and also requires that the Director of the Administrative Office be a Board member. Two circuit and three district judges, and one bankruptcy judge, are elected by the Judicial Conference (but, by statute, not *from* the Conference) for 4-year terms. The Board selects the Center's director. The Center is funded entirely by an annual legislative appropriation, a separate line item in the federal judicial budget. It can accept no private funds. Its budget for fiscal year 1986 was $9,187,000, and it had an authorized permanent personnel complement of 94 full-time positions, whose incumbents are joined from time to time by various temporary employees.

The Center was established to serve the federal judiciary only; it does no work directly for state courts. Nor does it serve the U.S. Supreme Court in any direct way; neither does the Administrative Office. Historically, the Supreme Court has been autonomous with respect to its administrative, technological, and training support needs.

The Center's work is the product of its five divisions, which operate independently of one another for the most part. The major functions of the divisions may be gathered from the statutory language that specifies the work the Center is to accomplish. There is the Division of Research, which responds to the mandate "to conduct research and study of the operation of the courts of the United States" (28 U.S.C. § 620(b)(1)). There is the Division of Continuing Education and Training and the Division of Special Educational Services, both in line with the requirement to "develop and conduct programs of continuing education and training for personnel of the judicial branch" (§ 620(b)(3)). There is the Division of Innovations and Systems Development, whose mission derives from a charge to the Center's Board to "study and determine ways in which automatic data processing and systems procedures may be applied to the administration" of the federal courts (§ 623(a)(5)). Finally, the Division of Interjudicial Affairs distributes the Center's publications and media programs, maintains a library on judicial administration and related matters, publishes a judicial-branch newsletter, and otherwise links the Center to other court-related organizations. Regardless of their location within the Center's structure, staff members may be called upon to fill another statutory responsibility, which is "to provide staff, research, and planning assistance to the Judicial Conference of the United States and its committees" (§ 620(b)(4)). This responsibility is an extremely important one, creating a major avenue of information flow between professional members of the staff and the governance structure of the federal court system.

Viewed from the inside, the distinctions between the Center's divisions seem large, even obvious; even more obvious is the distinction between the Center and the Administrative Office of the United States Courts. Viewed at any distance from Washington, however, even by federal judges and their staffs, these distinctions tend to blur, and the courts' "Washington bureaucracy" takes on a relatively monolithic character. This is a fact of more than passing interest, for its influences the kinds of communications that flow to or from any point in the center bureaucracy and some point in "the field." This is probably a feature common to all national bureaucracies, but in the federal court system its character is influenced by at least one fact that is very unusual, perhaps unique: No one in the Center or the Administrative Office has any management authority over anyone working elsewhere within the federal court system. But, while line management within the third branch of government is highly decentralized, budget and spending authority remains largely under the control of the Administrative Office in Washington. The reasons for this, and its costs and benefits, are both interesting and significant for the explanation of how the federal courts operate as an administrative institution. We mention it here without further exploration as a background fact that may aid the reader to form a more accurate understanding of how the structure of the institution influences communications that occur within it.

JUDICIAL EDUCATION PROGRAMS

Our focus in this chapter is on the educational and research activities of the Center, particularly as they address judges and adjunct judicial officers.

The "student body" contemplated by the Center's statutory mandate includes the almost 1,500 circuit, district, and bankruptcy judges and magistrates (as well as more than 15,000 supporting personnel located throughout the federal system). No statute or rule requires judges or other employees to attend the Center's educational programs, although almost all elect to participate in at least some of them.

The bulk of the Center's judicial educational budget goes to national and regional seminars and workshops for both orientation and continuing education. These include regional orientation seminars for small groups of new district judges; these programs are devoted to the basic sentencing, procedural, and case management tasks the new judges will soon face. A second, week-long orientation seminar attended in the first year of service presents the basic contours of substantive law in major areas of federal litigation, such as antitrust, civil rights, employment discrimination, and securities. Annual regional workshops, very much in the tradition of continuing legal education and shaped by the participants' expressed interests, deal mainly with updates on judicial and statutory changes in the law.

The Center also has a large media library of audiotapes

and videocassettes, some specially produced but most of lectures at Center programs. It also makes available tuition grants for courses at universities and other forums, although judges are among the least frequent users of these funds. Center educational monographs, written primarily by legal academics, cover both basic (e.g., employment discrimination litigation) and relatively esoteric (e.g., black-lung litigation) areas of federal law. The Center also publishes manuals directed at the immediate practical needs of judges. Some of these address topics addressed in the monographs (again, e.g., employment discrimination); others cover important matters of case management (e.g., a guide to appellate holdings dealing with recurring problems in criminal trial management); still others present useful administrative information (e.g., a desk book for chief district court judges).

In fact, the Center's growing reliance on audiovisual media programs and on educational publications led the Center's Board in 1986, to create a separate Division of Special Educational Services to develop and administer the publications and audiovisual programs as well as a few other types of programs. In this chapter, we have treated the Center's educational activities without regard to this divisional distinction.

EMPHASIS AWAY FROM SOCIAL SCIENCE

Given the goals of this chapter, it is important to stress at the outset that the curricula of Center programs are rarely based in social science. This circumstance does not reflect a deliberate curriculum choice by the Center, but rather the Center's decision that judges' perceptions of their needs should largely drive curriculum development. Thus, the curricula of the initial orientation seminars reflect the Center's accumulated experience and the advice of experienced judges as to those topics in which new judges feel (and are) most deficient. And subsequent programs for judges are structured in a semidemocratic fashion, based on surveys of those who will participate. The result in both cases is that programs are devoted primarily to legal substance and procedure, and to court and case management techniques.

This approach to curriculum development presents the common educational problem of determining whether to respond to needs or desires. In light of the quality, not to mention the status, of federal judges, the Center has consistently hewn to the view that, by and large, federal judges' wants reflect their needs. Judges seldom express a desire for sessions with explicit social science content, and therefore there is little explicit social science in the Center's curricula for judges.

Although most lawyers and judges do not realize it, much legal learnings rests implicity on empirical propositions. Typically, though, those propositions are not the judges' major concern. Take, for example, the Federal Rules of Evidence, to which orientation programs devote considerable attention. One exception to the rules' prohibition against hearsay statements allows introduction of a "statement describing or explaining an event or condition made while the declarant was perceiving the event or condition, or immediately thereafter" (Fed. R. Evid. 803(1)). This exception rests, according to the notes of the advisory committee of judges and lawyers that drafted the rules, on "[t]he underlying theory . . . that substantial contemporaneity of event and statement negative [*sic*] the likelihood of deliberate or conscious misrepresentation" (F. R. Evid. 803(1) advisory committee's note). However dubious this theory may be to social scientists, most new judges are less interested in its validity than in how they must behave in light of the evidence rule based on it.

There are at least four explanations for the general disinclination to focus on social science propositions. First, mastering the law (e.g., the Federal Rules of Evidence) is a task quite unto itself for many new judges; the specific shape of this challenge depends on a new judge's career before appointment, but no one comes to the federal bench without some learning needs.

Second, even judges with considerable experience have bemoaned the time constraints and workload pressures precluding the unhurried reflection and examination that judges seem to have enjoyed in an earlier era. Some have appropriated the term "bureaucratization" to describe a late-20th century judiciary in which the judging task is increasingly one of managing a caseload and directing a staff—a task in which exploration of underlying premises, including social science premises, has become a luxury (Rubin, 1980).

Third, expectations of the judicial role do not encourage judges—especially trial judges—to explore the social-scientific and other underpinnings of the legal policies given to them in the form of statutes, rules, and appellate holdings. Rather, the judicial role encourages judges to apply the law as given, rather than to debate the validity of underlying policy choices.

Finally, judges—whether newly appointed or long on the bench—are not inclined to want the benefit of social-scientific analysis to inform what they already perceive as common-sense questions to which experience provides the answer. For example, will a "mock jury" deliberate differently, depending on whether it knows that its verdict is not binding on the parties? To most judges interested in the question (which is raised in a Center educational video program), the answer is so clearly in the affirmative as to require no further analysis.

The pressures of time and the unstated skepticism regarding social science's potential contribution to the judicial process manifest themselves in various ways in Center programs. In January 1985, to give another example, the Center broadcast a 4-hour live video seminar by satellite on two October 1984 statutes that instituted major changes in federal criminal law and procedure (the Comprehensive Crime Control Act of 1984 and the Criminal Fine Enforcement Act of 1984). Approximately 170 judges and 2,000 supporting personnel in 30 major cities viewed it, and many more viewed videotapes of the broadcast. Circuit and district judges, a magistrate, prosecution and defense counsel, and others made brief presentations on aspects of the new law and then answered questions received by telephone from the viewing audience.

Social scientists might be struck by the degree to which this 4-hour program paid scant attention to the underlying propositions on which this controversial legislation was based—legislation that, for instance, modified the prior legislative assumption in favor of pretrial release of criminal defendants, drastically increased the fines for federal offenses, repealed provisions for separate treatment of youthful offenders, and significantly altered the defense of insanity. By contrast, judges were struck by the changes these two statutes (over 220 pages) required in their handling of criminal proceedings on a daily basis and by the need to conform their procedures to the changes. The immediate need to accommodate the legislation rendered contemplation of its underlying assumptions of distinctly secondary importance.

The Center also prepares special educational programs on topics ranging from juror utilization and calendar management to mandatory, nonbinding court-annexed arbitration. The emphasis in these programs is largely on informal discussion of techniques that judges' experiences have proven effective, not necessarily techniques that have been tested by social science research. (Of course, it is probably true that some judges internalize research findings into their experience, but the information as they present it to colleagues has a decidedly experiential base.) It is surprising that even this relatively simple type of information change can have dramatic impact. At one such session, a judge learned of a step in qualifying prospective jurors that could be accomplished without the need for a courtroom appearance—a step that is of major importance in districts such as hers, with large non-English-speaking populations. The change, when implemented, produced annual savings to the government of about $250,000.

PROGRAMS WITH SOCIAL SCIENCE EMPHASIS

Some Center programs present heavier emphasis on social-scientific information. For reasons discussed above, they are only a small part of the Center's judicial education work, and they do not comprise a generic category of programs. Rather, they are programs in a few select areas in which the judges themselves perceive the need to understand social science research in order to execute their judicial duties.

For example, there are the Center's periodic, regional "sentencing institutes," held pursuant to a 1958 statute that authorizes the U.S. Attorney General or (as is traditionally the case) a chief circuit judge to request the Judicial Conference to authorize an institute. Among the topics statutorily recommended for institute agendas is "the determination of the importance of psychiatric, emotional, sociological, and physiological factors involved in crime and their bearing upon sentences" (28 U.S.C. § 334(a)). Such concerns, however, do not constitute the bulk of all institute agendas; again, those agendas are set by planning groups of judges working with Center staff, and the judges' interests (and their perceptions of their colleagues' interests) will vary considerably.

Social science information was very prominent in a Center program held in the summers of 1984 and 1985 on statistics and expert testimony in the federal courts. The program was open to all district and circuit judges; fewer than 100 expressed interest in attending each session, and, both summers, fewer than 50 did so. (We offer this as no more than a crude, unobtrusive measure of judicial interest in statistical evidence; caseload and other pressures surely discouraged some from seeking to attend.)

Judges know better than anyone the increasing frequency with which they are faced with esoteric statistical proofs. Quantitative analysis is offered to establish the likelihood that observed racial patterns have occurred by chance. Arcane expert testimony comments on how market forces do or do not explain economic behavior. The Center's seminars focused on statistical and economic information as it is likely to be presented in evidence in economic litigation (antitrust and securities), employment discrimination suits, and damage claims involving calculations of the present, discounted value of future earnings. The seminars used mock cases to simulate the kind of testimony participating judges face, and they tried, through lectures and readings, to provide the judges with sufficient information on the underlying statistical theory that they could ask informed questions of those testifying. The program made no attempt, however, to offer enough information to put the judges on the same plane as those experts. In other words, with respect to communicating social science information to judges, the goal the Center has chosen is to equip judges to make the adversary system work for them.

PROTECTING THE INTEGRITY of JUDICIAL EDUCATION

Curriculum development for Center judicial education programs also raises the classic problems noted at the outset of this chapter: how to avoid contaminating the stream of adjudication, and how to avoid special pleading that may characterize some social science researchers (as it does some lawyers, law professors, and judges).

The problem has several manifestations. One is the danger that judges will learn legislative facts relevant to cases they are deciding, but learn it outside the boundaries of the adversary process. Center educational programs, by definition, do not treat cases that are *sub judice*. However, the Center is in no position to police conversations between judges and faculty members who gather for seminars, much less to regulate the telephone traffic that occurs after a seminar. One result of putting judges together in a seminar setting with first-rate academics—typically legal scholars, but social scientists on occasion—is that the judges may well seize the opportunity to explore questions that they believe parties' experts will not answer adequately during trial.

The Center's outside tuition support is sometimes sought when judges perceive a need that the adversary system is, in their view, not meeting. In the great majority of instances, the few judges who seek tuition support do so to learn about a relatively esoteric area of the law or procedure that regular Center programs do not cover. What if, however, a judge were to call the Center, explaining that he or she has a troublesome employment discrimination case in pretrial, and seeking Center support for a tutorial by a local university professor on the elements of statistics? The Center would probably be bound to respond that providing the judge with such education is a responsibility of the parties and that the Center cannot be a part of his or her learning about the issues in a case outside the bounds of the adversary process.

Another aspect of this problem is keeping Center programs free from biases and special pleading. In fact, one reason the Center offered the course on statistics in economic litigation, described above, was that many federal judges had been learning economics and statistics through an organization that, although university-based, was funded in part by corporate sponsors; this relationship caused some legislators and judges to fear that the instruction was biased.

There are few interest groups in legal and governmental environments that would not like a chance to tell judges the "real facts" of life. The Center, for example, is constantly approached by representatives of special-focus bar associations, prosecution and defense agencies, and public interest law firms, as well as by academics with particular interests, all volunteering to speak briefly to the class of new judges about their work. The Center could respond with an open-door policy, assuming that federal judges, in the business as they are of separating out the essence of an issue, can do the same when faced with this stream of volunteer experts. The Center's approach, however, has typically been to exclude such persons from its faculty except in carefully structured formats that guarantee equal time for all legitimate sides of a question.

There is, finally, a partial exception to this general principle—one that stems from the Center's role on the inside. When the Judicial Conference has taken positions on particular judicial administrative matters, those positions are prominent in any Center program dealing with the matter. For example, the Conference has implored judges to reduce the percentage of citizens who are called for jury duty but who neither serve on a jury nor are excused for service after challenge. The higher the percentage of such citizens is, the higher the unnecessary costs of the jury system and the degree of citizen frustration and wasted time become. Yet some judges are suspicious of this emphasis; they attach more importance to insuring the availability of ample numbers of jurors, just in case they may be needed, and are less concerned about a large percentage of citizens who may be called in for jury service but never become involved in the jury selection process. Despite this view by some judges, Center orientation programs emphasize the Judicial

Conference's stress on efficient utilization of jurors and urge judges to cooperate among themselves to avoid insufficient numbers of potential jurors. To give another example, Center orientation seminars present a particular approach to case management. It is an approach endorsed by many judges, and the Judicial Conference and it underlies the Federal Rules of Civil Procedure—active judicial involvement in case management and control from filing to disposition. It is not, however, an approach without its judicial critics.

Recall that the Washington bureaucracy has no line management authority over judges and supporting personnel. Even the Judicial Conference is limited in what it can mandate. And what it urges (as opposed to mandating) is not always noncontroversial, thus creating a delicate task for the Center in structuring educational programs: giving prominence to Conference positions without stifling alternative positions within the judiciary.

FEDERAL JUDICIAL CENTER
RESEARCH PROJECTS

From its inception, the Federal Judicial Center has conducted empirical inquiry to aid policy decisions affecting the rules and administration of federal courts. The location of the Center within the third branch provides a unique research perspective and favorable opportunities for data collection, verification, and analysis. But there are also risks associated with being a research organization inside the institution under study, for which the most obvious is the risk of being or appearing to be, less than totally independent of the policy positions or empirical beliefs held at the executive level of the institution. The risk is, if anything, enhanced when the research organization is embedded within the American legal system, because the typical and appropriate role of research in legal advocacy is to seek support for a position taken before the research begins (Jackson, 1977).

Providing such justification, is not, however, the role of research as practiced at the Center. The Center endorses and strives to conduct research according to the norms of objectivity and methodological rigor that characterize good applied social science. Certainly, the topics chosen for research will reflect questions and concerns from within the judiciary that empirical inquiry can answer or clarify. But once the questions are chosen, the subsequent methods, results, and interpretations are guided by the canons of social science research. Working these matters out in detail for each project is a self-conscious and important part of research at the Center. We present various examples below to illuminate this perspective on research within the courts. For other examples, and a somewhat different perspective on Center research, see Levin (1981).

How Research Projects Begin

Research at the Center begins with a question or concern within the federal judiciary. Often the question is triggered by legislative proposals about which the Congress has asked or will ask for Judicial Conference comment, or bills that the Conference itself may be considering proposing. Possible changes in procedural rules also give rise to research projects. In any case, institutional responsibility for studying the question is usually vested in a standing or an ad hoc committee of the Judicial Conference, and the committee turns to the Center for research support. Following a review by the Center's leadership, a decision to proceed with the project causes a research project team to be formed.

Once the team is formed, the researchers meet with the committee or a subcommittee thereof to clarify the required scope and depth of the research plan. This is a critically important stage of the process, because the researchers must be sure that the plan addresses the committee's questions in ways that are most likely to answer them. It may arise that the question as initially put is unanswerable by an empirical inquiry—if, for instance, a useful empirical answer first requires answers to questions that are normative or heavily policy-laden. This is true, for one example, in almost any research project designed (intentionally or not) to demonstrate variability in practices between judges or districts or circuits. Demonstration of variability per se, without standards anchoring the measurement to a normative baseline, may be interesting but are not useful as a guide to policy formation or change.

When the questions have been clarified, the staff and committee must agree that the research plan addresses the question meaningfully from the judicial perspective as well as the social science perspective. The researchers, for example, tend to be relatively more interested than judges are in quantification, and are prepared to be persuaded by quantitative arguments from the data. If the researchers rely too heavily on operational definitions and quantifiable proxy variables as stand-ins for concepts that judges think of primarily in qualitative terms, the judges may partially reject the research methods and findings as being irrelevant to their concerns. As noted above, judges are not generally disposed to believe that social science is required for the resolution of the problems they face. Also, they are frequently suspicious of social scientist's ability to comprehend and measure all the relevant variables. One research area that presents some problems for meaningful quantification, for example, is measurement of relative burdens that different kinds of cases impose on judges.

Not all research projects begin with requests from Judicial Conference committees. In some cases a committee of judges may be formed under the auspices of the Center itself, to work with Center staff on a topic that the Board and Director of the Center believe warrants the Center's research coverage. The Center's Advisory Committee on Experimentation in the Law (Federal Judicial Center, 1981), described below, is one example.

Individual courts or judges may work with the Center to develop ideas for research that lead to the organization of a project. Examples include the Center's research on the Civil Appeals Management Plan in the Second Circuit (Goldman, 1977; Partridge & Lind, 1983); a program of innovations in the Ninth Circuit (Cecil, 1985); and a description and review of the original "summary jury trial" procedure invented by Judge Thomas Lambros of the Northern District of Ohio (Jacoubovitch & Moore, 1982).

In short, much of the Center's research arises from an

interest expressed by one more of the Center's "significant others"—in particular, committees of the Judicial Conference or the Center itself, and individual judges and courts. But this does not mean that the Center research staff is always passive in the choice of research topics. Many members of the Center's staff are in frequent contact on a number of matters with judges, circuit executives, clerks of court, and other members of the court staff; from these contacts, the staff develops a sense of prevailing interests and concerns. The staff is also aware of developments in Congress that are likely to affect judicial activities and to have implications that can be understood more fully through the results of a research project. By staying current with legislative developments and informally expressed judicial interests, as well as by remaining abreast of academic interests and research in judicial administration and related legal fields, the Center often provides leadership in the choice of significant research topics.

RESEARCH GOALS

Research at the Center is performed to achieve one or more of several goals. No list of these goals is likely to be totally complete or accurate, but here we offer a set of three general goals that is reasonably comprehensive and true to the Center's research projects as we know them.

Description and Analysis

Center researchers have developed a strong familiarity with the details of the federal judicial process and its environment. This expertise allows the researchers to describe and analyze complex statutes and agency operations for the benefit of judicial officers.

For example, the laws governing federal criminal sentencing and the policies of the U.S. Parole Commission create an incredible labyrinth of choices for federal judges and magistrates to effectuate the sentences they wish defendants to serve. A regularly updated pamphlet, *The Sentencing Options of Federal*

District Judges (Partridge, 1985), explains how law and policies mix to limit those options. Judges are told immediately that when they sentence "a criminal offender to a term of imprisonment, one thing is nearly certain: The offender will not be imprisoned for the period specified in the sentence. The sentence imposed by the judge is a fiction" (Partridge, 1985, p. 1). (If, as expected, guideline sentencing takes effect in November 1987, parole will be abolished; in turn this new system will have its own complexities that will require analysis and explanation.)

Other examples of Center reports that clarify complex issues deal with judicial regulation of attorneys' fees (Willging, 1984), with problems in managing the numerous cases filed by victims of asbestosis (Willging, 1985), and with various alternative methods of dispute resolution (Shuart, 1984). Still another example shows how academic researchers may reach the judiciary through Center-supported publication of legal analysis. As part of an extensive project on the management of complex civil litigation, the Center asked Professors Luneburg and Nordenberg to prepare a thorough review and analysis of the law on expert juries and special tribunals (Luneburg & Nordenberg, 1981). This publication is but one of many that could be cited; all exemplify a mutually beneficial relationship between the Center and the legal academic community.

It is important to distinguish between these examples of analytic research and other legal research in which law, facts, and expert opinion are marshaled to support a position already held by the sponsor of the research. Though it would be a mistake to distinguish too strongly between the Center's research activities and the activity of a social scientist deploying arguments in favor of a strongly held hypothesis, the real differences between them are important. Indeed, the credibility of the Center, like that of any research organization within an institution whose prominent members have public opinions on researchable issues, depends on the research staff's ability to understand the differences and to stay on the proper side of the border between the two activities. As a rule, the norms governing this aspect of the Center's research activity are equivalent to those guiding its educational efforts, as described above in the section on protection of educational integrity.

Invention

Much of the Center's work in automation has been aimed at inventing software systems to aid the courts in their administrative activities. The analysis and design phases of this work are clearly research efforts, in that various approaches and alternatives may have to be tested and modified or discarded before a good solution is achieved. The methods applied to this work are not, however, the experimental and quasi-experimental methods of evaluation research. They are the methods of prototyping and change resulting from frequent, intensive communication with the courts that cooperate with the Center in specifying system requirements and testing the Center-developed software as "pilot courts." The eventual calculations of a system's costs and benefits are inevitably and appropriately based on understandings of the system's utility after it has been completed, rather than on predictions of its utility and effects before it has been built. The goal of the system (e.g., to replace the current paper dockets with an electronic docketing system) is either reached or not reached; the courts can utilize the system under their real-life budget constraints or they cannot; and so on. The criteria for evaluation normally do not require the heavy apparatus of experimental method (Weis & Bermant, in press).

Other research conducted in the context of invention could be subjected to the rigors of evaluation, but is not likely to be. Examples include the set of prescriptions for improving the quality of judicial voire dire that Chmielewski and Bermant (1982) made as part of an ongoing research project on federal voir dire practices, and the set of pattern jury instructions constructed under the guidance of judges serving on a Federal Judicial Center committee (Federal Judicial Center, 1982). The costs and other difficulties of conducting rigorous research on the validity of these recommendations seem out of proportion to the benefits that would be gained from it. Moreover, it is very important for the Center to be able to suggest innovation, and to pass along innovations suggested by judges, without always pausing to mount a major evaluation effort.

Evaluation

The development of a self-conscious discipline of evaluation research has encouraged the use of research designs and statistical analyses associated with "pure research" for evaluating the effectiveness of program alterations in ongoing institutional arrangements. The goals of the research are to bring as much inferential power as possible to the interpretation of the changes in behavior (whether individual or institutional) that follow program alteration, and to determine whether the changes correspond to the intentions or predictions of the officials who have been responsible for altering the program.

The history of research at the Federal Judicial Center reveals a long-standing commitment to conducting research with a goal of evaluation, either explicit or implicit, in the research design. The work of Partridge and Eldridge (1974) on judicial impositions of criminal sentences brought relatively controlled methods to bear on a very important question with potential policy implications: Is sentencing disparity a product of different cases or of different judges? And Goldman's (1977) study of the Civil Appeals Management Plan in the Second Circuit was a relatively early example of the introduction of random assignment of conditions into an ongoing program for evaluation purposes. Center research on court-annexed arbitration has also utilized random assignment procedures (Lind & Shapard, 1983).

The Center's research uses random assignment only after careful review of the alternatives. Because of its strong awareness of the ethical issues raised by the use of true experiments in justice system settings, the Center has sponsored and provided research support for a thorough critique of these issues. The methods and results of this project are described next as an example of a major Center project, and also as an illustration of how Center efforts can have value for agencies and institutions beyond the federal courts.

EXPERIMENTATION IN THE LAW

Basic to our concept of justice, or fairness, is that like cases are to be treated alike. Basic to our concept of scientific method is that causal relationships are best explored when like cases are treated differently and unlike cases are treated identically, and the outcomes are then carefully evaluated. Therefore, when we consider doing rigorous experimentation within ongoing justice system programs, there arises an immediate tension between the norms of justice and the norms of science. In some instances, the tension is easily resolved either in favor of or against experimentation, but in others—the more interesting ones—the problem does not yield easily to resolution.

In January 1978, Chief Justice Burger, as Chairman of the Center's Board, appointed the Federal Judicial Center Advisory Committee on Experimentation in the Law. The committee comprised 13 leading thinkers drawn from several professions and disciplines, including the judiciary, legal practice and law teaching, philosophy, and psychology. The mission of the committee was specified by the Chief Justice in his letter of invitation:

> The mission of the Committee will be to try to identify, define, analyze, and recommend resolution of issues bearing on the propriety, value and effectiveness of controlled experimentation for evaluating innovations in the justice system. Controlled experiments involve the random provision of disparate treatments. It is the most potent methodology for evaluative research—standard in medicine, education and psychology. We need to apply this concept to our problems even at the risk that its use in courts and other justice agencies may possibly raise constitutional and political questions peculiar to justice institutions. It is these questions with which the committee must deal. The ultimate purpose will be to provide guidance to researchers, judges and administrators who must decide what areas are appropriate for controlled experimentation. (Federal Judicial Center, 1981, p. 79)

The committee conducted its work through 10 sessions of 2 days each, and then prepared its report, which was published by the Center in September 1981 (Federal Judicial Center, 1981). Appended to the report is an introduction to the methods of empirical evaluation that may be used in relation to program experiments or other innovations in the justice system (Lind,

Shapard, & Cecil, 1981). Prepared specifically for the committee's use, this brief document has proved to be a very useful
brief introduction to research design and related issues.

The committee's report carefully distinguishes program
experiments from other forms of applied research: "A program
experiment is an alteration in the actual operation of the justice
system designed to show whether such an alteration would be
an improvement over the status quo" (Federal Judicial Center,
1981, p. 3). A critically important fact about the ethical analysis
of program experiments is that the experiment is always one
among a series of action alternatives that the agency may undertake. Experimentation in the legal system is never an issue
to be taken out of the context of ongoing action; the questions
raised about doing the experiment must also be raised about
doing any of the alternatives in the absence of an experiment.

The report proposes that four questions must be answered
during the process of deciding whether to conduct a program
experiment. First, do the circumstances justify resorting to a
program experiment? Second, what methods of experiment
(randomization, quasi-experimental methods, etc.) will be required? Third, what ethical problems arise from the application
of these methods in this context, and how are they to be resolved? And fourth, what authority and procedures are required to conduct the experiment?

The several chapters of the committee's report give thorough consideration to answers for each of these questions. In
response to the first question, the report concluded that experimentation is permissible only when the status quo requires
substantial improvement, when there is significant uncertainty
about the value of the proposed change, when experimentation
is the only feasible means to obtain the relevant information,
and when the experiment is aimed directly at determining the
correctness of moving to full-scale adoption of the innovation.

In response to the second question, the committee briefly
reviewed the various forms of research design and the inferential strengths and weaknesses that each presents, as well as
highlighting the ethical problems unique to each. The committee emphasized that the ethical costs of rigorous experimentation must always be balanced against the ethical costs of

proceeding with full implementation of a program in the absence of information of its effects, but that poor experimentation is not justified as a compromise between good research and no research at all.

The third question, about the ethical problems involved with applying a particular research design in a given setting, received the committee's most extended attention. The committee approached the question using the concept of balance; the task in each instance, they concluded, is to balance the benefits of conducting the experiment against the harms the experiment entails. But the degree of harm occasioned by the experimental manipulations must be very carefully considered, and in some instances an experimental treatment is to be considered harm per se. This applies, for example, when experimental participation is mandatory, whether in the treated or the untreated group. This is only one of the committee's very useful formulations; unfortunately, no summary in the space available can adequately capture the committee's major conclusions in this area, not to mention the richness of its commentary.

The fourth question concerned required authority and procedures. As to authority, the committee concluded, first, that legal authority to conduct a program experiment requires prior legal authority to implement the innovation on a nonexperimental basis. To put it differently, one may not introduce a program, as an experiment, that one would not have the legal authority to introduce as a fully operational program. Second, legal authority to introduce a program operationally may not be sufficient authority to introduce the program experimentally, if the experiment itself entails imposition of harm beyond the level of harm expectable in the program itself. This situation might arise, for example, as a result of random assignments to disparate treatments. In this case, the administrator must seek higher authority before proceeding with the experiment. And finally, as to required procedures, the committee concluded that agencies contemplating program experiments should establish advisory bodies within the organization for review and guidance of all research proposals, and that statements of justification for program experiments should be made part of a set of "informal precedents" for use in the developing body of material available on the ethics of program experimentation.

The work of this committee constituted an important landmark in the analysis of the ethics of applied social research in the justice system, and it is particularly appropriate that the committee and its report were sponsored by the Federal Judicial Center.

Two Further Case Studies of Research

The foregoing description of the work of the Center's committee on experimentation provides a glimpse of one kind of Center research product. In this section of the chapter, we present two further descriptions of the Center's research efforts, placing them in the contexts in which they arose and discussing them in the light of the issues that, it seems to us, will attend much of the policy research that is conducted by a research organization located within the institution it aims to study. The two studies have been chosen from among the dozens of studies published by the Center because they present issues worthy of description and also because we ourselves were closely enough involved with them to be familiar with their details. A complete list of Center publications, including its research reports, is given in its annual *Catalog of Publications*, and new items are reported in *The Third Branch*, a monthly bulletin available from the Center to all interested readers.

Quality of Advocacy in the Federal Courts

The quality of advocacy in the federal courts had been a matter of public concern to Chief Justice Burger for some time (Burger, 1973) when, in September 1976, he appointed a committee of the Judicial Conference to conduct an inquiry.

"Trial advocacy" refers specifically to lawyers' courtroom activities—examining and cross-examining witnesses, monitoring opponents' advocacy and objecting where necessary, and addressing the judge and jury. The immediate source of Chief Justice Burger's concern over trial advocacy was the possibility that the adversary system's trial component was not serving its factfinding function (it was acknowledged that most cases were not proceeding to trial). Inadequate advocacy could limit factfinding either because neither advocate was up to the task, or because there was imbalance between them. Inadequate advocacy could also contribute to other problems that Chief Justice Burger and others bemoaned more frequently. Poor courtroom advocacy, for example, could unnecessarily lengthen a trial and thus delay resolution of the litigation and squander the time of litigants, the instant parties, and the judge.

The committee appointed by the Chief Justice, the Committee of the Judicial Conference of the United States to Consider Standards for Admission to Practice in the Federal Courts, was composed of judges, prominent lawyers, and legal academics from throughout the country. One of its earliest actions was to appoint a subcommittee on procedures and methods, which in turn worked with the staff of the Federal Judicial Center to develop the appropriate research agenda. Research was conducted throughout 1977 and into 1978. The Center then prepared a report of its findings and presented it to the committee, as a regular part of the Center's research report series, in August 1978 (Partridge & Bermant, 1978).

The logic that the committee followed in commissioning the Center's research indicates the standard of objectivity to which applied research in the third branch aspires. Rather than assuming the existence of a significant problem of poor advocacy, the committee asked the Center to determine the actual rates of inadequate performance as accurately as possible. More particularly, the Center's research addressed three questions: (1) How important is the problem of inadequate trial and appellate advocacy? (2) Do some segments of the bar (e.g., public lawyers, young lawyers, house counsel) display more inadequacy than other segments do? (3) Are some segments of trial or appellate performance (e.g., pretrial preparation, oral argument before and during trial, direct and cross-examination techniques) more appropriate than others as targets for systematic efforts at improvement?

Obviously, a key ingredient for a successful research approach to these questions is a valid measure of adequate advocacy. The literature available at the time (and still today) does not inspire confidence that we can build general and objective measures of lawyering skills out of an analysis of behavioral samples. For the purposes of the study, therefore, the research relied for estimates of adequacy on the ratings given by judges of lawyers' performances. Thus, the Center asked every federal district and appellate judge to complete case report forms evaluating the performances of every lawyer appearing before the judge in trials, or appellate oral arguments, that ended during a specified 4-week period in 1977. The information requested on the forms was intended to allow the Center to attempt answers to the three questions that guided the research.

The case reports provided the major material material from which the committee drew its conclusions. But several additional research instruments also provided valuable information. To begin with, each district and appellate judge was requested to complete a relatively lengthy opinion questionnaire about the adequacy of advocacy. The lead question was framed to go to the primary focus of the committee's concern: "Do you believe that there is, overall, a serious problem of inadequate trial [appellate] advocacy by lawyers with cases in your court?" Subsequent questions repeated the substance of the first question for different segments of the bar and different aspects of the practice. The language of these categories overlapped with the language used in the case reports the judges filled out for each of the lawyers coming before them during the test period. The goal was to capture the degree of congruity between general opinions and actually measured performances occurring in the same settings. The research design called for judges to fill out the general opinion questionnaires before they undertook the evaluation required by the case reports.

Lawyers whose performances were evaluated during the study were requested to supply a small amount of biographical information so that these background characteristics could be tabulated against the judges' appraisals of the performances. In addition, a sample of highly experienced federal trial and appellate lawyers received opinion questionnaires including many of the same questions that were put to the judges on their opinion questionnaires. A final research instrument was designed to move one step beyond opinion polling and performance appraisals to assess the reliability of expert judgments of the adequacy of advocacy. Vignettes of trial and appellate performances were created from existing videotape archives of actual and realistically simulated trial and appellate performances. These vignettes were then shown to a number of judges and highly experienced trial lawyers, who evaluated the performances in terms of categories that were also used in the judges' case report forms.

One impressive feature of all Center research requiring data collection from judges is the response rate. In the present instance, 75% of the district judges either completed case report forms or reported that they had no trials ending during the 4-week window of observation; moreover, 81% percent of the trial judges and 75% of the appellate judges returned the opinion questionnaires. The published report contains a thorough analysis of the likely consequences of response rate for each of the research instruments that had been distributed.

The results of the research may have been surprising to at least some readers of the report. In the case reports, the judges reported 8.6% of the 1,969 rated performances to be "not quite adequate," "poor," or "very poor." (These were the bottom three categories of a seven-category scale that also included "first rate: about as good a job as could have been done," "very good," "good," and "adequate but no better.") At the appellate level, the measurements were more complex because performances had been rated by either one, two, or three members of a three-judge appellate panel. Variability among judges rating the same performance had to be respected in reporting the results. Thus, using the least favorable rating of 465 performances rated by three judges, 11.2% of the performances fell in the lowest three categories; using the most favorable rating for these same performances, only 2.2% of the performances were rated as less than adequate. The middle rating of the three, which was arguably the one to be preferred, generated a 4.3% return of ratings of less than adequate performance. On balance, one might reasonably conclude (at least tentatively) that the adequacy of appellate performances was generally evaluated as no worse than the adequacy of trial performance, and perhaps as somewhat better.

The general opinion questionnaires revealed that a sizeable minority of the responding trial judges, 41%, believed that there was a serious problem of inadequate advocacy in their trial courts. The equivalent percentage for the appellate judges was 32%.

The results of the videotape experiment were particularly interesting in three ways. First, there was considerable variability among judges and trial lawyers viewing these brief segments of advocacy. Judges used six of the seven categories to rate three of the performances, and all seven categories to rate the fourth. Second, there was a significant association between judges' ratings of videotaped performances and their response to general opinion questions about the existence of a significant problem of trial advocacy. Judges who believed there was a serious problem also tended to give lower ratings to the four performances. And third, judges as a group were less severe critics of the performances than were the trial lawyers who also assessed them.

One of the most interesting aspects of this research was the response to the report after its publication. The question facing the policymakers was, of course, whether the results justified the development of additional requirements for admission to the bar. Whether they did or not was not immediately discernible from the numbers themselves. For example, an 8.6% rate of inadequate performance, estimated nationally by these judges, did not imply the absence of particular districts with very serious problems of inadequate federal trial advocacy; perhaps litigation in these districts would benefit by increasing the entrance and continuing education requirements for membership in the federal bar. And indeed, some proponents of stiffer admission requirements argued that the 8.6% figure itself was cause for serious concern. One judge noted that when the percentage of "adequate but no better" ratings was added to the 8.6% in the three lowest categories, a full 25% of the performances were "less than 'good.'" This novel but literally correct reading of the data may stand as a lesson in how the semantics of research instruments may be turned to reflect different predispositions about the data's significance for policy.

Opponents of increasing admission requirements were not united in their responses to the report. Some decided that undiluted adversary advocacy was the way to approach it, so they assailed the report as the work of a captive research organization, finding whatever technical flaws they could. Others saw in the results a presumptive argument against increasing admission requirements, and therefore credited the report as objective and sound. Both sets of responses provide further education in the relationship between applied research and the rhetoric of policy formation.

The Judicial Conference committee accepted the report, and on the basis of it plus other activities, including public hearings around the country on the problems of advocacy and admission to federal practice, submitted its own report to the Judicial Conference as a whole. With a single dissenting vote, the committee concluded that the problem of advocacy adequacy in federal courts was serious enough to warrant the development of pilot projects in districts around the country to test different forms of admission requirements, peer review, and continuing legal education.

Evaluating Two Methods of Court Reporting

Some aspects of federal court operations are more closely controlled by explicit statutory language than one might initially imagine. One operation under relatively close control, for example, is the creation of the official record of courtroom proceedings and the official transcripts from those records—in short, what is normally called "court reporting." In this section, we describe how changes in the law involved the Federal Judicial Center in a major research project with requirements and implications that were surprisingly interesting and complex.

The Federal Courts Improvement Act of 1982 was a multipurpose statute with provisions governing such matters as the tenure of chief judges, postjudgment interest rates, and the creation and publication of appellate court rules. In this statute, however, Congress also enacted a prospective amendment to a provision then in place governing court reporting methods (28 U.S.C. § 753(b), 1976). The prospective amendment would permit use of "electronic sound recording" as an official means of creating the verbatim record of trial or other official proceedings (such as some in-chambers conferences). The statute then in force required the use of "shorthand or mechanical means" (i.e., stenotype), but allowed court reporters to tape-record the proceedings with their own equipment to help them in preparing transcripts when requested by the parties for review or submission to an appellate court. The statute also required that the official transcript of the record be limited to transcripts certified by the official court reporter and made from the records taken by the reporter. Under this stature, the official record was thus typically the bundles of narrow white paper containing the reporter's stenographic symbols. The official transcript was the transcript produced from this record, either by the reporter or by someone hired by him or her, using some combination of dictation, notes, and/or the auxiliary sound recording.

The prospective amendment introduced language referring to "the reporter or other individual designated to produce the record," either of whom could certify the record (which could be an electronic sound recording) and cause an official transcript to be made from it. The amendment left the method to be used in any specific proceeding to the individual district judge—subject, however, to regulations that the Judicial Conference could (but was not mandated to) promulgate. The regulations could not, in any event, be promulgated before October 1, 1983.

The tentative nature of this court reporting amendment came from the language of the final paragraph of the subsection, which held the amendment in abeyance for at least 1 year after the effective date of the Federal Courts Improvement Act itself (October 1, 1982) and directed further,

> During the one-year period after the date of the enactment of this Act, the Judicial Conference shall experiment with the different methods of recording court proceedings. Prior to the effective date of such regulations [i.e., those referenced above, which would guide district judges' selection of their reporting method], the law and regulations in effect

the day before the date of enactment of this Act shall remain in full force
and effect. § 401(b)

In other words, Congress authorized the Judicial Conference
to give effect to the prospective statutory amendment by issuing
the regulations. Whether it issued the regulations would presumably depend, at least in part, on whether the statutory mandated research provided grounds for believing that electronic
sound recording was adequate as a federal court reporting
method.

What was the operational significance of this congressional
action? There was, on the one hand, sincere congressional interest in allowing the federal courts and the litigants appearing
in them to benefit from the potential economies available from
an apparently proven technology (audiotape recording). On the
other hand, there was considerable caution in moving into a
situation that threatened or appeared to threaten, the livelihoods of the several hundred certified federal court reporters
who were fully employed in the use of stenotype for the pro-
duction of the record. Moreover, although audiotape recording
had been reported to be successful in some state courts and
elsewhere, numerous horror stories qualified these favorable
reports, and there was a general concern that the chief impetus
for using audio recording was to save money, albeit with a
decrease in quality. An earlier report by the General Accounting
Office (which evaluates government operations directly for the
Congress) had called for the replacement of stenographic records by electronic sound recordings (General Accounting Office, 1982), but this report had run into a firestorm of criticism
from the organized court reporters and some federal judges.
Hence, Congress put off its final decision for a year and called
for research to be conducted within the judiciary, and left it to
the judiciary (acting administratively) to allow the amendment
to take effect. Congress did not specify what the research needed
to demonstrate, and, of course, retained its prerogative to leg-
islate further.

The Center responded to the congressional mandate for
research in its role as research assistant to the Judicial Conference. Several requirements were clear from the outset of the
project. First, the research had to be completed by the end of

the 1-year waiting period—that is, by October 1, 1983. Second, the research had to deal directly with the comparative merits of electronic sound recording and the stenography that the recording could legally replace if the new law went into effect. It would be inadequate to limit research to studies of dollar costs of the two systems; questions of transcript accuracy and timeliness also required investigation. And third, the design and conduct of the research should be fully in the public eye and subject to scrutiny by any involved parties, including representatives of the court reporters and those who manufactured stenotype equipment (including auxiliary computer equipment that can be programmed to produce transcript from stenotype symbols).

Both court reporters and vendors were intensely concerned about adverse impact of the research on their livelihoods or on the correct functioning of the federal courts. Thus, what might have seemed from outside the system to be a straightforward research project on a mundane aspect of court function was, as accomplished from within the system, a much more complex and sensitive undertaking. Federal judges themselves were of at least two minds: Some were very suspicious of established court reporting procedures, while others were equally suspicious of any alternative.

The following description of method, results, and conclusions of the study is hardly adequate to convey the totality of the research product; the interested reader is referred to the published report for a complete discussion (Greenwood, Horney, Jacoubovitch, Lowenstein, & Wheeler, 1983). We hope to provide just enough of this material to support the commentary that we believe is of greater interest in the context of this volume.

The first step in the project was to assign responsibilities for tasks. The primary responsibility for the conduct of the study was assigned to the Center's Division of Innovations and Systems Development, and responsibility for handling external correspondence (i.e., with the court reporters' associations) and other communications (i.e., with the press) about the study was assigned to the Center's Assistant Director. This distribution of responsibility had the salutary effect of freeing the primary researchers from the considerable burdens of sustaining timely and full communication with a relatively small but intensely interested public. Assigning a single person to speak about the project also reflected the policy-charged environment in which the research was taking place, as well as the realization that primary researchers may not always be the persons most skilled at describing their work in such a setting.

A second key decision was to conduct the research as a field test—that is, to establish electronic sound recording systems in a dozen courtrooms around the country, side by side with on-going stenographic reporting (which, under the terms of the statute, remained the official court reporting method through-out the research). The implementation of this major research design decision required the cooperation of the Administrative Office of the United States Courts; the judges and clerks of court in the courts where the study would take place; and, to a lesser degree, the stenographers whose activities would be paralleled by the introduction of the tape recorders and op-erators. As part of a general strategy to explain the research design and objectives as openly as possible—and, in so doing, to encourage at least the necessary minimal participation by the court reporters—a fully descriptive plan of the research was distributed in June 1982 to all who requested it, in particular to members of a task force appointed by the two major court reporting associations. Based in part on comments received after this distribution, amendments to the June plan were dis-tributed in September 1982, and a final, binding plan was re-leased on November 19, 1982, less than 11 months before the research had to be completed and published.

Twelve courtrooms were used in the experiment; in them, and in adjacent chambers, all proceedings that the official court reporter recorded were subject also to electronic sound re-cording. The courtrooms, some of which were used by several judges during the experiment, were selected to include courts in most of the 12 federal geographic circuits (10 were finally represented). The sites included courts in large metropolitan as well as nonurban areas in all parts of the country (with greatly varying levels of transcript demand). Of the participating judges, a few were decidedly in favor of electronic sound recording, a few were decidedly skeptical, and the rest had no fixed opinion. Participating judges included one member of the Judicial Conference subcommittee responsible for court reporting matters, and one member of the Center's Board. Other considerations affected the choice of experimental courts, not the least of which was placing the experiment in the states or districts of senators and representatives prominent on the congressional judiciary committees. Appeals for legislative protection could surely be anticipated if the tests suggested in any way that it was feasible to use electronic sound recording. Legislators might want to know how judges in their jurisdictions perceived the technological shift and the Center's test of it.

The basic design of the research was relatively simple. Eleven experimental courtrooms were outfitted with four-track cassette recording equipment while one used reel-to-reel equipment. Trained audio operators supervised the recording of all proceedings that were subject to official reporting. Whenever transcripts were requested from the official reporter, transcripts were also ordered from the sound recording. The Center contracted with transcription companies around the country that had some experience in such work for state courts or other agencies. The project staff oversaw several comparative analyses of samples of the official and experimental transcripts, and gathered information as well on the comparative costs and speeds of the two methods.

A major task to be accomplished was the training of the audio operators for the experimental courtrooms. Earlier research and experience in state courts and administrative agencies suggested that audio recording proceeded best when operators were specifically trained for the task; of particular importance was the operators' attention to keeping log notes of speakers and key trial events in relation to their positions on the tapes. The Center had had no experience in this activity. It therefore contracted for training services with individuals who had extensive experience with training audio operators in state court systems. The operators themselves came from the ranks of individuals currently employed on court staffs.

The Center's objectivity was potentially subject to criticism throughout the study because of its position within the court system. To provide an extra measure of objectivity, therefore, study monitors from outside the federal court system were retained at each study site for the duration of the study. These monitors were respected persons in the legal communities where the study was conducted—for example, a retired state judge, a law professor, a psychology professor, several attorneys, a former Federal Bureau of Investigation agent, and a staff member of the National Center for State Courts. They had total access to the conduct of the study at all times, and they made periodic reports on the progress of the study in their districts.

The subtlest and most demanding aspect of the research was the comparative evaluation of the accuracy of transcripts based on stenotype and audiotape records. A multistage evaluation protocol was designed that finally involved the efforts of professional proofreaders; legal assistants who screened stenotype-based and audio-based transcript differences for legal meaningfulness; a professional editor who checked transcript against tape recordings for measures of overall accuracy; and panels of federal judges and federal court practitioners who made final decisions on the functional relevance of discrepancies discovered between audio-based and stenotype-based transcripts. In the search for functionally relevant discrepancies, it was acknowledged that some transcription errors would be meaningless to those using the transcript; for example, in most cases, it would be irrelevant to an appellate judge reviewing a transcript if the statement "I don't think so" were transcribed as "I do not think so." Transcript discrepancies held to be functionally relevant were finally resolved by checking them against the original tape recordings of the proceedings. When a tape recording could not resolve a discrepancy, the official (i.e., stenographic) transcript was deemed correct.

All the study materials used for these analyses were indexed and placed on file at the Center's library, where they were available for scrutiny. Much of this material was also copied and delivered to the private research firms that were retained by the court reporters' association to scrutinize the Center's effort.

The results of the comparative evaluation of accuracy were clear-cut. In respect to overall accuracy (transcript accuracy on all matters, not just those deemed to be functionally relevant), the audio-based transcript matched the audiotape in 56% of the 5,717 discrepancies evaluated. The stenotype-based transcript matched the audiotape in 36% of the discrepancies. Neither transcript matched the tape in 3% of the discrepancies, and the audiotape record could not resolve the remaining 5% of the discrepancies.

In respect to the analysis of functionally relevant transcript discrepancies, the audio-based transcript matched the audiotape in 62% of the 744 discrepancies evaluated. Thus, the accuracy of transcript based on the audiotape record, measured in either of two contexts, was at least as great as (and arguably greater than) the accuracy of transcript based on the stenotype record.

The financial analyses in the study, based in part on figures provided to the Center by the Administrative Office of the United States Courts, concluded that the average annual cost to the government of one audio-based system in a federal district court would be somewhat less than half the cost of a corresponding official stenographic court reporting system. The results of comparative evaluation of the timeliness of transcript deliveries were not as dramatic, but were clearly supportive of allowing judges to use electronic sound recording if they wished: The audio-based transcripts were delivered just as fast as, and perhaps faster than, the stenotype-based transcripts.

A complete report of the project's rationale, history, methods, and results was published in typescript form by the Center in July 1983, in advance of the congressional deadline, and later published as part of the Center's regular research series (Greenwood et al., 1983). The report's conclusion was brief and conservative: "Given appropriate management and supervision, electronic sound recording can provide an accurate record of United States district court proceedings at reduced costs, without delay or interruption, and provide the basis for accurate and timely transcript delivery" (Greenwood et al, 1983, p. xiii). On the basis of the information in the report, the Judicial Conference acted at the appropriate time to implement the delegation of authority that the Congress had given it in the language of the amendment. The Conference did this by allowing federal district judges to choose either method of creating the record of proceeding in their courtrooms. The amendment to the court reporting statute became effective on October 1, 1983, as scheduled, and the Conference regulations allowed judges to use electronic sound recording beginning January 1, 1984. As of February 1987, 32 active and 18 senior district judges and 67 bankruptcy judges were either using electronic sound recordings to create official records in the courtrooms or were preparing to do so pending installation of equipment and training of personnel.

What role did the elaborate and intensive research effort play in the Judicial Conference's decision to implement the amendment? It would be naive to think that the judges of the Judicial Conference, and the others who served on the Conference committees that recommended favorable action, acted as clean slates on which the Center simply wrote its favorable assessment of electronic sound recording. It would surprise us to learn that all of these judges read the report—at least in any great detail. Some were favorably disposed toward electronic sound recordings, and even a mildly negative report would probably not have changed that disposition; others were negatively disposed toward electronic sound recording, and probably no report by itself regardless of how favorable it was, would have changed their minds. All judges saw the issue through the lenses of their judicial experience and their relations with and perceptions of federal court reporters, vital members of the judiciary's support personnel; such relations and perceptions are rarely neutral. Judges, like all policymakers, act on the basis of various kinds of information, of which any sort of scientific research is only one. But the role that this particular item of research was intended to play influenced the impact that it had. In the final analysis, we suspect that the Center's findings convinced most Judicial Conference and Conference committee members that they could allow their colleagues the option of using electronic sound recording with confidence that the technology had been proven beyond any reasonable doubt to be at least as adequate as stenotype reporting; indeed, most would regard the technology as having met a much higher standard.

Giving effect to the amendment was not the end of the matter. Even before the Judicial Conference voted to give effect to the amendment, lawyers, auditors, and social scientists retained by the court reporting associations and stenotype machine manufacturers combed the Center's files and audiotape records to prepare documents of their own. Preliminary pleas were sent to the Judical Conference, and after the Conference acted, lengthier documents were forwarded by the court reporters' representatives to Congress—in particular to the members of the House Judiciary Subcommittee on Courts, Civil Liberties, and the Administration of Justice. To give full airing to the strenuous protests brought to their attention, the subcommittee held a hearing on March 8, 1984. Testifying at the hearing were representatives from the Federal Judicial Center, the major court reporter associations, and one of the two consulting firms retained by the associations to critique the Center's research and report. The full text of the hearing, including documents submitted for the record, covers 267 printed pages. We do not review the substance of the hearing here, but the interested reader is referred to the text (U.S. House of Representatives, Committee on the Judiciary, 1984) for interesting examples of adversary advocacy—some of it decidedly couched in social science terminology—applied against plain research findings. No further congressional action resulted from the hearing.

We realize, of course, that most readers of the current volume have no interest in the details of federal court reporting methods. Our purpose in this description has been to illustrate how even a relatively simple innovation within government, and courts in particular, may require elaborate research and justification. This is probably as it should be, for it is critically important that the courts operate, and appear to operate, according to rational policies in full public view. Given this legitimate concern for propriety and deliberation, we should not expect to achieve more radical changes in court operation, except as these are proven to be desirable following extended periods of research, reflection, and debate.

CONCLUSIONS: ADVANTAGES AND DISADVANTAGES OF WORKING WITHIN THE SYSTEM

We conclude this chapter with a list and brief discussion of what we believe are the advantages and disadvantages accruing to the social scientist who chooses to practice within the institutional framework of his or her theoretical or applied interest. We recognize that in the context of this volume, which is aimed particularly at the interests of those who would like to affect national policy in the area of child development and child welfare, our conclusions—indeed, the entire chapter—may seem tangentially relevant at best. We hope only that our presentation has provided some additional depth of contextual understanding of the processes by which federal courts are administered and the means by which federal judges may turn to their own institutional apparatus for useful information.

First, then, we find six advantages that are worth noting:

1. Educational materials and research reports coming to the judges between Center covers carry high source credibility: Judges have good reason to believe that these materials have been created with judicial interests foremost in mind. This credibility is a very valuable asset that the Center, properly, guards with extreme care, for it can be reduced or exhausted quite easily.

2. There are usually ample opportunities to clarify the required and desired substance of educational presentations and research projects before they are undertaken. These opportunities reduce the risks of subsequent wasted time and effort. When working from outside the system, the would-be educator or researcher may have to guess as to the interests of the judges and the best approach to capturing judicial attention.

3. There is unparalleled access to elite and expert communities required for the educational and research programs.

4. Doing research is a full-time job for staff members at the Center; there is therefore minimal distraction created by unrelated job requirements. Moreover, there is funding sufficient to do the work that needs to be done. (Providing contin-

uing judicial education is likewise a full-time task; however, it requires the skills not of teaching per se, but of educational administration.)

5. If the research or educational programs point to the advisability of change, opportunities to advocate and pursue the change are relatively close at hand. However, for reasons that may be inferred from what we have said above, the Center's educational apparatus is by no means an agent of its research apparatus. Those looking from the outside often assume that the Center's seminars teach what its researchers discover. This happens occasionally, especially in areas such as sentencing procedures. Typically, however, educational needs of judges and supporting personnel only partially overlap their needs for research and analysis.

6. The research work of the Center offers gratification to those who want or need to work in an active, policy-charged setting.

Four disadvantages of working from within the system are equally cogent:

1. As a social scientist with loyalties to professional norms that transcend loyalties to one's employer, one must guard against pressures, psychic or social, to conform to what might be convenient to teach or to discover. One must adhere to the absolute imperative to distinguish between legitimate procedures for deciding *what* topics will be studied and the standards for determining *how* they will be studied, interpreted, and brought to public attention.

2. Researchers working within the system are relatively insulated from professional peer pressure to conform to high professional standards; a desire to conform to these standards must be strong among the most senior management of the organizational structure. (We observe in passing, however, that private social science consultants, with less stable funding sources, appear to suffer far greater pressures than either of us has yet experienced. See, for example, the reports and testimony of the court reporters' consultants in the congressional subcommittee hearing cited above.)

3. Full-time commitment to the special areas of institutional interest restricts opportunities for broad professional

growth, including opportunities for funded travel to national conventions or conferences not related to the immediate project at hand.

4. Research from the inside may suffer a lack of credibility from peers outside the institution. Particularly within the sociolegal research community, "outsiders" may assume that "inside" research is based on the model of legal or justification research, in which the conclusions are reached before the research is begun. The only solution to this is to be sure that the assumption is false, and to guard the research process from the subtle but powerful corrosive effects to which it may be subject. We believe that it is to the significant credit of the leadership of the Federal Judicial Center over the two decades of its existence that this final disadvantage has been minimized.

REFERENCES

Burger, W.E. (1973). The special skills of advocacy: are specialized training and certification of advocates essential to our system of justice? *Fordham Law Review, 42,* 227–242.

Cardozo, B.N. (1921). A ministry of justice. *Harvard Law Review, 35,* 120–130.

Cecil, J.S. (1985). *Administration of justice in a large appellate court.* Washington, DC: Federal Judicial Center.

Chmielewski, D., & Bermant, G. (1982). Recommendations for the conduct of the *voir dire* examination and juror challenges. In G. Bermant, *Jury selection procedures in United States district courts* (pp.53–60). Washington DC: Federal Judicial Center.

Comprehensive Crime Control Act of 1984, Title II, Pub. L. No. 98–473, 98 Stat. 1976 (1984).

Criminal Fine Enforcement Act of 1984, Pub. L. No. 98–596, 98 Stat. 3134 (1984).

Federal Courts Improvement Act of 1982, Pub L. No. 97-164, § 401, 96 Stat. 25, 56–57 (1982).

Federal Judicial Center. (1981). *Experimentation in the law: Report of the Federal Judicial Center Advisory Committee on Experimentation in the Law.* Washington DC: Author.

Federal Judicial Center. (1982). *Pattern jury instructions: Report of the Federal Judicial Center Committee to Study Criminal Jury Instructions.* Washington, DC: Author.

Fed. R. Evid. 803.

General Accounting Office. (1982). *Federal court reporting systems: Outdated and loosely supervised*. Washington, DC: Author.

Goldman, J. (1977). *An evaluation of the Civil Appeals Management Plan*. Washington, DC: Federal Judicial Center.

Greenwood, J.M., Horney, J., Jacoubovitch, M.-D., Lowenstein, F., & Wheeler, R.R. (1983). *A comparative evaluation of stenographic and audiotape methods for United States district court reporting*. Washington, DC: Federal Judicial Center.

Jackson, D.W. (1977). Program evaluation in judicial administration. In L. Berkson, S. Hayes, & S. Carbon, (Eds.), *Managing the state courts: Text and reading* (pp. 346–356). St. Paul, MN: West.

Jacoubovitch, M.-D., & Moore, C.M. (1982). *Summary jury trials in the northern district of Ohio*. Washington, DC: Federal Judicial Center.

Levin, A.L. (1981). Research in judicial administration: The federal perspective. *New York University Law Review, 26,* 237–262.

Lind, E.A., & Shapard, J.E. (1983). *Evaluation of court-annexed arbitration in the federal district courts*. Washington, DC: Federal Judicial Center.

Lind, E.A., Shapard, J.E., & Cecil J.S. (1981). Methods for empirical evaluation of innovations in the justice system. In Federal Justice Centers *Experimentation in the law: Report of the Federal Judicial Center Advisory Committee on Experimentation in the Law* (pp. 81–121). Washington, DC: Federal Judicial Center.

Luneburg, W.V., & Nordenberg, M.A. (1981). Specially qualified juries and expert nonjury tribunals: Alternatives for coping with the complexities of modern civil litigation. *Virginia Law Review, 67,* 887–1007.

Partridge, A. (1985). *The sentencing options of federal district judges* (1985 ed.) Washington, DC: Federal Judicial Center.

Partridge, A., & Bermant, G. (1978). *The quality of advocacy in the federal courts: A report to the Committee of the Judicial Conference of the United States to Consider Standards for Admission to Practice in the Federal Courts*. Washington, DC: Federal Judicial Center.

Partridge, A., & Eldridge, W.B. (1974). *The Second Circuit sentencing study: A report to the judges of the Second circuit*. Washington, DC: Federal Judicial Center.

Partridge, A., & Lind, E.A. (1983). *A reevaluation of the Civil Appeals Management Plan*. Washington, DC: Federal Judicial Center.

Rubin, A.B. (1980). Bureaucritization of the federal courts: The tension between justice and efficiency. *Notre Dame Law Review, 55,* 648–659.

Shuart, K.L. (1984). *The Wayne County mediation program in the Eastern District of Michigan*. Washington, DC: Federal Judicial Center.

28 U.S.C. § 334 (1958).

28 U.S.C. § 620– 629 (1967).

28 U.S.C. § 753 (1976).

U.S. House of Representatives, Committee on the Judiciary, Subcommittee on Courts, Civil Liberties, and the Administration of Justice. (1984). *Federal court reporters and electronic recording* (House of Representatives

Hearing 4450, Serial No. 69), Washington, DC: U.S. Government Printing Office.

Weis, J., & Bermant, G. (in press). Automation in the federal courts: Progress, prospects, and problems. *The Judges' Journal.*

Wheeler, R.R. (1980, June). *The creation of the Federal Judicial Center as a case study of innovation, autonomy, and control in judicial administration.* Paper presented at the meeting of the Law and Society Association, Madison, WI.

Wheeler, R.R., & Jackson, D.M. (1976). Judicial councils and policy planning: Continuous study and discontinuous institutions. *Justice System Journal, 2,* 121–140.

Willging, T.E. (1984). *Judicial regulation of attorneys fees: Beginning the process at pretrial.* Washington, DC: Federal Judicial Center.

Willging, T.E. (1985). *Asbestos case management: Pretrial and trial procedures.* Washington, DC: Federal Judicial Center.

Getting Child Development Research to Legal Practitioners: Which Way to the Trenches?

THOMAS GRISSO
GARY B. MELTON

The results of psychological research on children must be disseminated in a way that will inform legal practitioners in the juvenile justice system. Little attention has been given to this dissemination objective. More often, the focus has been on informing legislators and higher-level policymakers who determine the basic rules that juvenile courts must follow in making decisions about children. Many a battle has been lost, however, not for want of adequate rules and plans sent forward from the command post to the trenches, but instead because of deficiencies in supplies, ammunition, or sound reasoning at the front line where orders are interpreted in action.

This chapter explores what must be done to assure that those in the "trenches" of juvenile justice are armed with current research information bearing on their deliberations about children and families. We first explain the importance of this dissemination objective, its target individuals, and general options for reaching the targets. Then we offer some observations concerning juvenile justice practitioners' current exposure and re-

Thomas Grisso. Department of Psychology, St. Louis University, St. Louis, Missouri.
Gary B. Melton. Department of Psychology and College of Law, University of Nebraska–Lincoln, Lincoln, Nebraska.

ceptivity to psychological research, including the results of a survey of their reading habits. Finally, we offer a case study of the dissemination of the results of one research project, followed by recommendations for dissemination and for further research on dissemination efforts targeting juvenile justice practitioners.

WHY TRY TO REACH THE TRENCHES?

Juvenile courts in most states are charged with making legal determinations in a wide range of matters influencing the welfare of children. Among these matters are abuse and neglect determinations; termination of custody; custody decisions in divorce; and decisions related to the detention, adjudication, and/or treatment of children who are identified by their delinquent or nondelinquent misbehaviors. The implications of juvenile courts' decisions for the welfare of children, therefore, are far-reaching.

A state's juvenile codes and appellate decisions provide juvenile courts with basic rules and procedures that must be followed in dealing with these matters. Modern juvenile justice seeks to protect three broad interests in the formation of rules and procedures: (1) children's and families' constitutional rights; (2) the welfare or "best interests" of a child; and (3) the welfare of the community in cases involving behavior of juveniles that might endanger others.

Historically, the second of these interests—that is, the best interests of a child—has been paramount in juvenile justice philosophy. Thus, until recently, the juvenile court was allowed to exercise broad discretion; few rules limited juvenile courts, since such restrictions were presumed to inhibit efforts to meet the individual circumstances and needs of children (Platt, 1977). Reforms in juvenile justice during the past two decades, however, have created new emphasis on protection of children and families from undue intervention by the state, as well as protection of citizens from violent crime by juveniles. These emphases have manifested themselves in recent years in juvenile codes that now offer more specific rules and procedures to be followed in juvenile cases.

Even recent juvenile codes, however, continue to allow much discretion for juvenile courts in making decisions about children. For example, statutes provide few limits and little guidance to courts in their determinations of the competency of children as witnesses in cases of alleged abuse (Melton, 1981). Juvenile codes prohibit pretrial detention of juveniles not charged with a delinquency, and they often require a determination of an allegedly delinquent juvenile's danger to self or others as a precondition of detention; yet they allow juvenile courts to decide their own standards for the nature of evidence that will support conclusions about dangerousness (Grisso & Conlin, 1984). Codes specify that juveniles must waive *Miranda* rights competently prior to confessions to be used in delinquency hearings; yet questions of the nature and sufficiency of evidence of a juvenile's competence are left to juvenile courts' discretion (Grisso, 1981). And many questions in family law continue to be guided merely by the directive that the decision (e.g., for custody, placement, or guardianship) must represent the "best interests of the child" (Mnookin, 1975).

The discretion that the "command post" of juvenile justice leaves to the front-line personnel is dealt with in the "trenches" in two ways. First, juvenile court judges, local prosecutors, and law enforcement agencies may establish formal procedural policies and decision rules that will apply in their own jurisdictions, as long as they are not in conflict with the law. Second, where neither state nor local policy and rules are explicit, juvenile court personnel are free to make whatever decisions are consistent with their own interpretation of a child's and the community's interests.

Juvenile codes will continue to change in the future, but the balance of determinative rules and discretionary decision-making in juvenile justice as characterized in the preceding description will probably not change. The law's general preference to refrain from automatic decision rules (Gordley, 1984) is clearly delineated in recent appellate cases involving children (e.g., *Fare v. Michael C.*, 1979), presumably on the grounds that such rules would not provide sufficient flexibility for juvenile authorities to meet the individual needs and circumstances of children or concerns of society.

Even if there is no direct impact of relevant research at the local level, trial lawyers' awareness of such research is often critical if it is to have credibility at the appellate level. Although there is no settled jurisprudence about the legitimacy of introduction of research at the appellate level (Melton, Chapter 9, this volume; Monahan & Walker, 1986), conservative judges often are reluctant to consider evidence that has not been "tested" through cross-examination at trial (see, e.g., *Ballew v. Georgia*, 1978; see generally Tremper, Chapter 8, this volume).

Therefore, it is important but not sufficient that legislators and national- and state-level policymakers be kept informed of new findings in child development research. Social scientists who wish to put their information to use in legal decisions about children must also reach juvenile court authorities who determine local policies beyond those demanded by state codes. Furthermore, the information must reach juvenile court personnel who decide many matters on the basis of neither legislative nor judicial policy, but of their own personal understanding and beliefs about children and their "best interests."

WHO ARE IN THE TRENCHES?

Any effort to disseminate social science information to juvenile courts must begin with an understanding of the roles of juvenile court personnel who have input into courts' decisions about children.

Juvenile court judges, of course, are ultimately responsible for many of the court's decisions. Their influence is at least twofold. In their administrative and policymaking role, they provide guidelines for decisionmaking throughout their own jurisdictions. In addition, they make decisions in many individual cases in which they hear and weigh the case facts to reach a conclusion. In both roles, they apply their own presumptions and knowledge regarding children in reaching conclusions regarding their best interests. Some juvenile court judges have specialized in juvenile justice through years of practice. In many jurisdictions, however, the juvenile court bench is occupied by a different judge each year or two, because of local policy that "rotates" circuit court judges through a tour of duty in the juvenile court. Increasing these judges' understanding of children, and updating the knowledge of specialized juvenile court judges, are clearly important objectives for disseminators of child development research.

Any plan to disseminate information to juvenile courts by targeting only judges, however, would be seriously deficient. This is because juvenile court decisions depend as much upon other juvenile court personnel as upon judges themselves. Many discretionary decisions in juvenile courts require no judicial review or only perfunctory approval, such as "informal case adjustments" early in the process of many minor allegations against juveniles. Furthermore, considerable discretion rests with other court personnel to determine whether cases will be petitioned for a judicial hearing or dismissed. In cases that reach formal judicial hearing, judges are largely dependent upon the decisions of other court personnel for the types of information about children that will be introduced for the judges' consideration. Thus many decisions about children in the juvenile justice system are not merely judicial decisions, but "juvenile court" decisions involving many nonjudicial personnel.

These personnel can be grouped into three basic types. First, prosecuting and defense attorneys, as well as guardians *ad litem*, play important roles in the juvenile court's use of information related to the interests of juveniles and the community. Attorneys' perceptions and understanding of children may influence their attention to, selection of, and use of information in addressing these interests. Second, juvenile court intake and probation officers in most courts are responsible for collecting and summarizing case information to be presented to judges and for making recommendations concerning judicial decisions in juvenile cases. Often these personnel also have direct or indirect control over diversion options, petitions for judicial decisions, and development of treatment plans. Third, almost one-third of juvenile courts in 127 of the largest jurisdictions in the nation now employ mental health professionals full-time, in order to perform psychological evaluations that provide specialized information for judicial decisions (Grisso, 1984).

The trenches of juvenile justice, therefore, are occupied by a wide range of professionals with varying degrees of autonomy and control in the decision process. Any attempt to assure that juvenile court decisions are informed by current child development research must consider all of these types of professionals as targets for dissemination.

WHICH WAY TO THE TRENCHES?

Having determined what personnel are in the trenches, one must consider potential supply lines that will provide them the resources that they might use in their front-line efforts. Some methods rely on direct communications, while others merely deposit information where it may be found by target individuals.

Direct communications require the researcher (or a representative of the researcher's field) to deliver supplies in person into the hands of personnel at the front line. For example, the juvenile court practitioner might be informed of child development research results at workshops, invited addresses, or continuing education seminars. Alternatively, the researcher might monitor the juvenile court's need for information and offer it to juvenile court personnel at the propitious moment in the form of a letter, consultation, or expert testimony. Examples are provided in a case study presented later in this chapter.

One major difficulty with the direct communication method lies in the type of commitment it requires of the child development researcher. Many researchers who produce information relevant to juvenile court decisions are not predisposed to embark upon interdisciplinary teaching activities or to endure the heat of battle in front-line interventions involving legal systems and processes. They may be excited about the application of their research; however, running the supply lines will often be perceived as extending their commitments too far beyond the laboratory, their own classrooms, and other endeavors that are integral to their traditional career plans and their continued commitment to produce further research.

An alternative is to deposit information where it is likely to be retrieved by juvenile justice practitioners—that is, to publish it in places where it will be discovered when it is needed. Dissemination by publication is probably more attractive to most researchers than the direct approach, because publication is an integral part of researchers' everyday activities. The effectiveness of this approach, however, requires special attention to how and where the information is published, so that it is most likely to be retrieved and used.

There are many potential resources for publishing child development research information relevant to legal issues so that it will be found by juvenile justice practitioners. Among them are the law review publications of law schools, social science journals and books, and a number of hybrid law-and-social-science journals that have been created in recent years (e.g., *Behavioral Sciences and the Law*, *Criminal Justice and Behavior*, *Law and Human Behavior*, *Law and Society Review*). In addition, national and state organizations have developed newsletters and "clearinghouse" publications (e.g., *Juvenile and Family Court Journal*) to keep juvenile court judges and other personnel informed of current issues in juvenile justice. Finally, newspapers and magazines in the popular press may be a source of social science research information for professionals outside the social sciences.

In selecting among these options, one consideration is whether one wishes to publish for active or passive discovery of the information. Active discovery occurs when legal practitioners engage in a search for social science information related to a problem encountered in their work. It is generally agreed that lawyers are more likely to discover social science information during legal research if the information has been published in a legal periodical. This is because many social scientific journals and books are not indexed in law digests and computer retrieval systems used by lawyers. Furthermore, many legal professionals are not familiar with social science indexes that will contain more extensive references to publications of child development research. Thus a publication strategy focused on active discovery places the ammunition in depots that are easy to find when circumstances at the front line give rise to a search.

In contrast, publication for passive discovery focuses on periodicals that are read customarily or "regularly" by juvenile justice practitioners. Thus researchers may deposit the ammunition "in their path," rather than relying on them to search for it in response to an immediate need. For example, later in this chapter we list many periodicals that have been designed especially for regular reading by juvenile court judges, attorneys, and intake and probation officers.

Plans to publish for either active or passive discovery, however, are based on a number of assumptions regarding the activities of juvenile court practitioners. How frequent is an active search for child development information in the course of juvenile court operations? Do juvenile court practitioners "regularly" read what has been published for them? In effect, is *either* publication strategy likely to meet one's objectives? These questions are addressed in the next two sections.

UNDERSTANDING LIFE IN THE TRENCHES

Systematic dissemination of information to juvenile court practitioners would be greatly facilitated by an understanding of the characteristics and "sociology" of juvenile courts. Most of what we know about these matters, however, discourages generalizations when describing juvenile courts nationally.

First, there appears to be no "typical" juvenile court. Stapleton, Aday, and Ito (1982) performed an analysis of juvenile courts in over 150 of the largest jurisdictions nationally. Factor analysis of various aspects of their structural organization and functions produced a typology involving at least four categories, three of which accounted for the majority of courts in the sample in about equal numbers. One set of courts tended to be entities unto themselves in relation to other criminal and civil courts in their jurisdictions. They could be characterized as highly specialized courts operating under relatively discretionary procedures and rules, depending more on decisionmakers' attempts to solve child and family problems than upon formal adversarial debate in arriving at legal decisions. A second type was not so distinct from other local courts in organization and functions, implying a greater emphasis on due process and formal legal rules in deciding juvenile cases. The third main type appeared to be in transition between the other two.

Such differences in organization, function, and philosophy are likely to make a difference in courts' active and passive discovery of social science information related to their decisions. For example, active legal research is more common in a due process system in which prosecuting and defense attorneys advocate different positions as vigorously as in criminal court proceedings. This system stimulates both parties to search more actively for information that will support their respective positions (Thibaut & Walker, 1978; Thibaut, Walker, & Lind, 1972). Thus one might expect active discovery of child development research to be more common in the more "legalistic" type of juvenile court described above. In contrast, passive discovery of child development information might be enhanced in the more highly specialized juvenile courts. When a court views its decisions not so much as legal conclusions but as solutions to individual and social problems, court practitioners may be stimulated to keep abreast of child development perspectives that could contribute to their special expertise.

Both of these characterizations, however, presume a proactive approach in both types of courts. More pessimistically, specialized juvenile courts may too often go unchallenged in their assumptions about children, thereby providing little stimulation for keeping abreast of developments in research on children. Courts oriented toward due process in turn, might encourage juvenile court practitioners to ignore child development evidence while attempting to win cases primarily on fine points of law. On the other hand, "activist" lawyers in due process courts might attempt to change law by using research to challenge the law's assumptions (Handler, 1978; Handler, Holingsworth, & Erlanger, 1978; Komesar & Weisbrod, 1978; Melton, 1986). Thus, active dissemination to lawyers in the few public interest law projects concerned with children's rights (see Mnookin, 1985) might be a time-efficient means of dissemination.

The urban versus rural jurisdiction of juvenile courts represents a second potentially salient dimension when considering dissemination strategies. Juvenile cases in rural jurisdictions frequently are heard one day a week by judges whose primary duties involve criminal and civil cases. Full-time staff for juvenile cases in rural jurisdictions may consist of one social worker. In contrast, many metropolitan juvenile courts consist of several full-time juvenile court judges and other hearing officers, a large staff of intake and probation workers, several assistant prosecutors and public defenders, and in some courts a clinical support staff of several full-time Ph.D. psychologists. The latter systems clearly offer the greater potential for passive discovery of child development research through casual sharing of information and publication sources. In addition, rural juvenile courts are outside the usual mainstream of workshops or other direct communication possibilities (Melton, 1983a). Their judges are less likely to have full-time clerks and secretaries who might free them from some administrative and clerical tasks so that they have time to read social science literature (Melton, Weithorn, & Slobogin, 1985). Simply because they have fewer cases and fewer potential sources of word-of-mouth transmission of information, rural legal actors are less likely to "hear the word" about new law quickly (Wasby, 1976); surely the same principle applies to extralegal information.

Finally, dissemination strategies must take into account the diversity of professional backgrounds of juvenile court practitioners. The more common fields of training represented in juvenile courts include law, social work, education, psychology, sociology, criminal justice, law enforcement, and business administration. Moreover, some personnel will have no specialized professional training at all. This diversity has at least two implications for dissemination efforts. First, it may be difficult to communicate one's research results clearly with a single publication, when readers represent a wide diversity of formal training in different systems, principles, and perspectives. Second, on may assume that juvenile court practitioners who read professional publications probably will choose from those to which they were exposed in their formal training. If so, then the diverse training backgrounds found in juvenile courts would suggest that no single periodical will be read by the full range of court personnel. On the other hand, it is possible that socialization processes inherent in juvenile court work itself may have focused juvenile court practitioners on a common set of periodicals, such as special "juvenile court journals" that are noted later in this chapter.

In summary, few generalizations can be offered concerning life in the trenches of juvenile justice from a national perspective. There appears to be no empirical information concerning either the active or the passive discovery of social science information by juvenile court practitioners. Moreover, the diversity of their professions and training defies easy answers to the problem of selecting periodicals in which to publish child development research for passive discovery. Consequently, we designed a survey study, relatively limited in scope, in order to provide initial information about the customary reading habits of juvenile court judges and juvenile court probation officers.

WHAT DO THEY READ IN THE TRENCHES?

In 1985, we administered a survey instrument to juvenile court judges and probation officers who attended workshops and conferences sponsored by the National Council of Juvenile and Family Court Judges. Table 6-1 describes the sample of 40 judges and 78 probation officers who responded to the survey questionnaire. The majority of the probation officers were from Southwestern and Northwestern states, while the judges represented a wider range of states geographically. The majority in both samples were from rural and small-city jurisdictions, although 22% of the judges and 37% of the probation officers represented larger jurisdictions. Both samples were from juvenile courts that heard a wide range of juvenile and family issues, and both samples had ample representation from courts in which judges are assigned only to juvenile/family cases versus courts in which judges are not likely to be involved in juvenile cases exclusively or for many years consecutively.

Respondents were given a one-page list of periodicals with check-mark response options to indicate which periodicals they read with what frequency. A composite of these responses pro-

TABLE 6-1. Description of Survey Samples of Judges ($n = 40$) and Probation Officers (POs) ($n = 78$)

Variable	Judges (%)	POs (%)
States		
Southwestern and Northwestern	15.0	73.6
North Central	20.0	13.1
Midwestern	10.0	0.0
Southeastern	50.0	9.2
Other	5.0	4.0
Size of jurisdiction		
Large city (500,000 and up) or large city plus suburbs (1,000,000 and up)	5.0	18.6
Medium-sized city and suburbs (250,000–1,000,000)	17.5	18.6
Smaller city in nonmetropolitan area (50,000–250,000)	35.0	32.0
Suburban only	5.0	6.6
Rural	37.5	24.0
Years in juvenile court		
1 or less	20.0	10.2
2–5	20.0	28.2
6–9	32.5	26.9
10 or more	2.5	34.6
Unknown	2.5	0.0
POs who manage juvenile cases		
Assigned to juvenile/family court only	95.0	83.7
Rotating or general jurisdiction	5.0	16.2
Number of judges in the court		
1	32.4	52.0
2–3	30.0	27.4
4 or more	37.4	20.5
Judges who hear juvenile cases		
Assigned to juvenile/family court only	60.0	61.5
Rotating or general jurisdiction	40.0	38.4
Issues heard in juvenile/family court		
Delinquency	97.5	96.1
Status offense/children in need of supervision	95.0	83.3
Child abuse/neglect	92.5	73.3
Child custody in divorce	45.0	29.4
Spouse abuse	47.5	12.8
Report that they read		
Some journal at least once a year	92.5	72.0
No journal at least once a year	7.5	28.0

vided the observation at the end of Table 6-1: About three-quarters of the probation officers and almost all of the judges reported reading some periodical at least once a year.

Table 6-2 describes the respondents' reports of their reading habits by periodical title and frequency. For convenience, the table groups the periodicals into four content categories. Our first observation was that apparently no single periodical was read by more than about 60% of the judicial sample with a frequency of at least once per year, nor by more than about 50% of the probation officer sample. Once-per-3-month reading of the most frequently read periodical in each sample (see rank orders of periodicals for the two samples in Table 6-2) dropped to 45% of judges and 24% of probation officers. These results alone suggest that the best one is likely to do in publishing research results in one periodical read most frequently by judges is to reach about half of the judges in the sample. And one will probably reach only one-quarter of the probation officers with an article in their most frequently read journal.

Table 6-2 also indicates that the six periodicals ranked highest in frequency on the basis of probation officers' reports publish sociological, criminological, or psychiatric/psychological reports specifically related to crime, delinquency, and child abuse. In contrast, the six periodicals read most frequently by judges tend to publish articles on family law or general law.

Five of the six periodicals most often read by probation officers were almost never read by judges, and five of the six periodicals most often read by judges were almost never read by probation officers. Were one to seek publication in a single periodical that has the greatest chance of being read by *both* judges and probation officers, the data suggest the *Juvenile and Family Court Journal*, which was the only periodical among the top six for both respondent samples. Even so, only about 20% of the probation officers and 45% of the judges would be likely to discover the article in the course of their customary reading.

One suspects that most child development researchers have rarely read and have never published in the periodicals with the highest rankings in Table 6-2. Moreover, the results suggest that 85–95% of the respondents almost never read professional periodicals with which most child development researchers would be familiar (i.e., *Child Development* and *Developmental Psychology*). The only periodical on the list that was read by at least a modest proportion of the respondents and might be considered "familiar" by a majority of child development researchers was *Psychology Today*. About one-quarter of the judges claimed to read this magazine (published for the general public by the American Psychological Association) at least once a year. We failed to include the magazine in our questionnaire list administered to the probation officers; however, about 15% of the probation officers mentioned this periodical in an open-ended invitation at the end of the questionnaire to "name a journal in the behavioral/social sciences that you read most frequently." It was mentioned more often than any other behavioral/social science periodical.

A breakdown of the results by size of juvenile court jurisdictions offered only a few observations that deviated from the results already described. First, nearly all of the judges who read *Psychology Today* at least once a year were from the two largest jurisdictional categories shown in Table 6-1. Second, there was a pronounced trend for judges in larger jurisdictions to report reading more of virtually every type of periodical (juvenile-court-oriented journals, law reviews, behavioral/social science periodicals, and criminology/delinquency journals) than did judges from rural jurisdictions. In contrast, virtually no differences between jurisdictional sizes were apparent among the responses of probation officers.

Recommendations based on these results must be made with due caution. The samples, of course, may not have been geographically representative of juvenile court jurisdictions or of judges and probation officers nationally. Furthermore, one suspects that some self-selection factors are at work in samples composed of juvenile court practitioners who choose to attend continuing education seminars.

Tentatively, then, the results suggest that child development researchers relying on a strategy of "passive discovery" must publish their results in "juvenile court journals," family law reviews, state bar journals (rather than "main-line" and more prestigious law journals), criminology and delinquency journals, or popular science periodicals if they expect their re-

TABLE 6-2. Frequency of Reading of Periodicals Reported by Judges (n = 40) and Probation Officers (POs) (n = 78)

Periodicals	Rank order for		At least 1 per 3 months[a]		At least 1 per year[a]		Never or less than 1 per year[a]	
	Judges	POs	Judges	POs	Judges	POs	Judges	POs
Criminology/delinquency								
Crime and Delinquency	—	1	2	24	15	20	85	56
Journal of Criminal Law and Criminology	—	6	5	11	5	9	90	80
Other criminology journals	—	2	5	17	7	11	87	72
Juvenile court/social services								
Juvenile and Family Court Journal	1	4	45	19	17	4	37	77
Child Abuse and Neglect	—	5	7	15	7	8	85	77
Social Work			0	9	5	8	95	83
Child Welfare			5	5	5	11	90	84
Family Advocate			7	3	7	3	85	94

	Law							
Any state bar journal	2	—	57	7	2	5	40	88
ABA Journal	3	—	37	4	7	6	45	90
Family Law Quarterly	4	—	25	4	7	4	67	92
Your state university's law review	5	—	12	5	20	3	67	92
Judicature	6		20	2	5	5	75	93
Journal of Family Law			15	2	7	5	77	93
Judges' Journal			12	5	2	2	85	93
Other law reviews			10	9	8	6	90	85
Yale Law Journal			0	0	3	2	97	98
Harvard Law Review			0	0	3	2	97	98
Behavioral/social science								
Psychology Today	—		7	—	15	—	77	—
Psychiatry/mental health journals		3	5	16	10	11	85	73
Child Development			0	7	7	9	92	84
Developmental Psychology			0	9	15	2	85	89
Law and Human Behavior			0	3	3	1	97	96

[a] Figures are percentages of total samples.

search to reach the desks of even a modest minority of juvenile court judges and probation officers. Publication in these periodicals, of course, offers virtually no career rewards for the tenure-conscious professor; other motivations are required. But clearly one should not expect a single publication to fulfill both one's desire to publish in highly respected scientific journals and one's desire to have juvenile justice practitioners receive and employ one's results in decisions about children.

Moreover, the results suggest that any "passive discovery" strategy must employ *multiple* publications outside the child development researcher's customary domain. Only one professional periodical was read by even a modest minority of both judges and probation officers, and it is possible that prosecuting and defense attorneys' reading habits might represent yet a third, nonoverlapping set of periodicals. The following case study in dissemination of a research project's results demonstrates one attempt to use a multimethod approach to the problem.

A CASE STUDY FROM THE TRENCHES

Between 1976 and 1980, one of us (Grisso) engaged in a series of research studies investigating the capacities of juveniles to understand *Miranda* warnings—that is, to comprehend advisements by law enforcement officers concerning their rights to silence and to consult an attorney prior to questioning. This is an important legal question, because statements made by juveniles about their delinquent behaviors cannot be used against them in delinquency hearings unless they have first waived their rights knowingly, intelligently, and voluntarily. Law enforcement officers, attorneys, and juvenile court judges often must decide whether a juvenile is able to meet this standard for "competent" waiver of rights. Furthermore, appellate judges and legislators have been in need of guidance when forming law that defines competent waiver and controls *Miranda* procedures and decisions in juvenile courts.

Developmental theory and basic research on children's cognitive capacities can be used to provide some guidance in questions concerning the probable abilities of children and adolescents to understand the concept of a "right" and to understand and process information in making decisions (Grisso & Vierling, 1978; Melton, 1980). In contrast, the project to be discussed here (funded with a grant from the National Institute of Mental Health) developed special methods for assessing juveniles' comprehension of the *Miranda* warnings specifically, as well as their appreciation of the significance of the *Miranda* rights and their reasoning about waiver of the rights. The performance of over 400 juveniles on these measures was described in relation to their age, intelligence, amount of prior experience with courts, race, and socioeconomic status. The research also provided comparative data from a sample of over 250 adults who were administered the same procedures.

The research demonstrated the significantly poorer capacity of juveniles below age 14 to comprehend the nature and significance of the *Miranda* warnings, and demonstrated how other variables (e.g., intelligence) could be used to determine which juveniles in the age range of 15–17 are less likely to have the requisite *Miranda* comprehension for competent waiver. Thus the research used developmental theory and special empirical research methods to produce information about juveniles' capacities specific to the *Miranda* questions, on which legislators, appellate courts, and juvenile courts were in need of decisionmaking guidance.

Dissemination of this information was targeted for other social scientists studying issues of children and the law, juvenile court practitioners, and juvenile advocacy attorneys. As described below, dissemination efforts included both direct and deposited methods. Furthermore, information was deposited in several ways in order to maximize both active and passive discovery. In most cases, it was difficult to determine the specific effects of each of the methods described here. That is, there was much evidence that the information was discovered by juvenile justice practitioners and by child development researchers; yet often it could not be determined specifically which of the several publications from this project produced the discovery.

Evidence that the dissemination effort met with some success is of several types. Between 1981 and 1985, the research was cited in seven appellate court opinions involving questions of juveniles' capacities to waive *Miranda* rights (Hafemeister & Melton, Chapter 2, this volume). Grisso also estimates that he received about 30–40 telephone inquiries per year during that 4-year period from attorneys and psychologists nationwide, requesting further information on the project's results.

About two-thirds of the inquirers were defense attorneys representing juveniles in delinquency cases. Several, however, were attorneys representing children in cases that involved questions of juveniles' capacities in contexts other than waiver of *Miranda* rights in delinquency proceedings. For example, one attorney was representing two children in a public school strip-search case. The case raised the question of 10- to 12-year-old childrens' capacities to have consented knowingly, intelligently, and voluntarily to the principal's request for a search while the children were in the school's athletic locker room. Another case involved a class action brought by Latin American minors against the U.S. Immigration and Naturalization Service. Part of the question addressed was whether the procedures employed by immigration officers (at the U.S.–Mexican border) for advising unaccompanied minors of their rights as illegal aliens were sufficient to assure minors' comprehension of their rights prior to a decision about waiver (usually resulting in immediate deportation).

Another one-third of the inquirers were clinical psychologists nationwide who had been asked by attorneys to evaluate their juvenile clients' capacities to understand *Miranda* warnings. During the time in question, requests for "*Miranda* evaluations" (using the research instruments in conjunction with other psychological tests) became a frequent referral request for certain clinical psychologists located in a few metropolitan areas on the East and West Coasts, especially in the Baltimore–Washington, D.C. area. Grisso himself has performed many such evaluations at the request of attorneys in the St. Louis metropolitan area.

The following discussion describes each dissemination effort in this project and offers comments on the known or potential values of each effort, as well as difficulties and issues that arose in employing each type of dissemination.

BOOKS

Books represent an important dissemination method for major research projects in child development. The present project resulted in a book (Grisso, 1981) that seemed to play an important role in the overall dissemination effort. One must understand, however, the limits to what one can expect from a book in the social sciences in the context of dissemination to juvenile court practitioners.

A book can serve two purposes for this dissemination effort. First, it may provide a source for active discovery when lawyers engage in research to locate social science information about children that is relevant to a legal question raised by their cases. Second, we suspect that books have a certain prestige that may be useful to lawyers in persuading judges of the importance of the discovered information when it is used in legal arguments. Most books reporting child development research, however, will be difficult for lawyers to discover in legal research, because very few of them will be indexed in digests and computerized search resources used by lawyers.

There are two basic ways for books to achieve indexing in these resources. One way is by being the subject of a book review in a law journal. Thus one may ask the publisher to supply certain law journals with review copies. Even so, there is no way to assure that a law journal's editor will perceive the book's content as warranting a review. The other way to achieve legal indexing is through the Library of Congress subject headings for classifying the contents of a book (located on the back of a book's title page). Unless substantial portions of the book's text apply the results to a legal question, however, the book's subject headings are not likely to promote its indexing in legal resources.

The book produced by the *Miranda* research project (Grisso, 1981) carries the following Library of Congress subject headings: "1. Right to counsel—United States. 2. Confession (law)—

United States. 3. Juvenile justice, administration of—United States. 4. Criminal psychology." These subject headings reflect the fact that the book, although reporting empirical research methods and results, focuses clearly from beginning to end on the relevance of the research to questions in juvenile law and the law of confessions. The research is reported according to scientific standards and traditions. As noted in the book's preface, however, it is meant to be used by lawyers, judges, and youth advocate groups. Thus the book de-emphasizes the implications of the research for the fields (developmental psychology, cognitive psychology, clinical psychology) that provided the empirical and theoretical tools for the project, while emphasizing the applications of the results in dealing with legal decisions about children. A book by a child development researcher is not likely to be discoverable in legal research unless it contains enough of this type of emphasis to warrant the assignment of law-related categories in cataloguing that contributes to legal indexing.

An additional benefit when one of a book's subject headings indicates its legal relevance is that it increases the likelihood that the book will be purchased by law school libraries, where practicing juvenile court lawyers frequently go for reference materials. One of the acquisition methods used by law school libraries is to deal with suppliers who screen and select new books from a wide range of publishers. The supplier then sends to the law library all books meeting the law library's prearranged subject heading specifications. Suppliers' screening processes themselves often employ the Library of Congress subject headings. Thus a social science book with at least one legally relevant subject heading may meet suppliers' screening criteria and increase its chances of purchase by law libraries.

In the present case, by mid-1982 (18 months after publication), the book was on the shelves of 208 U.S. university, law school, and other specialized law libraries (e.g., law firms); this number increased to 270 by early 1984. An author can discover such facts instantaneously if his or her university or law school library has the computer resources for accessing any of three nationwide networks used in interlibrary loan systems (e.g., the Online Computer Library Center). In the present case, Grisso used the system to obtain printouts showing all major libraries that had purchased the book. Then he was able to refer inquiring lawyers to the book quickly, no matter where they were located. This method was also helpful when psychologists telephoned to obtain the project's *Miranda* comprehension assessment instruments for use in their evaluations of juveniles, because the instruments were published in an appendix in the book.

Even if one's book is indexed for access to persons doing legal research, however, this does little to bring its attention to juvenile court judges and probation officers. The attention of these personnel may be drawn indirectly if one's book is well advertised among child and clinical psychologists who are likely to be consulted by judges and lawyers in juvenile courts. More directly, the author can make sure that the publisher submits copies of the book to relevant periodicals that publish book reviews. In the present case, the book was reviewed in the newsletter of the American Psychological Association's Division 37 (Child, Youth, and Family Services) (Weithorn, 1981), of which many psychologists in child welfare agencies associated with juvenile courts are members. It also received an article-length review in *Law and Human Behavior* (Melton, 1983b), increasing its exposure to psychologists providing consultation to legal practitioners. And it received a four-page review in *Crime and Delinquency* (Rubin, 1982), one of the journals read by at least some judges and probation officers in the survey samples reported earlier. Once again, however, the relevance of one's research to the concerns of juvenile court practitioners will have to be made fairly clear in the book in order to warrant its review in journals that publish for judges and probation officers. The minimum probably would be at least one chapter devoted entirely to legal implications of the research results.

JOURNAL ARTICLES

Various portions of the results of the present project were published in three journal articles (Grisso, 1980; Grisso & Pomicter, 1977; Grisso & Ring, 1979) and in two chapters in other authors' edited books (Grisso, 1983; Grisso & Manoogian, 1980). Each of the journal articles had several dissemination purposes that suggest strategies for other researchers.

The two earliest articles (Grisso & Pomicter, 1977; Grisso & Ring, 1979) did not report the main results of the project (which was not completed at that time), but rather the results of two secondary studies (frequency of juvenile interrogations, and parents' attitudes toward juveniles' rights to silence and counsel). Decisions concerning their publication and the choice of journals were based not only on the value of the results themselves, but also on the intention to inform the academic psychology–law community (in *Law and Human Behavior*) and psychologists in criminal justice, court, and correctional systems (in *Criminal Justice and Behavior*) of the main purpose of the project under way and the nature of its possible future contributions. In retrospect, a report also should have been submitted in different form to a journal such as the *Juvenile and Family Court Journal*, which the 1985 survey indicated was read with at least moderate frequency by juvenile court judges and probation officers. The results of the secondary studies would have been of inherent interest to juvenile court personnel, and the articles could have contained comments advising them of the type of information that the larger project hoped to provide in the future. (Nevertheless, some judges who read the *Juvenile and Family Court Journal* may have discovered the research through citations to it that appeared in other articles in that journal in subsequent years—e.g., Lawrence, 1983.)

For purposes of dissemination to lawyers, the publication of a condensed version of the project's main results in the *California Law Review* (Grisso, 1980) was the single most successful effort. Five of the appellate cases that used the research cited this article; only two cited the book, and none cited any other source (see Hafemeister & Melton, Chapter 2, this volume). Moreover, during the 4-year period following the project's completion (1981–1985), the great majority of lawyers making inquiries to Grisso indicated that they had discovered the research by way of this article. Most had discovered it through computer-assisted methods for searching information bases that index legal periodicals, through citation to it in other law review articles, or through other lawyers' referring them to the article. These observations support the extreme importance of publication in a law review periodical, resulting in indexing in services used by lawyers in their legal research, if one wishes to make lawyers in the juvenile justice system aware of one's research results.

There has been no evidence to determine the extent to which this publication was discovered by judges and probation officers. The logic in this case, however, was to target lawyers who would introduce the research as evidence presented in cases heard in juvenile courts. That is, the legal process itself was used to increase passive discovery of the information by judges; the objective was not their reading of periodicals, but their reading of attorneys' motions in pretrial hearings on the validity of a juvenile's waiver. Nevertheless, the results should also have been published in one of the "juvenile court journals" noted in the 1985 survey in order to augment this strategy. Researchers should also consider the value of publishing relevant child development research in law reviews focused entirely on juvenile and family law (see list of periodicals in Table 6-2).

Of course, many obstacles stand in the way of publication of child development research results in a law review. First, the relevance of the results to a legal question must be clearly described. In drafting the manuscript, the researcher must adopt the perspective that the research results are of virtually no value to the world except insofar as they are useful for addressing the applied, legal issue. This may be difficult for social scientists who are accustomed to treating the result of their research as an end in itself—that is, as a methodological "breakthrough" or as an important contribution per se to the understanding of children.

Second, the objective described above requires that the researcher either must know the law or must engage in a collaborative relationship (and probably coauthorship) with a professor or practitioner in law. Law reviews, of course, seek to inform lawyers of issues in the interpretation of law. Therefore, even articles reporting empirical studies must offer lawyers the citations to statutes and appellate cases that provide the legal context within which the empirical results can be interpreted and used. A colleague in law also can offer valuable information concerning how, when, and where to try to publish in law journals. For example, unlike the practice in social science publication, submission of manuscripts to several law journals simultaneously is standard procedure. In addition, the likelihood of acceptance by a "national" law review will vary depending upon the time of year, because each new student editorial board is limited in how many articles it can accept within a year.

Third, the researcher must be willing to relinquish some of the autonomy associated with authorship in social science publications. The events that took place in the case of the Grisso (1980) article are probably typical. Once the manuscript was accepted, law students on the editorial staff of the law review performed a thorough search of the law in juvenile waiver and confessions. Then they developed a number of ways in which the manuscript's legal relevance could be strengthened. In social science journals, the next step might have been to convey these to the author with the request to "rewrite and resubmit." In contrast, there began in this case a series of interactions between Grisso and the senior editor, which were designed to revise the manuscript.

The process included a redrafting of portions of the original manuscript by the editorial staff, primarily in the sections corresponding to the "Introduction" and "Discussion" sections of social science articles. The redraft was sent to Grisso for approval or further change, and was followed up by several lengthy telephone discussions between Grisso and the senior editor. These discussions always manifested the journal's respect for an author's ultimate responsibility for an article's content and interpretations. On the other hand, it sought to produce an article that used the research results to advocate as strongly as possible one position for juvenile justice policy regarding juvenile waiver. Thus the editorial staff favored interpretations of the results that went as far as legal logic and authorial adherence to scientific integrity would allow. Researchers embarking on such a venture should be prepared to struggle with the conflicts between this argumentative use of research and the more objective, nonpartisan approach to interpreting results in manuscripts for scientific journals.

DIRECT COMMUNICATIONS

The project's results were communicated in papers presented at several meetings of the American Psychological Association and the American Psychology– Law Society from 1976 to 1982. In addition, the results and their implications were presented at three meetings (1977, 1979, and 1981) of the National Conference on Juvenile Law Advocacy, a conference sponsored by the National Juvenile Law Center (then part of Legal Services, Inc.). Both of these efforts were responsible for several later contacts from psychologists and from attorneys with special practice in juvenile law.

Finally, an attempt was made to discover appellate cases concerning juvenile waiver while they were in process of litigation, in order to forward the project's results to attorneys in the cases for their consideration. This process was not successful, for several reasons. Grisso did not have the resources to do the task systematically, nor would most other social scientists in the normal course of academic life and other commitments. The two potential cases in which some inroads were made (both state supreme court cases) were resolved on other legal grounds.

The greatest potential opportunity, a U.S. Supreme Court case concerning juveniles' waiver of *Miranda* rights (*Fare v. Michael C.*, 1979), was missed. At that time Grisso was not familiar with means for early detection of upcoming U.S. Supreme Court cases. Data analysis was just nearing completion as the Court's deliberations were taking place. Had Grisso had earlier warning, the completion of certain analyses might have been given priority in order to be able to offer the results to attorneys in the case in time for them to be used.

Today child development researchers have a better chance of discovering cases for which their research is potentially relevant. They can watch the "Judicial Notebook" in the *APA Monitor*. Moreover, the American Psychological Association may discover relevant cases using its recently developed mechanisms for keeping the organization informed of cases that the organization might wish to enter as *amicus curiae*. Researchers themselves can avoid missing an opportunity like *Fare* by spending a few minutes each week reviewing the *United States Law Week* (available in any law library) to discover cases in which review (*certiorari*) has been sought of, or granted by, the U.S. Supreme Court. The minimal investment of time can have a double pay-off for psycholegal researchers: (1) alerting the researchers to cases in which their work might be used; and (2) identifying current empirical issues in the law.

CONCLUSIONS: INFILTRATING BEHIND THE LINES

Our data suggest some general strategies for reaching the trenches. Research should be published in journals indexed in the *Index of Legal Periodicals*, in order to facilitate its discovery by lawyers and judges actively seeking information on a particular topic related to child development. Ideally, researchers should aim for one of the high-prestige law journals included in LEXIS or other computerized legal data bases. For passive discovery, publication in multiple practitioner-oriented and popular sources is desirable.

These recommendations do not fit well with current practices in general, even among researchers who focus on socially relevant, interdisciplinary topics. Publication in *Juvenile and Family Court Journal* or even a prestigious law review is unlikely to be rewarded in research-oriented graduate psychology departments. Publication in multiple outlets, even when aimed at different audiences, may be perceived as padding one's *curriculum vitae* or even as an unethical exploitation of journals (see, e.g., Yankauer, 1985).

We believe that prevailing reward schemes and publication policies should be changed. In any event, we see no ethical violation in publication in multiple forms for diverse audiences. In fact, we believe that *failing* to pursue such avenues of dissemination may be unethical. Particularly when government agencies have supported the research, either directly or through the training of researchers (see Bermant, 1982), the researchers have an obligation to give their knowledge away in order to promote social welfare (American Psychological Association, 1981, Preamble and Principles 1 and 9; Weithorn, Chapter 10, this volume). Moreover, when researchers engage in particular lines of inquiry precisely because of their social relevance, it is difficult to understand why they would not want to take the additional step of active dissemination to insure that their efforts are not wasted.

Publications, workshops, and the like are not enough, though, to insure dissemination. The large literature on dissemination and use of knowledge (see, e.g., Havelock, 1968; Rogers, 1983) indicates that some people are much more likely than others to learn about and use new knowledge. Across professional groups, users are apt to be relatively venturesome, highly educated, specialized, upwardly mobile, and widely traveled. They tend to be at the middle of highly interconnected social networks, where they both receive and pass along information. Practicing professionals, including legal professionals (Wasby, 1976) and psychologists (Cohen, Sargent, & Sechrest, 1986), tend to learn not from journals, but instead by word of mouth from respected colleagues who are a bit *avant-garde* and who do seek new knowledge. Publication is important because it *starts* the multistep process of diffusion of knowledge, even though it reaches few practitioners.

Optimally, though, researchers trying to get their work to the trenches will infiltrate behind the lines. For example, researchers may seek to present their research at continuing legal education conferences. Here they may find that the major impact will come not so much from the formal workshop presentation as from getting to know well-connected legal practitioners. The real impact may occur more during the cocktail hour than during the workshop itself. Once one becomes accepted as an expert resource, requests for testimony may or may not increase substantially, but informal requests for information on diverse issues often do increase dramatically (Melton *et al.*, 1985). Thus one becomes a continuing source of information to the legal profession concerning not only one's own work but the rest of psychology's knowledge base in child development as well.

Thus, to bring child developmental research to the trenches, researchers may need to move actively behind the lines, infiltrating the intelligence network that leads to the front. They should use the best techniques of community psychology to insure that the network serves two important functions: as a supply route for information to the front, and as a means for the front to request new supplies that stimulate researchers to do new, legally relevant studies in child development.

REFERENCES

American Psychological Association. (1981). Ethical Principles of Psychologists. *American Psychologist, 36*, 633–638.

Ballew v. Georgia, 435 U.S. 223 (1978).

Bermant, G. (1982). Justifying social science research in terms of social benefit. In T. Beauchamp, R. Faden, R. Wallace, Jr., & L. Walters (Eds.), *Ethical issues in social science research* (pp. 125–143). Baltimore: Johns Hopkins University Press.

Cohen, L.H., Sargent, M.M., & Sechrest, L.B. (1986). Use of psychotherapy research by professional psychologists. *American Psychologist, 41*, 198–206.

Fare v. Michael C., 442 U.S. 707 (1979).

Gordley, J. (1984). Legal reasoning: An introduction. *California Law Review, 72*, 138–177.

Grisso, T. (1980). Juveniles' capacities to waive *Miranda* rights: An empirical analysis. *California Law Review, 68*, 1134–1166.

Grisso, T. (1981). *Juveniles' waiver of rights: Legal and psychological competence.* New York: Plenum.

Grisso, T. (1983). Juveniles' consent in delinquency proceedings. In G. Melton, G. Koocher, & M. Saks (Eds.), *Children's competence to consent* (pp. 131–148). New York: Plenum.

Grisso, T. (1984). *Psychological concepts in juvenile law.* (Final report of Research Grant No. MH-35090). Rockville, MD: Center for Studies of Antisocial and Violent Behavior, National Institute of Mental Health.

Grisso, T., & Conlin, M. (1984). Procedural issues in the juvenile justice system. In N. Reppucci, L. Weithorn, E. Mulvey, & J. Monahan (Eds.), *Children, mental health, and the law* (pp. 171–193). Beverly Hills, CA: Sage.

Grisso, T., & Manoogian, S. (1980). Juveniles' comprehension of *Miranda* warnings. In P. Lipsitt & B. Sales (Eds.), *New directions in psycholegal research* (127–148). New York: Van Nostrand Reinhold.

Grisso, T., & Pomicter, C. (1977). Interrogation of juveniles: An empirical study of procedures, safeguards, and rights waiver. *Law and Human Behavior, 1*, 321–342.

Grisso, T., & Ring, M. (1979). Parents' attitudes toward juveniles' rights in interrogation. *Criminal Justice and Behavior, 6*, 211–226.

Grisso, T., & Vierling, L. (1978). Minors' consent to treatment: A developmental perspective. *Professional Psychology: Research and Practice, 9*, 412–427.

Handler, J. (1978). *Social movements and the legal system: A theory of law reform and social change.* New York: Academic Press.

Handler, J., Hollingsworth, E., & Erlanger, H. (1978). *Lawyers and the pursuit of legal rights.* New York: Academic Press.

Havelock, R. (1968). *Bibliography of knowledge utilization and dissemination.* Ann Arbor: University of Michigan, Institute for Social Research.

Komesar, N., & Weisbrod, B. (1978). The public interest law firm: A behavioral analysis. In B. Weisbrod, J. Handler, & N. Komesar (Eds.), *Public interest law: An economic and institutional analysis* (pp. 80–101). Berkeley: University of California Press.

Lawrence, R. (1983). The role of legal counsel in juveniles' understanding of their rights. *Juvenile and Family Court Journal,* 49–58.

Melton, G.B. (1980). Children's concepts of their rights. *Journal of Clinical Child Psychology, 9,* 186–190.

Melton, G.B. (1981). Children's competency to testify. *Law and Human Behavior, 5,* 73–85.

Melton, G.B. (1983a). Community psychology and rural legal systems. In A.W. Childs & G.B. Melton (Eds.), *Rural psychology* (pp. 359–380). New York: Plenum.

Melton, G.B. (1983b). Making room for psychology in *Miranda* doctrine: *Juveniles' waiver of rights* [Review]. *Law and Human Behavior, 7,* 67–85.

Melton, G.B. (1986). Litigation *In the interest of children*: Does anybody win? [Review]. *Law and Human Behavior, 10,* 337–353.

Melton, G.B., Weithorn, L.A., & Slobogin, C. (1985). *Community mental health centers and the courts: An evaluation of community-based forensic services.* Lincoln: University of Nebraska Press.

Mnookin, R.H. (1975). Child custody adjudication: Judicial functions in the face of indeterminacy. *Law and Contemporary Problems, 39,* 226–293.

Mnookin, R.H. (Ed.). (1985). *In the interest of children*: Advocacy, law reform, and public policy.* New York: W.H. Freeman.

Monahan, J., & Walker, L. (1986). Social authority: Obtaining, evaluating, and establishing social science in law. *University of Pennsylvania Law Review, 134,* 477–517.

Platt, A. (1977). *The child savers: The invention of delinquency.* Chicago: University of Chicago Press.

Rogers, E. (1983). *Diffusion of innovations* (3rd ed.) New York: Free Press.

Rubin, H. (1982). [Review of *Juveniles' waiver of rights: Legal and psychological competence*]. *Crime and Delinquency, 28,* 627–630.

Stapleton, V., Aday, D., & Ito, J. (1982). An empirical typology of American metropolitan juvenile courts. *American Journal of Sociology, 88,* 549–564.

Thibaut, J., & Walker, L. (1978). A theory of procedure. *California Law Review, 66,* 541–566.

Thibaut, J., Walker, L., & Lind, E.A. (1972). Adversary presentation and bias in legal decision-making. *Harvard Law Review, 86,* 386–401.

Wasby, S. (1976). *Small town police and the Supreme Court: Hearing the word.* Lexington, MA: Lexington Books.

Weithorn, L.A. (1981). Building a knowledge base about the competencies of children and youth in legal settings. [Review of *Juveniles' waiver of rights*]. *Division of Child and Youth Services Newsletter, 4*, 6–7.

Yankauer, A. (1985). Prior publication, an ethical issue. *American Journal of Public Health, 75*, 341–343.

III

Procedures for Introducing Child Development Research into the Legal Process

Opportunities Lost: The Theory and the Practice of Using Developmental Knowledge in the Adversary Trial

MICHAEL J. SAKS

One might think that the trial courts are one of the best places to bring developmental research in order to have an impact on legal decisionmaking related to children. Here, the two most powerful engines of truth yet devised—empirical science and the adversary mode of trial—would appear to combine to yield well-informed, incisively tested conclusions. One might think this, but it is not so.

THEORETICAL ADVANTAGES OF TRIAL COURTS

Trial courts would seem to be an ideal place to bring knowledge, for a number of good and sound reasons. Courts, more so than any other official decisionmaking institution in our society, are rational and information-dependent. The sorts of political noises that pervade other institutions, such as legislatures, have been largely filtered out of the judicial process. The training and norms of the judiciary emphasize decisions based on principles of law and on relevant evidence, not on constituent preferences

Michael J. Saks. College of Law, University of Iowa, Iowa City, Iowa.

or exchanges of favors. Judges in all the federal courts and in many state jurisdictions are appointed or elected to serve for life, so that their decisions will be removed from the gusts and squalls of majoritarian political winds. In addition to such structural insulation, judges who feel they cannot in particular cases decide without bias are expected to excuse themselves and let such cases go to other judges. Juries similarly are insulated from external pressures, and means exist for excluding those with unacceptable biases. To the extent that such a thing can be achieved by a human institution, a judicial decision can be expected to turn more sharply on the evidence presented than is ever likely to be the case (or is supposed to be the case) in legislatures, executive mansions, or even administrative agencies.

While the factfinders are heavily information-dependent, the control of the presentation of that information is placed squarely in the hands of the parties. That is the *sine qua non* of the adversary process. The parties have a right to present any information they believe will persuade the factfinder that the outcomes they advocate should prevail. This is subject to provisions of the rules of evidence, such as the requirement that the evidence be relevant. These rules generally open a fairly wide gate, which has gradually been swinging open even further over the years (Giannelli, 1980). This control by the parties contrasts with the Napoleonic and Marxist models, which place most of the control in the hands of the judge, who serves as an inquisitor, a seeker of information, and a developer of the case facts. The factfinder in the Anglo-American system is largely passive, leaving it to the parties to develop and present their own cases (Thibaut & Walker, 1975).

Even if the parties leave out critical information about the specifics of the case before the court (i.e., "adjudicative facts"), the judge and jury are not permitted to seek out those facts through an investigation of their own. Should the parties omit or inaccurately present the law governing a case, the court does have an obligation to find and apply those principles. The general background facts of life, the kinds of information with which developmental research and other branches of science deal (labeled "legislative facts" by the law), have an uncertain status somewhere between those extremes (cf. Monahan & Walker, 1986, who argue that "legislative facts" should be, and for the most part are, treated as if they were law). Trial courts clearly may take judicial notice of them without adversary presentation (see Melton, Chapter 9, this volume). Appellate justices clearly may obtain them in the same way that they research the law. And both may receive legislative facts from the parties.

The parties have not only the primary role of presenting the adjudicative and legislative facts, but also strong motivation to do so. This is not a perfunctory chore; it is the way in which a case is won or lost. And, as every lawyer knows, winning is better than losing. Thus, one might expect the information presented to the court to be complete and appropriate, because those presenting it have the best of reasons to seek, to find, and to present the most germane and persuasive evidence they can.

Finally, if all of this fails, the court has both common-law and statutory powers to fill the information gap. Judges can appoint experts for the court (Fed. R. Evid. 706), can appoint special masters to develop or take evidence on specialized issues (Fed. R. Civ. P. 53), or can appoint advisory juries composed of experts in appropriate fields (Fed. R. Civ. P. 39(c)).

PRACTICAL FAILINGS

The vision described above does not usually materialize. As a result, the decisions of the courts infrequently reflect the best information available. In this section, I describe a number of the features of law practice that result in depriving the courts of developmental and other information that decisions might benefit from having. This discussion is, for the most part, derived from earlier work (Saks & Baron, 1980; Saks & Van Duizend, 1983a, 1983b), to which the interested reader may turn for richer detail.

FINDING AND UNDERSTANDING THE DATA

The people in charge of the case rarely if ever know the data and are unlikely to find them. On the one hand, lawyers are typically overextended and almost frenetically busy. And, on the other hand, they have learned a variety of skills, a body of workable knowledge, and a set of contacts, all of which usually perform adequately for them. None of this is conducive to realizing that a body of knowledge exists that is relevant but that they have not put to use. Indeed, when we are talking about new knowledge—the cutting edge of research on child development—this is almost by definition information that an attorney with a case will not be aware of. How is one to know what it is that one does not know? Many attorneys are unaware even of the existence of various fields or subfields. And all research psychologists are only too aware that even the educated public thinks that psychology equals clinical psychology.

One case that we (Saks & Van Duizend, 1983a) studied involved a suit against the city of San Francisco that sought massive reform of the city's money bail system. The plaintiffs relied on a good deal of sociological data to show that the assumptions on which the city's policies rested were unsound. Even in the face of this assault by data, the city's lawyer did not obtain expert help in challenging those data. After the case was lost, the next lawyer, on appeal, still thought he could challenge the empirical evidence effectively on his own without turning to expert help. In my interview with him, it became apparent that he was not aware of the sorts of challenges to empirical data that could be mounted, and he therefore did not think that help to do such challenging existed or could be obtained. So, although these lawyers and their client, the city, were strongly motivated to win the case, they failed to obtain expertise that— in my view, on having read the record—would have weakened the case against them.

Even when data are offered, attorneys often fail to appreciate their value. Accustomed as they are to traditional sorts of evidence and arguments, lawyers may not appreciate the potential value of research data even when they are made aware of them. Sometimes their resistance to realizing that the grounds on which a case will be decided is going to involve data reaches self-defeating levels.

The case of *Ballew v. Georgia* (1978) is familiar to social scientists. In that case, the U.S. Supreme Court halted its progressive reduction of the constitutionally required number of jurors at six. Justice Blackmun's opinion in the case was a virtual literature review of empirical research on the question. That the Court ostensibly turned for an answer to social science research should not have surprised readers of the cases that led up to *Ballew*, because in each of them the Court reasoned that its decision had to turn on the empirical question of how different-sized juries functioned, and it consistently cited research they believed to be relevant. When the case was granted review by the U.S. Supreme Court, Elizabeth and Tony Tanke—a social psychologist and lawyer, respectively—offered both sides of the case a recent bibliography of relevant literature and help in interpreting the literature (Tanke & Tanke, 1979). Having published a bibliography of empirical research on juries (especially effects of jury size), taken the trouble to contact both the attorneys for Ballew and those for Georgia, and generously made their offer of studies and expertise, what response did the Tankes get from counsel? Only one of the parties accepted the offer, and that party's brief still reflected only modest use of the studies. As it had done before, the Court relied on its own literature review and interpretations to guide its decision on the case.

Here, then, was just the sort of opportunity lawyers would be expected to look for. They have seen how the Court handles these cases; they can bring forward relevant studies and urge on the Court their favored interpretation of those studies. The alternative is to leave it to the Court to find and interpret the research by itself. Although this example is from appellate practice, I submit that much the same difficulties occur at the trial level. Having said that, I want to emphasize that considerable variation exists among attorneys, their backgrounds, and the circumstances of their practices. Data can be made known and used, but the use of the data will result more from the fortuities of an attorney's life than from the present structure of law practice (Saks & Van Duizend, 1983a). That is, attorneys are as likely to find evidence and experts through their informal friendship networks or through stumbling upon stories in the popular press as they are through a systematic quest for such information and expertise.

THE SEARCH FOR EXPERTISE

We must keep in mind that the larger goal that we have in mind is insuring that the system delivers the best information to the decisionmaker so that a reasonable opportunity exists for the best decisions to be made. The motivation to win is merely the energy that drives the process; winning obviously cannot be the goal of the process, except from the narrow viewpoint of one of the parties. If the preceding difficulties have been overcome, if an advocate is aware that a particular expertise exists, and if the advocate plans to present that expertise to the court, the advocate now has to find the expert through whose testimony the court will be informed. This process may contribute a certain amount of distortion to the information the court ends up receiving. First of all, because the advocate is motivated to win, he or she may approach a number of experts in search of one whose views are congenial to the needs of the case, or who is willing to modify those views. The result can be that a court hears from, let us say, one expert on each side of a particular empirical issue. The court will have no way of knowing how well those experts represent the population of such experts.

If our concern is that only a fraction of the experts in any given field are up to date on an issue, the search may not turn up the knowledge that is available and most needed. Although it is the knowledge that is really needed, the search is designed to pursue the experts, who, after all, are only potential repositories of the knowledge. This search for people is rarely conducted by examining the literature of a given field, to find the leading knowledge and the people who are contributing to that knowledge. The search almost invariably proceeds by way of "the grapevine" (cf. Coleman, Katz, & Menzel, 1966). This serves a number of purposes. It is easy; it follows an acquaintanceship network that inspires a certain amount of loyalty; and each expert nominated is also evaluated by the person providing the suggestion. Also, lawyers already have experts in various fields whom they have already used for a variety of routine matters and have established relationships with. They are likely to go back to "their psychologist" for any kind of psychological issue, even though this technique almost insures that their expert will not know about some new area that the new case needs. The result is that active practitioners or professional expert witnesses who are not well versed in the latest research—and who are not themselves the researchers involved in this work—are most likely to be called as the experts in such cases.

Trial Preparation

Even those attorneys who do find out about a relevant new body of knowledge are unlikely to prepare witnesses properly or to present testimony effectively. Again, there is great variation in this, depending upon the background and working lives of attorneys. The most common experience of experts, however, is of lawyers who, because of their workload and their constant collision with deadlines, do not have the necessary time. The legal textbook advice is to begin working on the substantive issues in a case with one's experts as soon as the issues become apparent. But for perfectly sound economic and business reasons, it rarely makes sense to do this. About 90% of an attorney's caseload will be settled before trial. A careful preparation of the case for trial makes sense only if the case is going to trial. (The pleadings on a case, for example, require a minimum of facts, but a reasonable grasp of the law.) Since the attorney cannot be sure which case in 10 it is that will go to trial, there is no point in getting down to business with the experts until he or she is fairly sure a case is going to be tried. Even when that is known, lawyers, like the rest of us, do not do today what can be left for tomorrow.

To give a telling example, I once helped organize an educational program for state trial judges on a particular scientific controversy. We decided to present it as a *voir dire* examination of an expert to establish the admissibility of the testimony. The attorney who would have to cross-examine the expert knew a full year in advance that this "trial" was going before the judge— indeed, before several dozen judges. She was more than a little aware that because of the audience, this exercise of only a few hours could have an inordinate impact on her reputation. We also made sure that she had, also for a full year, access to the expert she would cross-examine, as well as a consulting expert of her own to help her prepare. As it turned out, she did not speak with her own expert at all and did not speak with the opposing expert until he flew into town the morning of the "trial." In my opinion she did a mediocre job at best cross-examining the expert, thereby treating the judges to a more realistic presentation than the organizers hoped for.

Even routine, familiar, habitual presentations are done hastily and are not usually of prime quality. My basis for this assertion is our interviews with forensic scientists (toxicologists, medical examiners, ballisticians, etc.), as well as with the prosecutors who examined them on a regular basis in criminal trials. The experts complained of insufficient knowledge and preparation on the part of the lawyers, and the lawyers often felt that this was a corner they had to cut, given insufficient time to prepare their cases as well as they wished they could.

SHAPING THE EXPERT

On those occasions when attorneys do a conscientious and thor-ough-going job of working with their experts (most likely to occur in large, expensive civil cases, or when the attorney is a law professor who does an occasional case more for love than for money), they are likely to impose another kind of distortion on the information. I am interested here not in the ethical implications (see American Bar Association, 1980; Weithorn, Chapter 10, this volume) of this process, but in its effects on the image of knowledge that will reach the factfinder. Although the legal dictum holds that "a witness is not an advocate and an advocate is not a witness," an able advocate tries to win the expert witness over to the advocate's view of the case. Most of the experts we interviewed described this process and com-plained of it as "a constant negotiating process." A lawyer, of course, need not personally believe anything that is offered to the court (though the lawyer may not aid in perpetrating a fraud on the court); the lawyer's job is to give voice to the client's view of the controversy. The witness, not the lawyer, takes an oath to tell the truth, the whole truth, and nothing but.

The expert's job is to communicate a knowledge community's view of the relevant world. But it is perhaps inevitable that tensions emerge between what the expert can most conscientiously say and what the attorney wants the expert to say. And lawyers, being skilled persuaders anyway, practice a kind of minisocialization of expert witnesses, so that a shared view is held of who the good guys are and what the right outcome is. One result of that is that expert witnesses often find themselves in a role conflict, wherein the law and their own profession casts them as disinterested witnesses, but their clients see them as part of the advocacy team. The judges we interviewed uniformly expressed skepticism about experts, having done some shaping of their own experts not so long ago. As a result, judges may discount more than is warranted of the testimony of experts, while jurors may overvalue their testimony (Saks & Van Duizend, 1983a). And although most of our judge interviewees thought that calling the court's own expert witnesses was a good way to counter the "prostitution" of expert witnesses, they rarely if ever used that power. The theory of the Federal Rules of Evidence on this is that "[t]he ever-present possibility that the judge *may* appoint an expert in a given case must inevitably exert a sobering effect on the expert witness of a party and upon the person utilizing his services" (Fed. R. Evid. 706 Advisory Committee's note; emphasis in original). The litmus test for experts may be to imagine how they would feel and what they would do if asked by opposing counsel on cross-examination: "Tell me about all the missing pieces, all the defects, all the weaknesses in the testimony you have given so far; tell me everything you know that would be helpful to *my* client's case."

CROSS-EXAMINATION

Another source of distortion in the information presented is perhaps better characterized as misdirection. Some cross-examinations are cogent, incisive examinations of the flaws in and limits to the testimony given by the expert on direct examination. But, judging from the experiences of experts, far more cross-examinations are aimed not at testing the substance of the testimony, but rather at raising collateral doubts. These are the cross-examinations that focus on the witness and not the testimony. The fact that the witness lives in another state, or is not a "real" doctor, or cannot remember what page in a certain book something is on, become the issues, rather than the validity and applicability of the facts on which a rational decision will turn.

FACTFINDERS' BELIEFS

In addition, jurors, and probably judges as well, rely to some extent on their cultural stereotypes and personal contacts with members of a field in assigning weight to their testimony. We found that jurors judged psychologists to be about equal in competence and honesty to psychiatrists, and both about midway between the top of the rankings (occupied by physicians and chemists/toxicologists) and the bottom (occupied by polygraph and handwriting examiners) (Saks & Wissler, 1984). The better educated jurors were, the lower the ratings they gave to all experts. And, interestingly, while less educated jurors rated psychiatrists slightly above psychologists, the pattern was the reverse among the more highly educated jurors.

THE APPEARANCE OF ACCURACY

All of these practical problems reduce the likelihood that a factfinder will have all of the most relevant information needed to make the "best" decision in a case. Let me at least suggest the possibility that this is not necessarily a bad state of affairs. This conclusion must begin with the notion that decisions by a court are only in part exercises in technical accuracy. In larger part, they are exercises in justice. Scientific facts play only a supporting role in the rendering of an authoritative judicial decision. Such a role is best played by well-accepted facts uttered by well-respected experts. Thus, the appearance of accuracy may be more important than accuracy itself. One thing courts can do to further the appearance (if not the reality) of factual accuracy is to require that proffered facts enjoy a consensus of expert opinion. That is, if knowledge does not enter the courtroom until it has acquired a fairly solid professional following, and both parties respect the prevailing view (even though it is unavoidably at least somewhat out of date), then acceptance of the court's decision as an authoritative resolution of the dispute is more likely.

This, of course, is heresy to our scientific and technical selves, which fear nothing more than they do error and live in dread of not being up on the latest findings. But this may be in part what the *Frye* test of admissibility seeks to achieve. The *Frye* rule is the now-traditional test of admissibility of "novel" scientific evidence. It requires the court to admit only those scientific facts and theories that have become "sufficiently established to have gained general acceptance in the particular field" (*Frye v. United States*, 1923, p. 1014; see also *Dyas v. United States*, 1977). Thus a court will entertain scientific evidence only if the relevant community of experts has reached a consensus on it first. Adherence to such a rule of professional consensus cannot, as I have already suggested, insure up-to-the-minute accuracy, but it does afford the comfort of stability. Facts or theories widely accepted in a field may have the disadvantage of being a bit out of date, but they have the virtue of being unlikely to change tomorrow. Volatile facts can embarrass and undermine the authority of a court faster than erroneous or dated (but relatively constant) facts. Given the comfort of such a rule, it is of interest that the rule has been falling out of favor in recent years (Giannelli, 1983), and judges have more and more been willing to decide for themselves whether some proffered new knowledge is to be admitted or not (e.g., *United States v. Williams*, 1978). This strategy offers the potential benefit of allowing a factfinder to be more up to date, but also the risk of discovering shortly after the trial that the new knowledge has limitations not known to the court, or is simply nonreplicable (i.e., wrong).

The implication of these ideas for the present volume is that increased use by the courts of new developmental findings may be achieved by improvements in dissemination among members of the field and by periodic attempts to achieve consensus on the findings. This consensus needs to be scholarly and authoritative, and yet should not stifle researchers' freedom to disagree and seek still newer answers. The theme that appears to emerge is a tension between stability and accuracy, between being authoritative and being up to date. This delicate balancing act may betray a fundamental tension between the pursuits of science and the pursuits of courts.

Yet I can think of times when a court will want to—indeed, will need to—think like a scientist, and focus on the evidence and the methodology, rather than on who or how many people assert the truth of something. One clear example of such an occasion is when two trial courts have reached opposite findings with regard to the same legislative facts. This is an inconsistency that, when presented with it, an appeals court will have to resolve. And the only rational way to resolve it is through an examination of the data themselves. In a pair of cases reaching the U.S. Court of Appeals for the Fifth Circuit, one trial court had found that a link existed between liquor advertising and alcohol consumption (and therefore that a state's ban on advertising did not violate the First Amendment), while another trial court found no link (and therefore that a state's ban did violate the First Amendment)—no doubt because different experts produced different data. The Fifth Circuit Court's opinion noted:

> The degree to which an appellate court should defer to the "fact" findings of a trial judge as to the latest truths in the social sciences is an interesting question. The argument can be made that as long as the trial court applied the right legal test or the appropriate level of scrutiny . . . [the] decision should be upheld on appeal. . . . Should this finding be subject only to a clearly erroneous standard of review? Clearly not.
>
> In the first place, the issue of whether there is a correlation between advertising and consumption is a legislative and not an adjudicative fact question. It is not a question specifically related to this one case or controversy; it is a question of social factors and happenings which may submit to some partial empirical solution. . . . The specific issue here was undoubtedly considered by the . . . Legislature when local option and the curtailment of liquor consumption were being studied. Now the issue has moved to the judicial stage. If the legislative decision is not binding at this stage, at least it carries great weight. Certainly it cannot be thrust aside by two experts and a judicial trier of fact. (*Dunagin v. City of Oxford* 1983, p. 748)

One might think that, at least in those situations when appellate courts might have to focus on the amount and quality of the research evidence, trial judges and trial counsel would be prompted to pay similar, albeit anticipatory, attention to the amount and quality of the evidence. Once again, one might think this, but it is not so.

PROBLEMS OF LEGAL THEORY

The problems described above relate to the practical business of ferrying information from the field to the factfinder. Those problems assume that the legal theory is probably fine, but in practice does not deliver. In this brief section, I note a few instances where the legal theory (whether it gets translated into practice or not) creates problems of its own for the presentation of developmental research to trial courts.

LEGISLATIVE VERSUS ADJUDICATIVE FACTS

The distinction between legislative and adjudicative facts has been alluded to above. "Adjudicative facts" are those historical facts that describe the dispute at issue in the case now before the court. "Legislative facts" are the broader, repeatable findings that describe the nature of the physical and social world. While courts are eager to admit witnesses who can testify to adjudicative facts, they are not so eager to allow testimony on legislative facts. Though the courts seem not to realize it, all expert testimony is based to some extent on what really are legislative facts. Even an expert who examines an object or a person involved in a case can give opinions only by linking those current observations to a body of research, theory, and collective experience that makes the expert an expert. Indeed, it is this background (of legislative facts) that makes the expert useful to the court. But when an expert comes to court to speak directly to those underlying legislative facts—general background facts, social-scientific facts—then courts are wary. And this is just the sort of testimony that researchers usually come to court to give.

AGGREGATE DATA VERSUS PARTICULARISTIC EVIDENCE

The distinction between aggregate data and particularistic evidence comes close to being the empirical analogue of the legal distinction made above. As we all know, research gives us aggregate findings that allow us to make probabilistic applications to particular cases. When we go from inductive research to deductive application, we are always flirting with some very real uncertainty. Just because most children of a given age have achieved certain cognitive competencies (Melton, Koocher, & Saks, 1983), how do we know that *this* child has? In deciding the policy question of whether children are competent to consent to medical procedures (Weithorn & Campbell, 1982) or waive legal rights (Grisso, 1981), it is hard to imagine not paying serious attention to the research. But in deciding whether any particular child is competent to grant consent or to waive rights, especially in the retrospective glance of a court, the research data offer only the opportunity to make educated guesses. To know with certainty is impossible. Similarly, what are courts to do when asked to admit evidence that a parent accused of child abuse fits the profile of a battering parent? Or that a purportedly sexually abused child's demeanor is similar to that of children who are known to have been abused? Typically, courts have held that the research data are prejudicial or insufficiently probative, and therefore inadmissible, but that the testifying clinician's own judgments are admissible (e.g., *In re Cheryl H.*, 1984; *State v. Loebach*, 1981; *State v. Maule*, 1983; *State v. Saldana*, 1982).

Apparently, when the leap of theory, measurement, and deduction is made by an expert who is purportedly offering particularized testimony, the court is not bothered because it has more trouble noticing the leap in this form. The leap is implicit. At worst, the expert will be asked to explain the basis for the proffered opinion; the competent expert will mention the data, theory, and so forth; opposing counsel can argue the weight on closing; and the court will be satisfied.

Done the other way around—namely, the way a researcher will present it—the court is not so satisfied. Indeed, such evidence often is held to be either inadmissible or insufficient to support a verdict (Saks & Kidd, 1981; *Smith v. Rapid Transit,* 1945; Tribe, 1971). Most researchers will be comfortable presenting the aggregate data that are relevant, but will hesitate to extrapolate from them to the case at hand. If 78% of abusive parents have certain characteristics, does that mean that *this* defendant is also an abusive parent? The court will also hesitate, and often will not allow the evidence in. This is best illustrated in the psychology–law experience by the example of experimental and social psychologists' offering research on eyewitness identification testimony. Instead of clinical conclusions, they try to offer data on the general phenomena of perception and memory. They carefully avoid drawing connections to the specific case at hand, leaving that to the jury. And it is just this gap that persuades many courts not to admit the testimony at all. Meanwhile, predictions about the dangerousness of specific individuals by clinical psychologists and psychiatrists, whose accuracy is well known to be poor (leading to twice as many incorrect as correct predictions of dangerousness), have been held to be entirely admissible (*Barefoot v. Estelle,* 1983).

Suppose a judge does admit the presentation of research involving aggregate data and legislative facts. How effective is it likely to be? A dissertation recently completed by one of my students (Dondey, 1986) found that laypeople (and most likely scientists and statisticians as well) had a curious reaction to case study evidence, contrasted with more aggregated forms of data, such as correlational studies and experiments (of both the laboratory and field variety). First, they evaluated the studies in just the same order that scientists would with respect to both internal and external validity. They downgraded case studies as weak in both. They saw the other studies as benefiting from their larger n, and the experiments as leading to more unambiguous causal inferences than the correlational studies. To that extent, they "thought like scientists." But when Dondey measured the amount of attitude change the subjects experienced as a result of reading research summaries based on various designs, he found that the case study—notwithstanding its acknowledged defects—brought about the most attitude change.

POSSIBLE SOLUTIONS

I have no magic solutions to offer to these various problems. Those pertaining to the role conflicts created for experts and the consequent impact on the information received by the court have been with us for at least a century (Foster, 1897)—or, more likely, since the advent of adversary experts in the late 18th century (*Folkes v. Chadd*, 1782)—and are unlikely to abate in our lifetimes. My suggestions really center around continuing to do what our discipline and the legal profession have long been trying to do, and to keep trying to do those things better.

CONTINUING EDUCATION, BROADLY DEFINED

Nonacademic clinicians, as I have said, are more likely than researchers to be known and called by attorneys, more likely to be allowed to testify by judges, and more likely to be adverted to by factfinders. This is not a problem if the clinicians are reasonably up to date on research, reasonably sophisticated about the link between research and practice, and thoughtful about what they are doing (this includes being alert to their limits). Promoting such competence is not a new goal for psychology. Thus, I am suggesting that we can enhance the impact of research on the law by promoting good graduate education, good continuing education, and other means of making psychologists knowledgeable about their own field's capabilities and limitations.

Similarly, by encouraging better education and awareness among the public at large, and lawyers in particular, we increase the probability that they will be aware of the varieties of psychological knowledge, if not of particular findings. Thus, we can facilitate the impact of this knowledge by making ourselves and our knowledge available to the popular press, and trying to insist on faithful, not merely felicitous, reporting; we can also make ourselves and our knowledge available to law students and practicing lawyers through seminars and continuing education. We can let the two-step flow of communication work for us by conveying new knowledge to opinion leaders in the legal profession. And we ought to seek more informal contact with lawyers and judges, relying on a certain amount of osmosis to transmit information—or having ourselves become a part of their multiprofessional grapevine. When a case comes up that needs developmental expertise, they will know someone to whom to turn for testimony, consulting, or referral.

STRUCTURAL CHANGE

Part of the problem, as I have noted, is with the structure and pace of law practice in general. Most lawyers are too busy to do their jobs as well as we, they, and their clients would like. We are unlikely to be in a position to do much to change that, but as citizens we can do our part. Kalven and Zeisel's (1966) data show, for example, that prosecutors are far more likely to bring virtually every kind of expertise before a court than defense counsel are. This is just one reflection of the imbalance of resources available to the prosecution compared with the defense. Public defenders are more overworked than prosecutors and are less able to find and pay for experts. For example, they do not have the investigators the prosecution does (i.e., the police) or the forensic scientists (i.e., those at the police laboratory). This applies as well to the more exotic kinds of experts—for example, psychologists with developmental expertise. As citizens, we can support the greater distributional justice that is a precondition for the kind of justice that depends upon well-prepared and well-presented cases by both sides.

INVOLVEMENT IN TRIALS

When it comes to their involvement in particular cases, expert witnesses need to realize the potential practical importance of what they offer at trial. While appellate courts have the power to seek legislative facts on their own, many are reluctant to do so, and none have the time to do it particularly well. In common practice, the record that is constructed at trial, and the "Brandeis briefs" submitted to appellate courts, are the most controllable vehicles for offering such information to the courts for the eventual purpose of setting policy. This is one of the lessons to be drawn from Mnookin's (1985) intense examination of major children's test cases. A clear example is provided by the state's strategy in *Bellotti v. Baird* (1976), in which a Massachusetts statute requiring parental consent for minors' abortions was under attack:

> [Assistant Attorney General Garrick] Cole believed that to win before the U.S. Supreme Court, a different approach was essential. He had to develop a record that illuminated the *policy* issues. Using the usual tools of a litigator, he would try to build a record that would show the complexity of the teenage pregnancy problem and the importance of parental involvement. He wanted to convince the Supreme Court that, as construed, the Massachusetts legislation was a reasonable approach to a difficult policy problem. To this end Cole aggressively sought to discover evidence usable in court and to force a new trial, at which he could create a whole new record. (Mnookin, 1985, p. 198)

In Cole's own words, "We're trying to develop, basically, a record composed of legislative fact. . . . in an adversary way, . . . but one upon which fundamental judgments of constitutional law are going to be made" (quoted in Mnookin, 1985, p. 201).

Each stage of the legal process offers the parties and their attorneys different opportunities to shape and control the outcome. At the trial level, it is building the record that may eventually go to the appeals courts. For the expert, the opportunity to contribute directly to the factfinder's and judicial policymaker's comprehension of the relevant legislative facts (i.e., the research findings) usually ends with the trial. Thus, to do a sound, scholarly, and effective job, the expert must overcome some of the problems discussed earlier in this chapter.

Sometimes the expert witness must find the lawyers involved in the right case, and not the other way around. (The *APA Monitor's* "Judicial Notebook" is a vehicle to help psychologists do just that.) The expert may have to prepare the lawyers by pressuring them to take the time to learn and understand the research findings and theoretical concepts, and by practicing direct examinations and cross-examinations. And in court, the expert may have to resist the not always sure-footed lead of counsel on either side, in trying to offer to the court an accurate, complete picture of the state of the relevant knowledge.

REFERENCES

American Bar Association. (1980). *Model Code of Professional Responsibility.* Chicago: National Center for Professional Responsibility and the ABA.

Ballew v. Georgia, 435 U.S. 223 (1978).

Barefoot v. Estelle, 103 S. Ct. 3383 (1983).

Bellotti v. Baird, 428 U.S. 132 (1976).

Coleman, J., Katz, E., & Menzel, H. (1966). *Medical innovations: A diffusion study.* Indianapolis, IN: Bobbs-Merrill.

Dondey, M. (1986). *Research design as an attitude change variable.* Unpublished doctoral dissertation, Boston College.

Dunagin v. City of Oxford, 718 F.2d 738 (5th Cir. 1983).

Dyas v. United States, 376 A.2d 827 (App. D.C. 1977).

Fed. R. Civ. P. 39, 53.

Fed. R. Evid. 706.

Folkes v. Chadd, 3 Dougl. 157, 99 E.R. 589 (1782).

Foster, W.L. (1897). Expert testimony—prevalent complaints and proposed remedies. *Harvard Law Review, 11,* 169–186.

Frye v. United States, 293 F. 1013 (D.C. Cir. 1923).

Giannelli, P.C. (1980). The admissibility of novel scientific evidence: *Frye v. United States,* a half century later. *Columbia Law Review, 80,* 1198–1250.

Giannelli, P.C. (1983). *Frye v. United States:* Symposium on science and the rules of evidence. *Federal Rules Decisions, 99,* 188–218.

Grisso, T. (1981). *Juveniles' waiver of rights: Legal and psychological competence.* New York: Plenum.

In re Cheryl H., 153 Cal. App. 3d 1098 (1984).

Kalven, H. & Zeisel, H. (1966). *The American jury.* Boston: Little, Brown.

Melton, G.B., Koocher, G.P., & Saks, M.J. (Eds.). (1983). *Children's competence to consent.* New York: Plenum.

Mnookin, R.H. (Ed.). (1985). *In the interest of children: Advocacy, law reform, and public policy.* W.H. Freeman.

Monahan, J. & Walker, L. (1986). *Social Science in Law.* Mineola, NY: Foundation.

Saks, M.J., & Baron, C.H. (1980). *The use/nonuse/misuse of applied social research in the courts.* Cambridge, MA: Abt.

Saks, M.J., & Kidd, R.F. (1981). Human information processing and adjudication: Trial by heuristics. *Law and Society Review, 15,* 123–160.

Saks, M.J., & Van Duizend, R. (1983a). *The use of scientific evidence in litigation.* Williamsburg, VA: National Center for State Courts.

Saks, M.J. & Van Duizend, R. (1983b). Scientific evidence in litigation: Problems, hopes, accommodations, and frustrations. *State Court Journal, 7,* 5–7, 23–28.

Saks, M.J. & Wissler, R. (1984). Legal and psychological bases of expert testimony. *Behavioral Sciences and the Law, 2,* 435–449.

Smith v. Rapid Transit, 317 Mass. 469, 58 N.E.2d 754 (1945).

State v. Loebach, 310 N.W.2d 58 (1981).

State v. Maule, 35 Wash. App. 287 (1983).

State v. Saldana, 324 N.W.2d 227 (1982).

Tanke, E.D., & Tanke, T.J. (1979). Getting off a slippery slope: Social science in the judicial process. *American Psychologist, 34,* 1130–1138.

Thibaut, J., & Walker, L. (1975). *Procedural justice: A psychological analysis.* Hillsdale, NJ: Erlbaum.

Tribe, L.H. (1971). Trial by mathematics: Precision and ritual in the legal process. *Harvard Law Review, 84,* 1329–1393.

United States v. Williams, 583 F.2d 1194 (2d Cir. 1978).

Weithorn, L.A. & Campbell, S.B. (1982). The competency of children and adolescents to make informed treatment decisions. *Child Development, 53* 1589–1598.

The High Road to the Bench: Presenting Research Findings in Appellate Briefs

CHARLES R. TREMPER

Including child development research in appellate briefs could be an effective way of interjecting social science into the policymaking process, but a number of factors limit the potential for substantial influence. In some respects, appellate courts are ideally suited for policymaking based on research. For example, judges, who serve as *de facto* policymakers, are usually few in number, well educated, insulated from partisan politics, and obliged to rest their decisions on rational grounds. Though with these characteristics they might be expected to embrace the empirical sciences as a ready source of knowledge upon which to base decisions, they generally prefer other sources of authority. The equivocal role social science plays in jurisprudential theory manifests itself in various obstacles to judges' relying upon extralegal sources. Nonetheless, judges have sometimes drawn upon psychology and other social sciences in reaching landmark decisions. In any given case, the impact of research on the result will depend on the nature of the issue, the quality of the available studies, and a host of less easily identifiable factors.

This chapter examines how social science research has been and could be used in the appellate process. Because written briefs, both of parties and of other interested individuals and

Charles R. Tremper. College of Law and Department of Psychology, University of Nebraska–Lincoln, Lincoln, Nebraska.

organizations participating as *amici curiae*, are the primary vehicles for placing information before the appellate courts, the
discussion focuses primarily on their use. The scope must be
somewhat broader, however, because research reaches appellate courts through other channels as well, and the effects of
those alternatives have implications for researchers and attorneys.

In line with the theme of this book, the inquiry into use of
social science in the appellate process is devoted almost exclusively to child development research. The particular child development topic used here for illustration is the competence of
minors to make decisions about abortion. As that topic has been
developed in a series of U.S. Supreme Court cases on minors'
rights to abortion, it includes concepts of maturity, decisionmaking capacity, and family dynamics that are within the province of or closely associated with developmental psychology.

The methodology used to study how empirical research
presented in parties' and *amici*'s briefs affects appellate decisions
consists of a comparative content analysis. The six U.S. Supreme
Court cases (through 1985) dealing with minors' access to abortion, and their associated briefs, are examined. The opinions
are reviewed to determine what empirical statements they contained and how those propositions were supported. A similar
analysis of the briefs is conducted to determine whether the
briefs supplied sources or ideas used in the opinions. Compar-
isons among all briefs for one case and across cases are also
made to determine how briefs of parties and *amici* were related
and to see whether the use of research changed over the time
between the earliest and the most recent cases in this series.

From this analysis of the use of social science in appellate
briefs, two sets of recommendation are offered. The first set
deals with effectively incorporating research in briefs. The second concerns conducting research of maximal value to appellate courts.

POTENTIAL FOR CHILD DEVELOPMENT RESEARCH
TO INFLUENCE APPELLATE OPINIONS

Of the various methods discussed in this volume for interjecting
social science research findings into the policy process, inclusion

in appellate briefs is the most Byzantine. This section describes the mechanics of incorporating research findings into appellate briefs and getting those briefs before a court. It then discusses characteristics of the legal process that limit the effects research is likely to have on the law that emerges from appeals courts.

APPELLATE BRIEFS IN GENERAL

The value of appellate briefs as instruments for interjecting social science research into the policy process derives from their function in the process of communicating with appellate judges. Appellate judges, whether state or federal, hold concentrated authority to effect legal change. In contrast to the dozens to hundreds of legislators (and the thousands or even millions of voters) needed to change a law, two to five votes among members of the appellate bench are typically sufficient to achieve the same result. Providing these policymakers with research findings is, therefore, a significant method of influencing the policy process. For an appropriate issue—generally one that presents a narrow legal question—the appellate route may be the most suitable method of affecting policy.

The appellate brief is the principal means available for advocates to supply judges with information (Stern, 1981). The primary function of an appellate brief, however, is not simple transmission of information. The brief must be more rhetorical than expository (Springer, 1984). The only informational requisite of a brief is to discuss the pertinent law, whether or not it supports the position advocated in the brief (Weinstein, 1966). Beyond that, a brief should combine facts, law, and logic as needed to present the most compelling possible argument for the position advocated.

In part because briefs do subordinate informing to persuading, appellate judges do not rely on them as their exclusive source of knowledge. Invariably judges have before them the written record of the trial, which may total many thousands of pages. In most cases, they will also hear oral arguments from the opposing attorneys. In addition, judges or their clerks can conduct independent library research into any matter of interest (Marvell, 1978, p. 180). Off the bench, judges receive background information continuously through extralegal channels such as judicial conferences and the nightly television news. Attorneys submitting briefs must take these alternative sources into account in choosing what to include.

AMICUS BRIEFS

Briefs may be, and in major cases frequently are, filed not only by the parties, but also by *amici curiae,* literally "friends of the court" (O'Connor & Epstein, 1982). The *amicus* brief provides a mechanism for interested individuals and organizations to supply the court with information they consider important to deciding a case. Participation is generally permitted whenever the *amicus* has a legitimate interest in some aspect of the case that is distinct from the interest of the parties. In a right-to-counsel case appealed by an indigent defendant, for example, the professional bar would have interests and perhaps insights beyond those of either the defendant or the state. Consequently, the American Bar Association would probably be permitted to file an *amicus* brief that could inform the court about such topics as lawyer availability, customary practices, and effects of various rules on the legal profession. In such a situation, the court may request participation by *amici* even if none have petitioned to become involved.

Originally the *amicus* appearance was intended as a neutral contributor to the court's store of knowledge (Krislov, 1963). Over time, however, the neutrality of *amici,* if it ever existed, gave way to a predominantly adversarial posture (Keenan, 1982; Wiggins, 1976). In the U.S. Supreme Court, the tradition of neutrality has been undermined by a rule requiring *amici* to file in support of one of the parties (Sup. Ct. R. 36.2). Along with the tendency toward advocacy in submitting *amicus* briefs has come a great increase in the frequency and importance of their use (O'Connor & Epstein, 1983b). In some circumstances, *amici* virtually supplant the parties they support. Rather than being "at best only icing on the cake . . . [*amicus* briefs] are often the cake itself" (Ennis, 1984, p. 602).

Since *amici* can potentially enter any case in which they

have an interest, some organizations submit appellate briefs as part of an orchestrated campaign to change the law through whatever means they can (O'Connor & Epstein, 1983a). Sophisticated participants coordinate filing of their briefs with those of the parties they support in complex cases to provide comprehensive treatment of all the issues (Shapiro, 1984). This relatively new use of the *amicus* brief as an advocacy instrument has led to greatly increased filings. Whereas the *amicus* appearance was once fairly rare, it has now become almost a standard feature of major precedent-setting cases (O'Connor & Epstein, 1982; cf. Hakman, 1966).

Social Science Literature in Appellate Briefs

The increase in *amicus* participation during the last quarter of a century has paralleled another change in appellate briefs: greatly increased use of social science research (Alpert, 1984). Since appellate courts, especially the U.S. Supreme Court, may at times revise the law, brief writers have some incentive to extend their arguments beyond black-letter law to all manner of policy considerations (Stern, 1981). Despite the reservations of some observers (Rehbinder, 1972; Thibaut & Walker, 1978), social science research, including research on child development, is relevant to resolution of some cases and is increasingly being placed before appellate courts for their use. Rationales and procedures for using social science research in briefs, however, place some constraints on the practice. These derive principally from the uncertain role of "legislative facts" in the law (K.C. Davis, 1942; Melton, Chapter 9, this volume; Saks, Chapter 7, this volume). Although prevailing legal theory now recognizes the legitimacy of introducing material pertaining to "legislative facts," disagreement persists regarding, among other things, how such material ought to enter the legal process and what weight it should receive (Levine & Howe, 1985; Monahan & Walker, 1986).

For parties or *amici* desiring to present judges with social science research, submitting a "Brandeis brief," as research-laden briefs have come to be called, offers several advantages over introducing the material at trial (Korn, 1966; Marvell, 1978). First, submitting research findings in briefs reduces the time and complexity of the trial, allowing the trial attorneys to concentrate on other matters that cannot be handled exclusively on appeal. Second, the presentations can be tailored to circumstances that have changed since the trial, either in the case law or in the available research. Third, limiting the presentation to a written format eliminates distractions and irrelevancies attendant to the expert witness system (Wolfgang, 1974). Cross-examination of experts frequently runs more to their qualifications than to the substance of what they are presenting. This process contributes little to either making a coherent presentation or assessing the validity and relevance of the research (Bersoff, 1986; Levine, 1984).

Despite the advantages of "Brandeis briefs" over introducing social science findings at trial, the appellate process is at best an imperfect alternative. Critics point out that allowing research findings to be presented on appeal deprives trial judges of the opportunity to see how the sources would fare under cross-examination and bypasses the other processes the legal system uses to test factual assertions (Black, 1972; Miller & Cavanaugh, 1975). The following excerpt from the *Ballew v. Georgia* (1978) opinion of Justice Powell, in which he expressed his dissatisfaction with Justice Blackmun's extensive analysis of social science findings in the majority opinion, expresses the view that appellate courts should be circumspect in their use of research.

> I have reservations as to the wisdom—as well as the necessity—of Mr. Justice Blackmun's heavy reliance on numerology derived from statistical studies. Moreover, neither the validity nor the methodology employed by the studies was subjected to the traditional testing mechanisms of the adversary process. The studies relied on merely represent unexamined findings of persons interested in the jury system. (p. 226)

Notwithstanding criticisms and reservations, appellate courts have come to use social science in some circumstances, and advocates are by and large free to introduce it. The best strategy for interjecting research findings into the judicial process has received much less discussion in the legal literature than has the debate over the role of science generally in the courts. Considerations regarding introduction at trial or on appeal, by parties or *amici*, may be more practical than theoretical. To a great extent, attorneys may choose the approach they think most likely to achieve a favorable result, and *amici* can participate however they see fit.

Necessary Conditions for Introducing Social Science Research

If child development research is to be put before an appellate court, several conditions must appertain. While some of these are common for any policy forum, others are unique to the court system. They can be especially constraining for *amicus* participation. Most importantly, the individuals or organizations wishing to present materials must work in coordination with an attorney and must adhere to the filing procedures for appellate briefs (Martineau, 1983). This collaboration may prove uneasy, because the two professions have fundamentally different methods and styles (Haney, 1980). To be effective, researchers must accustom themselves to the formalistic, precedent-bound nature of the law. Attorneys must assemble the available research so that it properly supports legal propositions. Ultimately, only an attorney may submit a brief (Sup. Ct. R. 33.2(a)(7)).

The first set of formal conditions for participation concerns getting an appropriate case to the appellate court. Since courts do not decide issues in the abstract, a case must not only be brought; it must be litigated in such a way at trial that the issues for which social science research might be pertinent are preserved on appeal (Martineau, 1983). Unless some person directly affected by the law or practice at issue is willing to bring suit, there will be no trial, no appeal, and no use of social science (O'Connor & Epstein, 1983a).

Once a case is brought, attorneys must attempt to frame at least one of the issues so that social science research will be relevant to its resolution. This aspect of the process requires attention to the legal bases for challenging or defending the status quo. Stating an equal protection claim will almost always make social science presentations appropriate. Suitability for other purposes may depend on how an issue is analyzed. In cases dealing with the permissibility of empaneling criminal juries with fewer than 12 members (*Ballew v. Georgia*, 1978; *Williams v. Florida*, 1970), for example, arguments based on what the framers of the U.S. Constitution meant by a "jury" would have created little opportunity for introducing empirical data. Focusing instead on the the functional equivalency of various-sized juries in these cases made social science data all but essential (Diamond & Zeisel, 1974). If psychological studies are to be introduced, they are more likely to be useful for contradicting assertions of certainty, simplicity, and "normality" than for any other purpose (Katz, 1971).

Framing the issue in constitutional cases is especially problematic because the legal question presented may mask a host of unstated issues that lie behind the controversy. This shadow game can become extended to the resulting opinions as judges use the legal arguments to justify results reached on other grounds (Marvell, 1978, p. 115). Particularly in landmark constitutional cases, the case itself becomes little more than a vehicle for court pronouncements. According to one commentator discussing the Supreme Court's role in desegregation, "[t]he specific case often became merely the vehicle for the announcement of a set of new rules to guide all those subject to the Court's general supervision" (Forrester, 1977, p. 1216).

The other conditions for participation are mostly technicalities. Every appellate court has certain rules for filing briefs and making oral arguments (Martineau, 1983). These typically include time periods within which various legal documents must be filed, page limits on briefs, time limits on oral argument, and such picayune details as acceptable font sizes for printing briefs (Stern & Gressman, 1978). In the U.S. Supreme Court, attorneys for the parties are limited to 30 minutes of oral argument; their briefs must be filed within 45 days after the Court accepts the case; and they must not exceed 50 pages without express permission (Sup. Ct. R. 34.3, 35.1, 38.3).

Additional and generally more stringent rules apply for participation by *amici*. Unlike the parties, *amici* cannot seek extensions of any of the time limits for filing (Ennis, 1984). They must follow the schedule established by the parties. In general, they are provided no opportunity for oral presentation. They may not be permitted to participate in oral argument, and if they do, the time may be subtracted from the allotment to the party on the side the *amicus* favors. If filing a brief with the Supreme Court, they must adhere to a 30-page limit (Sup. Ct. R. 36.2). In addition to these relatively minor differences for *amici* and parties, there is one major distinction: Participation of *amici* is discretionary rather than automatic. In the Supreme Court, *amici* may participate either if they receive permission from all parties in the case, or if the Court grants authorization (Sup. Ct. R. 36.1). This determination is made independently of whether the *amici* participated in the original trial of the case.

SUITABILITY OF SOCIAL SCIENCE RESEARCH

In part, the debate over the role social science research should have in the judicial process stems from the nature of the research itself. Newer fields, with psychology and child development certainly among them, are looked upon with some suspicion by practitioners of a legal system steeped in tradition and precedent (Haney, 1980). Commentators who caution against resting judicial decisions on social science research point to the instability of findings and the disagreement among experts on virtually every issue (Rosen, 1972). The lack of certainty in the social sciences conflicts with the need for finality and definiteness in judicial decisions (Murphy & Pritchett, 1978).

To date, the social sciences have had a greater impact on the justice system through avenues other than the appellate courts. Psychology, for example, has had a major influence on the juvenile justice system and corrections (Ryerson, 1978). At the trial level, expert testimony by psychologists has become commonplace in child custody disputes (Litwack, Gerber, & Fenster, 1979–1980). To a great extent, however, forensic psychologists rendering judgments based on clinical experience have predominated, and their influence has been limited to dispositions in individual cases rather than formulation of judicial policy (Melton, 1984).

Regardless of how little appellate courts currently use social science research, the potential for such use is great. Many commentators have examined the issue and concluded that the social sciences can make substantial contributions to a just system of law that reflects our understanding of the world (Diamond, 1982; Kalven, 1968; Melton, 1983; Saks, 1974). These commentators typically note that for research to be useful, it must be less theoretical and more applied than scholarly standards have traditionally favored. Studies must also be methodologically rigorous and clearly related to a legal issue (Bersoff, 1987). Increasingly, child development research studies, as well as those in other fields, have met these criteria.

SOCIAL SCIENCE ON APPEAL TO THE SUPREME COURT: MINORS' ABORTION CASES

To examine the use of social science in appellate briefs in more detail, and to explore further the impact of those submissions on the courts, this section focuses on the U.S. Supreme Court cases (through 1985) dealing with abortion rights of minors. The first portions of this section provide background about the minors' abortion cases to establish the context for the ensuing analysis. The background discussion includes an overview of the cases and a more detailed examination of the role the concept of maturity played in those cases. The subsequent analysis examines how the briefs and opinions used social science research findings about maturity.

Several characteristics of the minors' abortion cases make them ideally suited for illustrating appellate use of social science. Most importantly, the pertinent cases accorded constitutional stature to the developmental concept of maturity, providing a logical context for interjecting child development research. Moreover, the high visibility of the issue attracted the *amici* participation of many interest groups that might be expected to supplement the parties' use of social science findings. Those interest groups made various uses of research literature, with some on each side ignoring it and others submitting citation-laden briefs.

In addition, the research available for use by the interest groups and ultimately by the Court has progressed concurrently with the case law. When the first case reached the Court in 1976, few relevant studies were available. Researchers subsequently have conducted sophisticated multidisciplinary studies and are continuing to add to the store of knowledge on topics pertinent to the Court's reasoning in these cases. Since this line of cases is still evolving, research yet to be conducted and briefs yet to be submitted may influence the nascent standards.[1]

DEVELOPMENT OF THE SUPREME COURT'S CONCEPTION OF MATURITY

The minors' abortion cases grew logically out of the Court's seminal *Roe v. Wade* decision in 1973 granting women a limited right to abortion choice. While clearly holding that states could not prohibit all abortions, *Roe* left many questions about permissible regulations unanswered. Among these, since Roe was an adult, was the entire range of abortion issues for minors. The cases that subsequently dealt with minors' rights are difficult to interpret because the Justices rarely agreed on how to resolve the major issues; when they did agree on the outcome, they differed about the rationales to support their decisions (Dembitz, 1980).

The first two cases brought by minors reached the Supreme Court 3 years after *Roe*. In one of those cases, *Planned Parenthood of Central Missouri v. Danforth* (hereinafter referred to as *Danforth*) (1976), a divided Court invalidated the portion of Missouri's abortion statute that gave parents an "absolute, and possibly arbitrary, veto" (p. 74) over their daughters' decisions to have an abortion. In the other case that year, *Bellotti v. Baird* (hereinafter referred to as *Bellotti I*) (1976), the Court simply withheld judgment pending state supreme court clarification

---

1. In 1986, another case dealing with minors' access to abortion went before the Supreme Court (*Thornburgh v. American College of Obstetricians and Gynecologists*, 1986). However, the Court failed to resolve the issues presented about minors and instead remanded these to the district court. The Court may reach these issues in *Hartigan v. Zbaraz* (1986).

of the statute at issue. After the state court interpreted the statute to impose an unqualified requirement of parental consent, the Supreme Court, in *Bellotti v. Baird* (hereinafter referred to as *Bellotti II*) (1979), ruled it too unconstitutional.

At the same time that these cases sent the clear message that states could not prevent all minors from obtaining abortions without parental consent, they explicitly reserved judgment as to whether "every minor, regardless of age or maturity, may give effective consent for termination of her pregnancy" (*Danforth*, 1976, p. 75). Some of the plurality opinions contained advisory statements about the different rights of mature and immature minors, but none were definitive because the facts of neither *Danforth* nor *Bellotti I* placed the issue properly before the Court.

Maturity of individual minors became a condition of constitutional entitlement for the first time in *H.L. v. Matheson* (hereinafter referred to as *H.L.*) (1981). The statute at issue in *H.L.* requires doctors to notify a minor's parents before performing an abortion. To challenge the constitutionality of that law, attorneys brought a class action suit on behalf of all minor girls who wished to obtain an abortion without having their parents notified. Although attorneys for both sides argued the case as if that entire class of minors was represented, the majority opinion dealt with the statute only as applied to immature minors. The majority reasoned that any girl like H.L. who "is unmarried, fifteen years of age, resides at home and is a dependent of her parents" (1981, p. 406) could not suitably represent any group other than immature minors. As to immature minors like H.L., Utah could constitutionally require parental notification.

If *H.L.* left any doubt about the constitutional significance of maturity, subsequent developments dispelled it. In the companion cases of *City of Akron v. Akron Center for Reproductive Health* (hereinafter referred to as *Akron*) (1983) and *Planned Parenthood of Kansas City v. Ashcroft* (hereinafter referred to as *Ashcroft*) (1983), the Court emphasized that "demonstrably mature minors" have greater rights than their immature sisters. Akron's ordinance failed the constitutional test because it did not afford every mature minor seeking an abortion an adequate alternative to parental consent. The Akron City Council could "not make a blanket determination that all minors under the age of 15 are too immature to make this decision" (*Akron*, 1983, p. 2498). In contrast, the option for girls in Kansas City to have their maturity assessed by a judge, and to proceed autonomously if found mature, was deemed constitutionally sufficient in *Ashcroft*.

SUBSTANCE OF THE COURT'S CONCEPTION OF MATURITY

In ascribing constitutional import to maturity, members of the Court were aware of the concept's inherent ambiguity. Justice Powell observed in one opinion that it is "difficult to define, let alone determine, maturity" (*Bellotti II*, 1979, p. 643–644, note 23). Perhaps in recognition of that difficulty, the Court to a great extent avoided attempting either task and left the determination of maturity in individual cases to the discretion of trial judges. Defining "maturity" was not wholly necessary, both because the Court assumed general knowledge of the concept and because none of the cases raised the issue in such a way as to require a definition. Instead of defining "maturity" or establishing a test for determining whether an individual possesses it, the fractionated opinions in the minors' abortion cases made oblique references to it (cf. detailed test for obscenity, *Miller v. California*, 1973). The following review distills from the several opinions the attributes of maturity that a majority of the Justices endorsed.

The clearest proposition about maturity to emerge from the opinions was that individuals do not attain it at any particular age. Although Justice Stevens initially indicated a willingness to consider age a constitutionally permissible proxy for maturity (*Danforth*, 1976, pp. 104–105), he too acknowledged that age can be no more than a convenient approximation, not a true indicator of maturity.

Beyond recognizing that individuals do not uniformly mature after a given number of years, the Court also noted that minors may be mature for some purposes but not others. As the Court observed in *H.L.*, "There is no logical relationship between the capacity to become pregnant and the capacity for mature judgment concerning the wisdom of an abortion" (1981, p. 408). Additional references to differences between physical and psychological maturation, as well as to types of emotional maturity, appeared throughout the opinions (e.g., *Bellotti II,* 1979, pp. 643–644, note 23). The requirement of individualized judicial determinations of maturity in place of a chronological dividing line rested upon the Court's acknowledgment of developmental variability.

The actual attributes the Court identified in these cases as essential to maturity fall roughly into two categories. One set of qualities has to do with cognitive capacities and rational decisionmaking. The other concerns the worldliness or sophistication of the individual. In combination, these qualities negate the "peculiar vulnerability" of minors.

Regarding mental capacity, the Court required that minors be able to make decisions in the rational manner presumed of adults. To be judged mature, minors must be able "to make critical decisions in an informed, mature manner" (*Bellotti II,* 1979, p. 634). Alternatively stated, they must possess the "ability to make fully informed choices that take account of both immediate and long-range consequences" (*Bellotti II,* 1979, p. 640). Though the linguistic formulation is different here, the concept resembles the requisite rationality for the "reasonable person" standard in tort law (Prosser & Keeton, 1984). Interestingly, this "maturity test" requires more mental competence than minors must possess in order to be held responsible for criminal acts (Gardner, in press) or to waive their constitutional protection against self-incrimination (*Fare v. Michael C.,* 1979).

In addition to adequate cognitive capacity, a mature minor must be somewhat savvy about the ways of the world. The opinions' most complete statement of this quality would have minors possess "the experience, perspective, and judgment to recognize and avoid choices that could be detrimental to them" (*Bellotti II,* 1979, p. 635). They must have sufficient experience with the world to know what options they have available and what the likely consequences of their choices would be. The underlying desire to protect children from their own imprudence has been a major consideration in other contexts as well for justifying special rules for minors (*In re Gault,* 1967; *Ginsberg v. New York,* 1968).

Particularly in *Danforth* and *Bellotti II,* the concepts that the Justices associated with maturity resemble characteristics a developmental psychologist might list. Although the Justices overlooked some important distinctions between mature and immature youths, and in *H.L.* they failed to apply their own criteria for judging maturity, the characteristics that *were* mentioned in these cases accord with psychological evidence. As discussed in the next section, however, the Justices derived these propositions in a manner quite different from the way a research psychologist would proceed.

THE BRIEFS, THE OPINIONS, AND THE REAL WORLD

Identifying the sources the Justices used in developing their concepts of maturity requires some familiarity with the strategies advocates used for influencing the Court's abortion opinions. Each case was a class action initiated as part of an orchestrated campaign to test restrictions on minors' access to abortion services. Although the governmental defendants differed in each case, national organizations opposed to abortion intervened in some manner each time, thus providing a measure of uniformity and continuity that might not be expected in discrete cases.

Amicus Participation

If cases carried the names of *amici* rather than parties, the course of this litigation would be known as *Americans United for Life v. Planned Parenthood Federation of America.* Each time the issue of minors' consent to abortion has reached the Supreme Court, these two organizations have filed briefs. Both organizations operate nationwide to promote their respective views on abortion choice. Their participation as *amici* is but one technique in their arsenal of strategies for influencing public policy.

In addition to these two ever-present *amicus* filers, 69 other organizations and hundreds of individuals joined the *amicus*

briefs for these six cases. Almost all of the participating organizations fit into one of five categories. Of these groups, the
largest is composed of 19 professional associations, including 7
consisting primarily of women members of various professions.
The American Medical Association and the California Women
Lawyers Association typify the professional group. Participation
of these associations was warranted both because their members
provide services affected by the contested regulations and because they could provide the Court with specialized knowledge.

The next largest categories of organizations are two groups
of organizations with substantial advocacy orientations. Organizations in one of these groups take positions on many issues,
generally with some common theme such as civil rights or family
integrity. These include the National Organization for Women
and the United Families Foundation. The other group of policy-
oriented organizations consists of those limited primarily to
advocacy on the abortion issue. Joining Americans United for
Life and Planned Parenthood in this group are the National
Abortion Federation and the Legal Defense Fund for Unborn
Children. Generally, several of these groups submitted a joint
brief in a case. A few on each side of the issue formed a core
group filing repeatedly, with the others joining only once.

Another 11 filers are broad-based organizations operated
primarily for reasons other than advocacy. Many of these are
convocations of religious orders, such as the United States Catholic Conference and the American Jewish Congress. Others
include the Young Women's Christian Association (YWCA) National Board and, in somewhat of a class apart, the U.S. government. Each of these entities filed in only one case. The
remaining group of *amicus* filers consists of the five named
abortion service providers that had an obvious and direct interest in the cases. All but one of these clinics and associations
joined a brief in more than one case.

Together, these 71 organizations submitted a total of 44
briefs in the six cases. The three most active organizations filed
a brief on the minors' abortion issues in each case. A few of the
other organizations filed briefs limited to issues other than minors' abortion rights. Those organizations and briefs are in-

cluded at this stage of the analysis on the interest of comprehensiveness.

Social Science in the Briefs

With so many briefs filed in these six cases, and coordinated submissions of some parties and *amici*, ample opportunity existed for the introduction of social science research findings. The Court might then have drawn upon that research in developing its conception of maturity. The ensuing analysis of the use of research is limited to literature germane to child development aspects of a minor's right to choose an abortion. The introduction of research on other topics, such as procedures to be followed in performing an abortion, is not discussed here.

Most of the parties' and *amici*'s briefs cited few research findings pertaining to minors' ability to make abortion decisions. Parties' briefs used a smattering of social science sources, but none at all support assertions about maturity. Several factors weighed against including extensive social science discussions in the briefs for the seminal cases. The multiple issues in the cases restricted the available space that could be devoted to discussing minors' competence. More significantly, the parties on both sides wished to deal with the class of minors' seeking abortions as an undifferentiated whole (Luker, 1984). The arguments treated maturity as a red herring, with some briefs asserting that by virtue of becoming pregnant, a girl gains a presumptively superior claim to anyone else for deciding how her pregnancy will end, and others contending that minors always need parental assistance. Furthermore, little relevant research was available.

Extensiveness of research in *amici*'s briefs varied considerably, as Table 8-1 shows. The table layout provides columns for the total number of briefs and the number dealing with minors' rights. Pure social science sources appeared in only about half of the briefs, and just three of those might be considered "Brandeis briefs." Some of the briefs undoubtedly downplayed research on maturity because they were coordinated with the parties and sought to avoid the issue.

The briefs favored two techniques over citing research.

TABLE 8-1. *Amicus* Briefs in the Supreme Court's Minors' Abortion Cases

Case	Total	On minors' issues[a]	Research on minors[b]
Danforth	6	6	3
Bellotti II	3	3	1
H.L.	4	4	3
Akron	23	6	2
Combined	36	19	9

Note. The table excludes reference to *Bellotti I* because no briefs were filed and to *Ashcroft* because the briefs in that case overlapped with the briefs for *Akron*.
[a] Briefs with a section devoted to minors' issues.
[b] Briefs containing relevant social science citations.

Most commonly, they left broad, common-sense statements about minors unsupported. Alternatively, the briefs cited case law, often to support the proposition that minors are different from adults. References to medical sources were also fairly abundant, but mostly for substantiating statements about physical rather than psychological differences between older and younger females.

In each of the most research-oriented briefs, some indication of collaboration between attorneys and social scientists was apparent. The National Right to Life Committee brief for *Akron* mentioned that a professor of family relations assisted in drawing together the social science literature. The social science elements of the other two briefs were developed primarily by the research staff of Planned Parenthood. Those researchers were sufficiently familiar with the literature that they could include a citation in their brief for *H.L.* to an article in press at the time.

Use of research pertaining to minors did not vary appreciably among the various types of organizations that filed briefs, but the narrowness of the analysis in this chapter may obscure a general trend. This possibility is suggested by the rationales for participation given in the introductions to the briefs of professional organizations. For example, the reason the American Psychological Association (1983) offered for submitting a brief in *Akron* was to "bring to the Court's attention relevant professional standards and empirical studies that will not be addressed by the parties" (p. 2). The brief did indeed cite empirical sources, but none specific to the minors' issues encompassed by the primary analysis here.

Social Science in the Opinions

Much like the briefs, the opinions themselves contained extremely few citations to social science literature, and fewer still that appeared in the briefs. Despite the recurrent emphasis on maturity, none of the opinions referred to studies having to do specifically with maturity, adolescent decisionmaking, or cognitive functioning.

In the earliest cases (*Bellotti I*, 1976; *Bellotti II*, 1979; *Danforth*, 1976), the portions of the various Justices' opinions dealing with minors contained no empirical citations of any kind. The corresponding sections of the most recent cases (*Akron*, 1983; *Ashcroft*, 1983) cited a few articles about abortion in the medical literature, but did not include any references for child development propositions. The only case with any empirical citations pertaining to developmental topics was *H.L.* (1981). Even there, Chief Justice Burger's majority opinion made only limited and inappropriate use of empirical research. The single instance occurred in a footnote containing the assertion that "emotional and psychological effects of the pregnancy and abortion experience are markedly more severe in girls under 18 than in adults" (*H.L.*, p. 411, note 20). The two psychiatry journal articles cited to support that statement made no comparison of minors and adults.

More extensive and suitable citations appeared in Justice Marshall's dissent. Almost all of those citations, though, were to medical or psychiatric literature discussing the probable medical consequences of requiring minors to obtain parental consent before getting an abortion. This opinion, making the greatest use of research in any of the six cases, drew only minimally on child development.

When the Justices did choose to support a factual statement about children with a reference to some source of authority, they favored previous cases over scholarly journals. Most often cited for this purpose was Justice Stewart's concurring opinion in *Ginsberg v. New York* (1968), which itself contained no empirical references. Justice Stewart's discussion of the differences between youths and adults that justify differential application of the First Amendment provided much of the rationale needed for distinguishing between mature and immature minors. The citations to *Ginsberg* and other cases as authority for statements about extralegal matters constitute a peculiar example of the status the law accords to the contents of prior opinions. Much as a statement of law becomes binding by virtue of the Court's announcing it, a statement of fact gains a certain measure of validity in the legal world by appearing in a precedent-setting opinion (Monahan & Walker, 1986; Perry & Melton, 1984).

Aside from the Justices' awareness of what they said before, other sources of information about maturity evident from the opinions were insubstantial. *Bellotti II* typifies the lot (Mnookin, 1985). The preamble to *Bellotti II* (1979) noted that evidence at trial led to a finding "that many, perhaps a large majority of 17-year olds are capable of informed consent, as are a not insubstantial number of 16-year olds, and some even younger" (p. 632). The majority opinion also contained one citation to a sociologically oriented law review article (p. 639, note 17; reference to Hafen, 1976), but the reasons why it was cited are unclear. Since the citation was offered in support of a speculative statement about the beneficial effects of legal restrictions on children, the article may have been cited for its philosophical aspects rather than its substantive content.

Like the briefs, the opinions contained many unsubstantiated statements about minors, few of which mirrored what was offered in the briefs. Whereas the briefs generally treated the class of minors monolithically, the opinions noted differences based on maturity. The Justices apparently felt that maturity is a topic of such common knowledge that no citations were needed. They may have considered themselves sufficiently competent "amateur psychologists," on the basis of having been children and raised children themselves, to offer some general statements about the qualities of maturity necessary for the constitutional entitlement to autonomous abortion choice.

The insubstantial use of child development research in cases that predicate constitutional entitlements on maturity may be surprising, yet perhaps understandable in light of the way maturity came to be an issue and the particular function it serves in the case law. Participants supporting the minors in the early cases took the position that once a minor became pregnant, discussion of her maturity to make the abortion decision was irrelevant. Denying her decisionmaking authority would leave her with the default "choice" of having a baby. On the other side, the leading advocacy groups sought to require parental consent before any minor could obtain an abortion, as a means of reducing abortion availability (Luker, 1984). To acknowledge maturity as a relevant criterion would have been to accept that some minors would be able to obtain abortions autonomously. Although the Court ultimately rejected both of these alternatives, it did so in a peculiar fashion.

   In all of the cases except *H.L.*, the Court dealt with maturity only in the abstract. Even in *H.L.*, when maturity of the minor named in the case was an issue, the matter received short shrift. Rather than attempt to elaborate upon and apply the explicit criteria for maturity developed in previous cases, the Court simply presumed the girl immature, solely on the basis of her age and family circumstances. Because none of the cases featured a minor who alleged that she had been incorrectly ruled immature, the need for precise standards did not arise. A future case may yet present that issue, and the Court may turn to social science in resolving it.

The Available Research Base

Had the brief writers or the Justices been inclined to draw upon developmental research, they could have discovered pertinent materials. Although little research pertaining specifically to minors' abortion choices was available at the time of the first cases, the early decisions stimulated researchers to conduct more legally oriented investigations (Melton, 1987). Much as in the cases involving jury size, the Court might have found later research sufficiently valuable to warrant careful examination (Kaye, 1980).

   Because the study of maturation is central to child development, there has been no shortage of literature on the subject. Detailed information and refined theory about adolescent development are available from Erikson (1968), Offer (1969), and other researchers investigating various aspects of adolescence.

Research on how individuals make decisions has been available since the investigations of Piaget in the first quarter of this century (Inhelder & Piaget, 1923/1958). Piaget's studies of mental processes established a framework that other researchers have subsequently used to explore a range of related issues. Before the Court heard the first minors' abortion case, this topic had been studied extensively (Blasi & Hoeffel, 1974). Lessing's (1972) study of adolescents' ability to conceptualize their lives at times in the future would have been particularly apropos to these cases. In another study highly relevant to deciding whether pregnant minors are less capable than adults of making abortion choices, Tomlinson-Keasey (1972) compared decisionmaking strategies of females aged 11 to 54.

In addition to investigating the abilities of adolescents to make decisions, researchers have studied the context within which abortion decisions are made. The perception during the decade before the minors' abortion cases of a "generation gap" stimulated abundant research on the topic. Articles such as the ones by Balswick and Macrides (1975) and Newman and San Martino (1975) would have been excellent sources to confirm or refute assumptions about family harmony.

Although all of this research was available at the time of *Danforth* and *Bellotti I,* it was not ideally suited for use in the courts. The primary deficiency, from the perspective of appellate judges, was that it did not deal directly with abortion. Many of the studies also suffered from laboratory rather than real-world settings.

Stimulated in part by the Supreme Court's decisions in cases touching upon the developmental characteristics of adolescents, psychologists have focused increased attention in the past decade on developing an adequate research base for legal purposes (Melton, Koocher, & Saks, 1983). The work of Lewis (1980) epitomizes this law-targeted research. Lewis studied patients at an abortion clinic, getting as close as a researcher's methods and ethical standards would permit to the actual decisionmaking process. The research of Lewis and others who have used similar techniques (see citations in Lewis, 1987; Melton, 1986) provides the Court with a suitable source of information about maturity for making abortion decisions.

CONCLUSIONS AND RECOMMENDATIONS

In the series of U.S. Supreme Court decisions concerning minors' abortion rights and giving constitutional stature to the developmental concept of maturity, psychological and other social science research played an extremely limited role. Only a few briefs offered much of the available research on cognitive capacity, decisionmaking, and other relevant topics. The Court's majority opinions did not cite any relevant research. While the opportunity for interjecting research findings may have been less than one might think because of the way the Court handled the maturity issue, the almost complete lack of reference to social science does suggest judicial discomfort with infusing developmental psychology into constitutional decrees. That reluctance to draw upon psychological studies may be overcome in the future by better research and more appropriate presentation in briefs. On the other hand, the appellate system may remain relatively impervious unless the decisionmaking structure is altered—a very unlikely prospect.

INFLUENCE OF CHILD DEVELOPMENT RESEARCH

At least three factors contributed to the dearth of social science citations in the minors' abortion cases, and each of these three can limit the use of research in other cases as well (Bersoff, 1987; Monahan & Walker, 1986). First, though the law has warmed to importation of social science knowledge, the theoretical union of law and science is incomplete. Second, the procedures for communicating with the Court are not well suited for presenting social science research credibly. Third, the research available when the Court heard the seminal cases was inadequate and flawed. The discussion below examines each of these factors and considers their implications for other contexts.

As discussed at greater length in other chapters of this book, as well as elsewhere (A.L. Davis, 1973; Horowitz, 1977), the dissimilarities of law and social science have mediated against the latter's substantially influencing the former. For law and psychology, the disjunction is especially severe, despite the frequently articulated assertion that psychology has the *potential* to make significant contributions to law (Diamond, 1982; Haney, 1980; Melton, 1983). The minors' abortion cases manifest the schism between law and psychology in their citations of developmental propositions to precedent rather than to research literature. Whereas a psychologist asserting that children generally lack the rational capacity of adults would be likely to cite Piaget, a judge might think first of *Ginsberg v. New York* (1968).

Accentuation of the jurisprudential over the empirical pervades judicial opinions. Particularly on appeal, broad assumptions about the world can substitute for specific facts. Some of the statements about maturity that were made in the minors' abortion cases go so far in this direction that they defy refutation. No amount of research, for example, will disprove the observation that "minors often lack the experience, perspective, and judgment to recognize and avoid choices that could be detrimental to them" (*Bellotti II*, 1979, p. 635). Though the statement is nearly vacuous, because the same may be said of adults, it did serve in the case to justify the Justices' conclusion that minors are not competent to make major decisions. Without anyone having ferreted through the research literature for findings about maturity, the statement suffices as indication that its author took real-world circumstances into account in reaching a decision. Statements like this one serve their purpose well in the appellate decisionmaking process—not because they are grounded in the best available knowledge, but because judicial custom favors reliance on common sense as an adequate basis upon which to rest an opinion.

Legal controversies simply are not often structured in a way that makes social science research (especially child development studies) relevant, much less essential. Moreover, the course of litigation may not suggest the appropriateness of introducing social science prior to the appellate court's decision, or the parties may want to downplay the empirical aspect of the case. In *H.L.* (1981), for example, the individual minor's maturity was not an issue in the lower courts, and her attorneys sought to minimize the importance of her personal characteristics. The Supreme Court did not indicate relevance of the girl's maturity until rendering its final opinion. By then, the opportunity for attorneys to cite research had passed.

Mechanics of the appellate process also limit the introduction and use of research. The entire process into which submitting briefs fits was designed long ago for the resolution of legal issues without reference to social science research, and its features reflect that orientation. Therefore, if social science is to be introduced, it must be channeled through a conduit that is imperfectly suited for providing appellate judges with empirical research.

Unlike evidence adduced at trial or legal propositions presented in briefs, research presented to an appellate court carries no assurances of veracity (Cleary *et al.*, 1984). Facts are subjected to the adversarial trial process of cross-examination so as to assist judges in determining the truth. Although statements of law do not receive the same treatment, ethical canons require attorneys to make their discussions of law accurate and comprehensive (Weinstein, 1966). Research findings, on the other hand, come to the appellate judge without having been scrutinized by the opposing party at trial or sworn to by an attorney. Not even research in briefs of *amici* carry any assurances of comprehensiveness or neutrality. Consequently, judges tend to distrust briefs' discussions of research and to conduct independent reviews of the literature when they do want to draw upon research findings (Marvell, 1978).

As the appellate process is currently structured, research findings in briefs are likely to remain somewhat suspect. Treating them the same as either law or fact, however, would introduce a new set of problems. Dissatisfaction with the strictures that apply if research is treated as fact have given way only in the last century because of the inadequacy of that approach. Going back to the old arrangement now is unlikely. Requiring full discussions of all pertinent research, as is done for law, would be difficult if not unworkable because, unlike the source volumes of law, the body of research literature is virtually boundless. Creative proposals have been offered (K.C. Davis, 1986; Monahan & Walker, 1986), but the system will probably remain unchanged, and research presented in appellate briefs will continue to lack the authoritativeness it may deserve.

A final reason why research literature may not get into appellate briefs, and from there into opinions, is that the quality of the available studies may not warrant their inclusion. Having been criticized for relying upon poor research, judges may find the easier and safer course to be that of avoiding any citation at all (Miller & Barron, 1978). They may derive information from social science sources, but refrain from explicitly acknowledging their reliance on a particular publication. Perhaps a judge will have read some material, formed an impression of its validity, and subsequently used it in an opinion without recalling the source of the information. As one commentator has put it, "the Brandeis brief is important, but not so much for the case in which it is used as for some later case when its analysis has been accepted by the community" (Levi, 1949, p. 61).

Getting information before appellate judges and into general circulation may not have direct, immediate effects on the outcome of a single case, but may nonetheless shape the law over the long run. Increasing the chances that the appellate courts will use research findings, either directly or indirectly, requires continued attention to the needs of the judiciary and to improving the reputation of the social sciences for scholarliness and impartiality.

APPELLATE BRIEFS OF TOMORROW

As Rosen has noted, "Although the Court uses social science, it does not logically follow that social scientists will be able to use the Court" (1972, p. 225). The collaboration of researchers and advocates will be most potent if they keep the constraints of the appellate process in mind while undertaking to disseminate findings not only in briefs, but through law reviews and other media that may reach the judiciary. In a specific case, the influence of research on an appellate decision may depend on the quality and suitability of the research, as well as the manner of presentation.

Appellate judges may pay more attention to research if they develop a higher regard for its validity and suitability for their purposes. Because the qualities of research that make it useful to the courts have been discussed at length elsewhere, they are not belabored here. In general, if research is to have a greater influence on appellate courts, either directly or indirectly, it will need to satisfy jurists' criteria for utility. These differ from traditional academic standards primarily in being more applied than theoretical. How subjects respond to hypothetical questions may interest a researcher, but it will not have much effect on the Supreme Court.

Given high-quality research to cite, brief writers still must attend to presenting it in ways that suit the courts. How much better those presentations can be than the sophisticated strategies of the parties and *amici* in the minors' abortion cases, though, is hard to imagine (Tremper, in press). Several of the following suggestions are drawn from tactics used by the participants in those cases.

One effective technique for brief writers is to cite types of literature most favored by the Court. Law journals, of course, are first on the list of literature sources a court will cite. While the legal literature does not provide a forum for standard research studies, many journals do print articles that have a heavy social science orientation. Next most likely to be cited, at least in the type of case that has been reviewed here, are medical and psychiatric journals. Favoritism for these sources may be rooted in the fairly long history of medical experts testifying in court. Psychological and sociological sources, which are newer to the judicial process, have received mention only infrequently. An implication of this preference hierarchy for researchers seeking to have their studies noticed by judges is that, if possible, they should publish in legal and medical journals.

In choosing what research to include in briefs, attorneys may more routinely collaborate with knowledgeable experts in the fields of interest. Attorneys and social science professors joined forces on several of the "Brandeis briefs" in the minors' abortion cases. Increased collaboration may lead to professional standards in the social science disciplines for researchers' participation in litigation. Application of those standards, and perhaps a special set of rules for *amicus* participation, may eventually give judges more confidence that research discussions in briefs bear some assurance of quality.

In terms of litigation tactics, cases are too diverse for many general suggestions to be valuable. In any case, though, consideration should be given to introducing some of the research at trial, or at least to clearly raising issues for which research is relevant. In this way, presentation of research on appeal will not violate the prohibition against going beyond the record in the case (Shapiro, 1984).

The final suggestion requires the greatest expenditure of effort by the brief writer: It is to tailor the presentation of research findings to the specific interests and biases of the judges (Ennis, 1984). This may be impossible in the lower courts because judges' preferences may not be publicly known, but at the Supreme Court level, a great deal of information about what the Justices find valuable is available (Friedman, 1978; Woodward & Armstrong, 1979). Taking judges' preferences into account is one peculiar form of targeting a presentation to a specific audience.

Justice Blackmun is regarded as the most research-oriented member of the Supreme Court at present (Schlesinger & Nesse, 1980). His strong background in scientific research methodology, which includes serving as counsel to the Mayo Clinic for 10 years and studying mathematics as an undergraduate, enables him to feel more comfortable than the other Justices in reviewing empirical material. Although no other member of the Court has as much familiarity with empirical research, they all have areas of special interest and idiosyncrasies to which presentations might be directed.

If the past predicts the future, the introduction and use of social science in the appellate process will continue to increase. Each successive use further reduces the threshold of resistance to the next use as judges become accustomed to finding empirical citations in briefs and incorporating them in opinions. An ever-expanding supply of pertinent, well-designed, and properly conducted studies addressing specific legal issues will reduce objections based on the quality of research. The primary remaining impediment to more complete integration of research into the appellate process is the unsuitability of the appellate brief as a means of drawing research findings to judges' attention. Perhaps the advent of a method that will give judges greater assurance they are receiving an accurate and comprehensive survey of the available research is not too far in the future.

ACKNOWLEDGMENTS

I gratefully acknowledge the assistance of Don Bersoff and Gary Melton in conceptualizing this chapter. Appreciation is also due Jill Hinds and Perry Gregg for their research assistance.

REFERENCES

Alpert, G.P. (1984). The needs of the judiciary and misapplications of social research. *Criminology, 22*, 441–456.

American Psychological Association. (1983). [*Amicus curiae* brief in the case of *City of Akron v. Akron Center for Reproductive Health.*] Washington, DC: Author.

Ballew v. Georgia, 435 U.S. 223 (1978).

Balswick, J., & Macrides, C. (1975). Parental stimulus for adolescent rebellion. *Adolescence, 10*, 253–266.

Bellotti v. Baird (Bellotti I), 428 U.S. 128 (1976).

Bersoff, D.N. (1986). Psychologists and the judicial system: Broader perspectives. *Law and Human Behavior, 10*, 151–165.

Bersoff, D.N. (1987). Social science data and the Supreme Court: *Lockhart* as a case in point. *American Psychologist, 42*, 52–58.

Black, D.J. (1972). The boundaries of legal sociology. *Yale Law Journal, 81*, 1086–1100.

Blasi, A., & Hoeffel, E. (1974). Adolescence and formal operations. *Human Development, 17*, 344–363.

City of Akron v. Akron Center for Reproductive Health, 462 U.S. 416 (1983).

Cleary, E.W., Broun, K.S., Dix, G.E., Gelhorn, E., Kaye, D.H., Meisenholder, R., Roberts, E.F., & Strong, J.W. (Eds.). (1984). *McCormick on evidence* (3rd ed.). St. Paul, MN: West.

Davis, A.L. (1973). *The United States Supreme Court and the uses of social science data*. New York: Irvington.

Davis, K.C. (1942). An approach to problems of evidence in the administrative process. *Harvard Law Review, 55*, 364–393.

Davis, K.C. (1986). Judicial, legislative, and administrative lawmaking: A proposed research service for the Supreme Court. *Minnesota Law Review, 71*, 1–18.

Dembitz, N. (1980). The Supreme Court and a minor's abortion decision. *Columbia Law Review, 80*, 1251–1263.

Diamond, S.S. (1982). Growth and maturation in psychology and law. *Law and Society Review, 17*, 11–20.

Diamond, S.S., & Zeisel, H. (1974). "Convincing empirical evidence" on the six member jury. *University of Chicago Law Review, 41*, 281–295.

Ennis, B.J. (1984). Effective *amicus* briefs. *Catholic University Law Review, 33*, 593–609.

Erikson, E. (1968). *Identity, youth, and crisis.* New York: Norton.

Fare v. Michael, C., 442 U.S. 707 (1979).

Forrester, W.R. (1977). Are we ready for truth in judging? *American Bar Association Journal, 63*, 1212–1216.

Friedman, L.M. (1978). *The Justices of the U.S. Supreme Court.* New York: Bowker.

Gardner, M.R. (in press). Punitive juvenile justice: Some observations on a recent trend. *International Journal of Law and Psychiatry.*

Ginsberg v. New York, 390 U.S. 629 (1968).

H.L. v. Matheson, 450 U.S. 398 (1981).

Hakman, N. (1966). Lobbying the Supreme Court—an appraisal of the political science "folklore." *Fordham Law Review, 35*, 15–50.

Hafen, B.C. (1976). Children's liberation and the new egalitarianism: Some reservations about abandoning children to their "rights." *Brigham Young University Law Review, 1976*, 605–658.

Haney, C. (1980). Psychology and legal change: On the limits of a factual jurisprudence. *Law and Human Behavior, 4*, 147–199.

Hart, H.L.A. (1968). *Punishment and responsibility: Essays in the philosophy of law.* New York: Oxford University Press.

Hartigan v. Zbaraz, 710 F.2d 393 (3rd Cir. 1984), *appeal docketed*, 85-673 (Oct. 16, 1985).

Horowitz, D.L. (1977). *The courts and social policy.* Washington, DC: Brookings Institute.

Inhelder, B., & Piaget, J. (1958). *The growth of logical thinking from childhood to adolescence.* New York: Basic Books. (Original work published 1923).

In re Gault, 387 U.S. 1 (1967).

Kalven, H. (1968). The quest for the middle range: Empirical inquiry and legal policy. In G.C. Hazard (Ed.), *Law in a changing America* (pp. 56–74). Englewood Cliffs, NJ: Prentice-Hall.

Katz, M. (1971). The unmasking of dishonest pretensions: Toward an interpretation of the role of social science in constitutional litigation. *American Sociologist, 6*, 54–58.

Kaye, D. (1980). And then there were twelve: Statistical reasoning, the Supreme Court, and the size of the jury. *California Law Review, 68,* 1004–1043.

Keenan, D.C. (1982, June). Forum: Revitalizing the true *amicus* appearance. *Trial,* pp. 74–77.

Korn, H.L. (1966). Law, fact, and science in the courts. *Columbia Law Review, 66,* 1080–1116.

Krislov, S. (1963) The *amicus curiae* brief: From friendship to advocacy. *Yale Law Journal, 72,* 694–721.

Lessing, E. (1972). Extension of personal future time perspective, age and life satisfaction of children and adolescents. *Developmental Psychology, 6,* 457–468.

Levi, E.H. (1949). *An introduction to legal reasoning.* Chicago: University of Chicago Press.

Levine, M. (1984). The adversary process and social science in the courts: *Barefoot v. Estelle. Journal of Psychiatry and Law, 12,* 147–181.

Levine, M., & Howe, B.S. (1985). The penetration of social science into legal culture. *Law and Policy, 7,* 173–198.

Lewis, C.C. (1980). A comparison of minors' and adults' pregnancy decisions. *American Journal of Orthopsychiatry, 50,* 446–453.

Lewis, C.C. (1987). Minors' competence to consent to abortion. *American Psychologist, 42,* 84–88.

Litwack, T.R., Gerber, G.L., & Fenster, C.A. (1979–1980). The proper role of psychologists in child custody disputes. *Journal of Family Law, 18,* 269–300.

Luker, K. (1984). *Abortion and the politics of motherhood.* Berkeley: University of California Press.

Martineau, R.J. (1983). *Modern appellate practice: Federal and state civil appeals.* Rochester, NY: Lawyers Cooperative.

Marvell, T.B. (1978). *Appellate courts and lawyers.* Westport, CT: Greenwood Press.

Melton, G.B. (1983). Minors and privacy: Are legal and psychological concepts compatible? *Nebraska Law Review, 62,* 455–493.

Melton, G.B. (1984). Developmental psychology and the law: The state of the art. *Journal of Family Law, 22,* 445–480.

Melton, G.B. (Ed.). (1986). *Adolescent abortion: Psychological and legal issues.* Lincoln: University of Nebraska Press.

Melton, G.B. (1987). Legal regulation of adolescent abortion: Unintended effects. *American Psychologist, 42,* 79–83.

Melton, G.B., Koocher, J.P., & Saks, M.J. (Eds.). (1983). *Children's competence to consent.* New York: Plenum.

Miller, S.I., & Barron, J.A. (1978). The Supreme Court, the adversary system, and the flow of information to the Justices. *Virginia Law Review, 61,* 1187–1245.

Miller, S.I., & Kavanagh, J. (1975). Empirical evidence. *Journal of Law and Education, 4,* 159–171.

Miller v. California, 413 U.S. 15 (1973).

Monahan, J., & Walker, L. (1986). Social authority: Obtaining, evaluating, and establishing social science in law. *University of Pennsylvania Law Review, 134,* 477–517.

Mnookin, R.H. (1985). *Bellotti v. Baird:* A hard case. In R.H. Mnookin (Ed.), *In the interest of children: Advocacy, law reform, and public policy.* New York: (pp. 149–264). W.H. Freeman.

Murphy, W. F., & Pritchett, C.H. (1978). *Courts, judges, and politics: An introduction to the judicial process* (3rd ed.). New York: Random House.

Newman, M.B., & San Martino, M.R. (1975). Adolescence and the relationship between the generations. *Adolescent Psychiatry, 4,* 60–71.

O'Connor, K., & Epstein, L. (1982). *Amicus curiae* participation in U.S. Supreme Court litigation: An appraisal of Hakman's "folklore." *Law and Society Review, 16,* 311–320.

O'Connor, K., & Epstein, L. (1983a). Beyond legislative lobbying: Women's rights groups and the Supreme Court. *Judicature, 67,* 134–143.

O'Connor, K., & Epstein, L. (1983b). Court rules and workload: A case study of rules governing *amicus curiae* participation. *Justice System Journal, 8,* 35–45.

Offer, D. (1969). *The psychological world of the teenager.* New York: Basic Books.

Perry, G.S., & Melton, G.B. (1984). Precedential value of judicial notice of social facts: *Parham* as an example. *Journal of Family Law, 22,* 633–676.

Planned Parenthood of Central Missouri v. Danforth, 428 U.S. 52 (1976).

Planned Parenthood of Kansas City v. Ashcroft, 462 U.S. 476 (1983).

Prosser, W.L. & Keeton, W.P. (1984). *Prosser and Keeton on torts* (5th ed.). St. Paul, MN: West.

Rehbinder, M. (1972). The development and present state of fact research in law in the United States. *Journal of Legal Education, 24,* 567–589.

Roe v. Wade, 410 U.S. 113 (1973).

Ryerson, E. (1978). *The best laid plans: America's juvenile court experiment.* New York: Hill and Wang.

Saks, M.J. (1974, June). Ignorance of science is no excuse. *Trial,* pp. 18–20.

Schlesinger, S.R., & Neese, J. (1980). Justice Harry Blackmun and empirical jurisprudence. *American University Law Review, 29,* 405–437.

Shapiro, S.M. (1984, Spring). *Amicus* briefs in the Supreme Court. *Litigation,* pp. 21–24.

Springer, J.R. (1984). Some suggestions on preparing briefs on the merits in the Supreme Court of the United States. *Catholic University Law Review, 33,* 593–602.

Stern, R.L. (1981). *Appellate practice.* Washington, DC: Bureau of National Affairs.

Stern, R.L., & Gressman, E. (1978). *Supreme Court practice* (5th ed.). Washington, DC: Bureau of National Affairs.

Sup. Ct. R. 33.2, 34.3, 35.1, 36.1, 36.2, 38.3.

Thibaut, J., & Walker, L. (1978). A theory of procedure. *California Law Review, 66,* 541–566.

Thornburgh v. American College of Obstetricians and Gynecologists, 106 S. Ct. 2169 (1986).

Tomlinson-Keasey, C. (1972). Formal operations in females from eleven to fifty-four years of age. *Development Psychology, 6*, 364.

Tremper, C.R. (in press). Organized psychology's efforts to influence judicial policy-making. *American Psychologist, 42*.

Weinstein, J.B. (1966). Judicial notice and the duty to disclose adverse information. *Iowa Law Review, 51*, 807–824.

Wiggins, G.S. (1976). Quasi-party in the guise of *amicus curiae*. *Cumberland Law Review, 7*, 293–305.

Williams v. Florida, 399 U.S. 78 (1970).

Wolfgang, M.E. (1974). The social scientist in court. *Journal of Criminal Law and Criminology, 65*, 239–247.

Woodward, B., & Armstrong, S. (1979). *The brethren*. New York: Simon & Schuster.

Judicial Notice of "Facts" about Child Development

GARY B. MELTON

THE DOCTRINE OF JUDICIAL NOTICE

Judicial notice is perhaps the most common means of introduction of knowledge about child development into the legal
process. Through "notice" of facts, a judge may take cognizance
of information without its formal introduction into evidence.
As a result, almost any time that a case involving children is
being considered, there is the possibility of a judge's basing his
or her opinion on assumptions about child or family behavior.
As I have noted elsewhere, the scope of information admissible
through judicial notice is broad: "indisputable truth, common
knowledge, readily verifiable facts, social science authority, social fact assumptions—through a variety of mechanisms—brief
of counsel, independent judicial research, judicial experience,
judicial imagination—both on and off the record, explicit or
implicit in opinions" (Perry & Melton, 1984, p. 634, note 7).
Thus, almost regardless of the source (and, therefore, almost
regardless of the veracity), information about child development can enter into legal decisionmaking through judicial notice.

Some reliance on what is generally assumed without hear-

The discussion in this chapter is based on my previous article on a related topic with
Gail S. Perry (Perry & Melton, 1984). Ms. Perry's research has contributed substantially
to the chapter.

Gary B. Melton. Department of Psychology and College of Law, University of Nebraska–
Lincoln, Lincoln, Nebraska.

ing evidence, and the doctrine of judicial notice itself, can be traced far back into civil and canon law (Thayer, 1890). Indeed, were there not a formal judicial-notice doctrine, there would inherently be one *de facto*. The legal process would be hopelessly bogged down if it were necessary to prove every proposition that is involved in a decision. The very fact of how a judge knows what he or she knows—the experience that shapes perception of the meaning of the evidence—would otherwise be subject to proof. Other facts are so commonly known that to require their proof would be absurd. For example, if an eyewitness's credibility is in question because of poor lighting at the time of the event in question, it should not be necessary to submit evidence that people cannot see well in the dark, or that it is dark outside at midnight. The absence of a judicial-notice doctrine would require a legal fiction that judges sit as *tabulae rasae* with no knowledge beyond the trial record and the law itself.

Despite the ancient origins of the judicial-notice doctrine and the clear need for it, its breadth is a relatively recent jurisprudential phenomenon. Historically, "notoriety" has been the general criterion for proper use of judicial notice. Bentham (1825), for example, concluded that a judge "may pronounce on a question of fact, according to his own knowledge, without other evidence . . . when the facts are too notorious to require a special proof" (p. 46). Thus, facts could be noticed if they were known to be true (*Ricaud v. American Metal Co.*, 1918, pp. 308–309), either by the court or by "every informed individual," (*Bone v. General Motors Corp.*, 1959; *Carroll v. United States*, 1925, p. 160; *United States v. Butler*, 1935, p. 61). Because the requirement that *everyone* know a fact was felt to be so stringent as to be impractical, the standard evolved to "matters familiar to the majority of mankind" (*Leach v. Burr*, 1903)—the "common-knowledge" test. Ultimately, the standard stretched from "common knowledge" to a "readily verifiable certainty" (McCormick, 1951). Thus, although most people might not be knowledgeable about a fact, it could still be noticed if authorities were in agreement.

The modern version of the judicial-notice doctrine incorporates this expansion of the notoriety requirement. The Federal Rules of Evidence provide that a "judicially noticed fact must be one not subject to reasonable dispute in that it is either (1) generally known within the territorial jurisdiction of the trial court or (2) capable of accurate and ready determination by resort to sources whose accuracy cannot reasonably be questioned" (Fed. R. Evid. 201(b)). To compensate for the slip in the stringent notoriety requirement, a party may present evidence to challenge a judicially noticed fact (Fed. R. Evid. 201(e)), although the court may take judicial notice at any stage of the proceeding (Fed. R. Evid. 201(f)) without request by the parties (Fed. R. Evid. 201(c)).

However, the major expansion of the notice doctrine—the virtual collapse of the notoriety requirement—did not occur through the addition of notice of readily verifiable certainties. Rather, the huge exception to the rule is that it expressly applies only to "adjudicative facts" (i.e., case facts) (Fed. R. Evid. 201(a)). There are no evidentiary limitations to notice of "legislative facts" (i.e., social facts), a distinction initially suggested by Davis (1942). Legislative facts are defined by one authority on evidence as

> that great body of information and expository material which contributes to rationalization by capable, intelligent and objectively thinking people in the process not only of ascertaining what the common law and social concepts are but also in promoting their improvement and development. It is not concerned with specific facts that are relevant to the resolution of a disputed factual situation in a given case. (Gard, 1972, § 2:9).

The lack of a standard for judicial consideration of facts about how the world operates, apart from the facts of the immediate case, reflects a marked evolution in the prevailing theories of jurisprudence. The "adjudicative fact" criterion in Federal Rule of Evidence 201 was based on an assumption that judges need to have relatively free rein to consider social context when making policy (Fed. R. Evid. 201(a) advisory committee's note). Although judges are assumed to be finding facts when they notice adjudicative facts, they are considered to be making or pronouncing policy when they notice social facts:

> [I]n substance the growth of the law is legislative. And this in a deeper sense than that what the courts declare to have always been the law is in

fact new. It is legislative in its grounds. The very considerations which judges most rarely mention, and always with an apology, are the secret root from which the law draws all the juices of life. I mean, of course, considerations of what is expedient for the community concerned. Every important principle which is developed by litigation is in fact and at the bottom the result of more or less definitely understood views of public policy; most generally, to be sure, under our practice and traditions, the unconscious result of instinctive preferences and inarticulated convictions, but none the less traceable to views of public policy in the last analysis. (Holmes, 1881/1963, pp. 31-32).

The wide-open approach to notice of social facts follows, then, from the recognition that judges do make policy. To insure that they do so rationally, it is desirable to promote the integration of social reality into the law. Policy analysis would be likely to be constrained by strict reliance on the evidence presented by the parties (cf. Mnookin, 1985).

The desire to facilitate judges' policymaking is a remarkable reflection of the changes that occurred in American legal thinking during the early and middle 20th century. With the U.S. Supreme Court's acceptance of Brandeis's brief in *Muller v. Oregon* (1908) came a new era in jurisprudence and a new approach to judicial notice. The "Brandeis brief"—now the term for a genre of appellate briefs citing extralegal authority— contained an enormous amount of medical and social science opinion about the dangers to women of long hours of factory labor. Not only did the Court's attention to the Brandeis brief signal a new willingness to consider the social rationales for the law; it also legitimated the use of social science treatises at the appellate level, even when they had not been subjected to the rigors of the adversary process and the rules of evidence at trial. This action was consistent with the developing "sociological jurisprudence" (Pound, 1908) and the soon-to-develop legal realism movement, which advocated the broadening of legal reasoning to consider the potential contributions of the other social sciences to policy and the consequences of legal decisions for social welfare.

Still another major development in the use of social facts in the appellate process came with the U.S. Supreme Court's landmark decision in *Brown v. Board of Education* (1954). With the fabled footnote 11 and the acceptance of a brief that con-

tained nothing but social science (Allport *et al.*, 1953), the Court
sanctioned the use of social science to attack the constitutionality
of state action. *Brown* led to a sharp increase in notice of social
science authorities by the Supreme Court, although still most
commonly in the opinions of liberal Justices (Hafemeister &
Melton, Chapter 2, this volume; Rosen, 1972). The Warren
Court's social activism was facilitated by its willingness to consider social analyses that called into question the rationality of
state intrusions on liberty and equality.

PROBLEMS WITH JUDICIAL NOTICE

Although the 20th-century acknowledgment of the realities of
the law's origins and influence may be largely a welcome phenomenon, the law's treatment of broad reliance on extralegal
authorities and observations has been ambivalent, perhaps with
good reason. The most basic problem is that the validity of
judicial notice of social facts is dependent largely on the quality
and quantity of judges' (or their clerks') own knowledge and
research. The free judicial rein is not simply in informed policymaking, but "in finding, recognizing, ignoring, and distorting
otherwise legitimate social facts" (Perry & Melton, 1984, p. 641).
Thus, the same doctrine that allows courts to be more rational
in decisionmaking—to consider the empirical validity of assumptions underlying the law—also permits courts to pronounce their prejudices as if they were reality, or simply to err
in perception of reality without the parties' having the opportunity to present rebutting evidence.

Broad use of judicial notice raises other potential problems.
Each time that a judge injects facts into the decision, the parties
lose some control over the process. This judicial intrusion within
an adversary system may increase the appearance of unfairness
and diminish the parties' perception that justice is being done
(Thibaut & Walker, 1978).

A related but less compelling concern is that judicially noticed facts have not been "tested" in the adversary process.
Because of the legal assumption that the process of confron-
tation and rebuttal results in more reliable findings, some jurists

are skeptical of any information about social facts that has not been admitted into evidence of trial (see, e.g., *Ballew v. Georgia*, 1978, opinion of Justice Powell, joined by Chief Justice Burger and Justice Rehnquist, concurring in the judgment). Although the assumption that the trial process results in a closer approximation of the truth than nonadversary inquiries is dubious (Thibaut & Walker, 1978), such a concept is axiomatic in Anglo-American jurisprudence.

These problems are exacerbated by the fact that judicially noticed social facts may come to take on a life of their own through citation by subsequent courts (Perry & Melton, 1984). Thus, the risk of distortion of social facts is magnified. Insofar as the social assumptions of an appellate court are basic to its analysis, lower courts may feel bound by the principle of *stare decisis* to accept the "reality" perceived by the superior court, whatever the empirical reality. Although reliance on precedent is an illogical method of establishing the truth of an empirical proposition, social science authorities and assumptions about social facts cited in judicial opinions are often drawn from previous opinions, especially those of the U.S. Supreme Court (Marvell, 1978; see also Tremper, Chapter 8, this volume).

As a result of these considerations or simply a narrow vision of the courts' role, some judges resist taking notice of social facts that do not fit within the traditional notoriety requirement. Although some judges undertake independent investigation of the social reality, others rely only on authorities introduced at trial or cited by parties in appellate briefs (Marvell, 1978). As already noted, some Supreme Court Justices are still leery of serious consideration even of extralegal authorities, if the relevant information was not introduced into evidence at trial (see *Ballew v. Georgia*, 1978). On the other hand, some of the Justices—notably Justice Blackmun (Schlesinger & Nesse, 1980)—are "users" of scientific authority (cf. Weiss, Chapter 3, this volume), who frequently investigate such treatises on their own. The finding of a substantial negative correlation between Justices' citation of prior cases and their citation of secondary authorities (Hafemeister & Melton, Chapter 2, this volume) is illustrative of this dichotomy between users and nonusers of extralegal sources.

Judges can rely, of course, on mechanisms other than judicial notice when the validity of social facts is critical to their opinions. For example, the advisory committee that drafted the Federal Rules of Evidence suggested that judges might wish to remand cases in order to take evidence on relevant social facts (Fed. R. Evid. 201(a) advisory committee's note), although this procedure is rarely used.

The point is that, although the standard for judicial notice of adjudicative facts is clear, there is no parallel rule for consideration of social facts. As Monahan and Walker (1986) have lamented, judicial notice of social facts has been essentially lawless and arbitrary, subject to each judge's philosophy of his or her role, as well as to mere judicial whim and caprice. Even judges who purport to apply notice rules to social facts and sometimes expressly do so still commonly rely on "facts" that would not fit the notoriety requirement (Marvell, 1978). Indeed, as we shall see, some of the Supreme Court Justices most suspicious of "untested" social science evidence have been especially prone to rely uncritically on intuition and weak social science evidence in reaching conclusions about processes of human development and family life.

SPECIAL PROBLEMS WITH "FACTS" ABOUT CHILD DEVELOPMENT

The problems with the notice doctrine acquire special significance when applied to children's cases. Indeed, some commentators (e.g., Melton, 1984b; Wadlington, 1967; Wadlington, Whitebread, & Davis, 1983, p. 182) have suggested that the courts may often be incapable of considering family law cases logically and dispassionately. Opinions about child and family issues often are obfuscated by a wealth of dicta that make for pithy quotes but ambiguous, ill-informed policy.

Judges in family law cases often seem compelled to use their opinions as fora about the nature of the family as a social institution. These discussions are often mythological, expounding the nature of *the* child and *the* family. The general picture of the child that emerges from recent U.S. Supreme Court opinions is of a creature who is vulnerable and incompetent and, therefore, properly subservient to the authority of parents and state. At least since 1979, decisions in children's cases have been typified by a passing (begrudging?) acknowledgment that minors are "persons" entitled to the protection of the Bill of Rights, and then by extended discussion of why these rights should not be fulfilled (see, e.g., *H.L. v. Matheson*, 1981; *New Jersey v. T.L.O.*, 1985; *Parham v. J.R.*, 1979; *Schall v. Martin*, 1984). To reach this conclusion, the Court has often had to adopt a curiously narrow vision of minors as vulnerable to all sorts of threats—except threats to their liberty or privacy. The Court also has had to ignore the differences between the competency of adolescents and that of younger minors, a distinction largely ignored in the law (Melton, in press-a, in press-b, Zimring, 1982).

Partially because of the lengthy discussion common in family law opinions, they are typified by relatively numerous citations of secondary sources, including writings of social scientists (Hafemeister & Melton, Chapter 2, this volume). However, the courts have rarely looked to child development research for systematic analysis of social facts underlying family law. Thus, although Chief Justice Burger commonly cited extralegal authorities in children's cases (see Hafemeister & Melton, Chapter 2, this volume), the authority for his most questionable and most central assumptions was often merely his intuition. Burger often asserted that his conclusions about child development and family life were derived from "the pages of human experience" (*Parham v. J.R.*, 1979, p. 601), "the reality of human experience" (*Globe Newspaper Co. v. Superior Court*, 1982, p. 617), or "the ordinary course of human experience" (*Wisconsin v. Yoder*, 1972, p. 232). As "facts" known by everyone, these conclusions were in effect beyond question and, as presented, well within the scope of the traditional notice doctrine.

Therefore, formidable obstacles may stand in the way of consideration of child development research by the judiciary. First, even clearly mistaken conclusions may be believed to be so intuitively correct that no evidence is needed to support them and no evidence will be sufficiently strong to rebut them. Second, although stated empirically, statements of social fact about children and families may be more normative than descriptive. The U.S. Supreme Court's conclusions about children's vulnerability and incompetency may reflect more their concepts of how children *ought* to behave (dependent upon and deferent to their parents and adults who stand *in loco parentis*) than how they do behave. The assumptions embedded in the Court's opinions in children's cases may describe a *hypothetical* legal construct of a child rather than real children.

Third, even if their assumptions are truly empirical, the legal philosophy of some judges precludes their analyzing the validity of social science findings in order to determine what is known and with what certainty. Even Brandeis, the originator of judicial notice of social science, never intended extralegal authorities to be used to attack the rationality of state action (Rosen, 1972). Instead, he introduced social science treatises to show the *existence,* not the *validity,* of social facts. By citing extralegal authorities (but not analyzing their logic), Brandeis purported merely to inform the judiciary that authoritative sources existed on which the legislature might have based its action. Therefore, regardless of the validity of the observations of these extralegal authorities, the legislature's action was not wholly irrational or arbitrary.

Conservative jurists still apply such a theory. Therefore, Chief Justice Burger and his successor, then Associate Justice Rehnquist, have been caustic in their attacks on their brethren for reliance on social science as a foundation for conclusions that certain state statutes are unconstitutional (see, e.g., *Ballew v. Georgia,* 1978; *Craig v. Boren,* 1976; *Lockhart v. McCree,* 1986; *Schall v. Martin,* 1984). Nonetheless, they have been quite willing to rely on social science in arguments that state legislatures' judgments should be upheld, even when the research that is cited in poorly designed or simply inapposite (Melton, 1984a).

If my analysis is correct, it implies that judges often may be uneducable about the reality of child development and family life. Even though their decisions ostensibly rest on psychological foundations, these assumptions actually may never have been empirical, or at least may never have been applied critically. Thus, careful diffusion of relevant child development research to the courts may realistically be more for the purpose of insuring intellectual honesty than for that of reforming the law. If relevant research is systematically brought to their attention, judges may be forced to identify the real bases of their decisions. For example, if research on adolescent abortion is before the court, judges may find it necessary to argue straightforwardly that some limitation on minors' access to abortion is defensible because of historic deference to parental authority, rather than to construct a ruse of "grave emotional and psychological consequences" of adolescent abortion (*H.L. v. Matheson*, 1981, pp. 412–413).

A change in the form of judicial argument is obviously a more limited goal than alteration of the holdings. Nonetheless, it is not a trivial purpose. In recent children's cases alone, the Supreme Court made clearly erroneous findings of social fact in numerous contexts: adolescent abortion (see Melton, 1983; Melton & Pliner, 1986); civil commitment (see Melton, 1984c; Melton & Spaulding, in press; Perlin, 1981; Perry & Melton, 1984); detention of juveniles (see Ewing, 1985); interrogation of juveniles (see Grisso, 1981); school searches (see Hyman & D'Alessandro, 1984; Ianni, 1980; Melton, 1983; Ornstein, 1982; Rosenberg, 1985); and testimony by child witnesses (see Melton, 1984a). Relevant social science research was often not presented in briefs by the parties or *amici curiae* (see Tremper, Chapter 8, this volume). Even if the results had not changed, better-reasoned, more accurate opinions in this wide range of cases would have clarified their actual meaning for the public and subsequent courts. Diversion from erroneous, mythical statements of social fact may also have positive indirect effects on children's rights. Much of children's law is symbolic (Melton, 1987), and expansive verbiage in judicial opinions about children's incompetency and vulnerability often may do more damage to their status than adverse holdings may.

Finally, even if social science is unlikely to change judges' minds about social reality, it is important to have it available when judges are ready to perceive child and family life more accurately. Whether "noticed" in library research or briefs or formally presented into evidence at trial, social science evidence is unlikely to influence a judge who finds it counterintuitive, no matter how rigorous the methods that generated it (cf. Weiss,

Chapter 3, this volume). On the other hand, a judge considering an innovative analysis may find the case easier if his or her intuition is corroborated by expert opinion. A change in social reality is the most common basis for overruling precedent (Marvell, 1978).

MAKING CHILD DEVELOPMENT RESEARCH NOTICEABLE

If we assume that judicial notice is a common way of introducing social science into the legal process, and that judges are sometimes willing to consider such evidence in their decisions, questions remain about how to make child development research more noticeable. How can we best diffuse research so that judges will learn about it and use it appropriately?

TESTIMONY

Perhaps the most obvious answer by someone schooled in the law is to avoid the problem. Conservative jurists are most likely to feel comfortable in relying on social science if it is introduced through testimony at trial. Such a strategy treats social facts like adjudicative facts and averts the problem of determining the appropriate threshold for judicial notice. It also best preserves the adversary process and perhaps minimizes the possibility of an uninformed or arbitrary assumption by the judge.

However, total reliance on testimony at trial may be neither practical nor desirable. In keeping with the assumptions that guided the expansion of the notice doctrine, we may want to insure that the court can pursue its policymaking role independently when the parties do not fully develop evidence about pertinent social facts. Such activism in factfinding is especially significant in cases in which the public interest is at stake (Chayes, 1976).

More generally, expert testimony may be poorly suited to determination of social facts. The adversary system tends to result in distortion of the evidence (Thibaut & Walker, 1978).

Effective cross-examination about social science research may serve more to obfuscate the findings and attack the expert's credibility than to illuminate the limitations of the study (see Saks, Chapter 7, this volume). Therefore, written briefs, as used in the appellate process, may be more appropriate than trial testimony in informing the court about social facts (see Monahan & Walker, 1986).

Regardless of the merits of testimony at trial versus briefs in the appellate process, the issue may never be posed. The key issues in regard to social facts may not become apparent until the court—indeed, the appellate court—begins its own analysis. Obtaining expert testimony and argument on relevant facts (essentially, reopening the trial) is uneconomical at that point in the process.

A middle ground may be to invite comment on the conclusions that have been reached:

> One thing seems certain . . .: Counsel are unlikely to supply empirical data with this purpose in mind [of educating judges about social facts], for they are unlikely to know the judges' social fact assumptions ahead of time. Judges may not be self-constrained and industrious enough to do independent research aimed at attacking their assumptions. Judges should, therefore, notify counsel, at least in important appeals, of social facts they think important to their decision, giving counsel a chance to present empirical data attacking their assumptions. The judges could even give counsel a tentative draft opinion that specifies the important social facts; counsel would then know not only what facts are important but how the court proposes to use them. (Marvell, 1978, p. 204)

Although the option that Marvell suggests should be (and is) available to judges, it is problematic as a general strategy. First, it requires judges to determine which assumptions are not *so* obvious that they require no scrutiny. Second, it assumes that counsel are sufficiently motivated and skilled to develop a rapid but comprehensive response to the judge's assumptions of social fact. I have heard several judges lament that counsel rarely follow through in those instances in which the court requests argument on problems of social fact. Because the judge's conclusions about social facts may have effects beyond the immediate case, we should not constrain his or her independent research for "social authority," just as we do not restrict his or her search for relevant precedents in case law (Monahan & Walker, 1986). By the same token, though, we should not constrain the judge's attempts to obtain assistance from the parties or *amici curiae* in analyzing the nature of social reality.

IN-HOUSE EXPERTS

The major risks, of course, in giving judges free rein to notice social facts are that their experience or their independent research will be incomplete or distorted and that their interpretations of social science will be incompetent. Although careful application of common sense will illuminate many of the flaws of social science studies (see Monahan & Walker, 1986), it is also true that some key methodological or conceptual problems are apt to be beyond the ken of persons untrained in social science. For example, the meaning of base rates is a subtle problem that arises frequently in the application of social science findings to legal decisionmaking. If 90% of child abusers fit a particular profile and 90% of other adults do not, what is the meaning of a positive finding? If one is not trained to remember that 90% of child abusers is probably a substantially smaller figure than 10% of adults in general, erroneous conclusions can be reached easily.

Perhaps the most obvious way of insuring that judges have access to skilled review and analysis of social science is to provide such a service within the court itself or through organizations serving the judiciary (e.g., National Center for State Courts, National Council of Juvenile and Family Court Judges). The major problem (other than simply the availability of funds for such a resource) is that judges' consultation of experts on an *ex parte* basis (outside the presence of one or both litigants) violates the usual position of judicial neutrality in an adversary system (see Bermant & Wheeler, Chapter 5, this volume). The relevant section of the Code of Judicial Conduct does permit the judge to "obtain the advice of a disinterested expert on the law applicable to a proceeding before him if he gives notice to the parties of the person consulted and the substance of the advice, and affords the parties reasonable opportunity to respond" (Canon 3(A)(4)).

However, the commentary to the relevant canon indicates that it is not intended to preclude consultation with "court personnel whose function is to aid the judge in carrying out his adjudicative responsibilities." Therefore, the canon appears not to bar a judge's selecting a clerk on the basis of his or her psychological expertise and then delegating the task of researching social science literature to that clerk (see Monahan & Walker, 1985, p. 293). The canon also may not prohibit consultation of psychologists employed by the court, a common occurrence in juvenile and family courts (see Grisso & Melton, Chapter 6, this volume). Perhaps, as Judge Jerome Frank argued, "Competently to inform ourselves, we should have a staff of investigators like those supplied to administrative agencies" (*Triangle Publications v. Rohrlich*, 1948, dissenting opinion, p. 976).

Nonetheless, the problem of relying on in-house experts is that the risk remains of unbalanced, unrebutted presentations by individuals who may not even be specialized in the specific subject at issue. At the same time, insofar as judges are permitted or even encouraged to engage in independent research, the assistance of staff members familiar with social science methods and findings seems to be preferable to a completely naive approach to the literature. Just as judges seek clerks who are the best young scholars in the law, they might seek the best assistance available in researching extralegal sources.

CONTINUING JUDICIAL EDUCATION

An alternative means of insuring that judicial notice is informed is to provide judges with training in social science methods and education about relevant development in child development research. When judges are in trial courts of general jurisdiction or appellate courts, this approach to increasing judges' sophistication about child development may be unrealistic. Judges obviously cannot become experts or even "quasi-expert" specialists in every type of case that they hear.

However, it is both realistic and reasonable to expect specialized juvenile and family court judges to become acquainted with social science research relevant to their work. (The issue may be more one of insuring that the social scientists most knowledgeable about juvenile and family law are involved in judicial education for juvenile court judges.) Because they encounter the same questions repeatedly, consultation with experts is less problematic. It is not likely to be focused on a *particular* case currently being litigated, and therefore is clearly not subject to the prohibition of *ex parte* consultation of experts without notice to the parties.

Although judges in courts of general jurisdiction may find that learning about child development is not an efficient use of their time, increased knowledge about social science methods may help them to understand a broad range of cases, including child and family issues. For example, discussion of social science in law has been a useful, well-received part of the curriculum in the University of Virginia's graduate law (LL.M.) program for appellate judges (Meador, 1983).

CONCLUSIONS

The final point is one that is made in several chapters of this book. Social scientists interested in increasing judges' sophistication about child development should be sure to publish their work in places where judges either will see it in the course of their general reading (whether in the mass media or professional journals) or will find it when they look for references on a particular topic (see Grisso & Melton, Chapter 6, this volume). Judicial notice is most commonly based on the conventional wisdom spread throughout the culture or on the information available in law reviews (see Hafemeister & Melton, Chapter 2, this volume).

At a time when the range and content of litigation are more complex than ever and when children's law remains largely unsettled, there are no signs that the limits of judicial notice will be constricted, either in general or in children's cases specifically. Judges' images of children and families may be the most powerful influences on and of their opinions. To make children's law more informed and rational, child development researchers need to make their work more noticeable.

REFERENCES

Allport, F.H., Allport, G.H., Babcock, C., Bernard, V.W., Bruner, J.S., Cantril, H., Chein, I., Clark, K.B., Clark, M.P., Cook, S.W., Dai, B., Davis, A., Frenkel-Brunswick, E., Gist, N.P., Katz, D., Klineberg, O., Krech, D., Lee, A.M., MacIver, R.M., Merton, R.K., Murphy, G., Newcomb, T.M., Redfield, R., Reid, I.D., Rose, A.M., Saenger, G., Sanford, R.N., Sargent, S.S., Smith, S.B., Stouffer, S.A., Warner, W., & Williams, R.M. (1953). The effects of segregation and the consequences of desegregation: A social science statement. *Minnesota Law Review, 37*, 429–440.

Ballew v. Georgia, 435 U.S. 223 (1978).

Bentham, J. (1825). *A treatise on judicial evidence.* London: J.W. Paget.

Bone v. General Motors Corp., 322 S.W.2d 916 (Mo. 1959).

Brown v. Board of Education, 347 U.S. 483 (1954).

Carroll v. United States, 267 U.S. 132 (1925).

Chayes, A. (1976). The role of the judge in public law litigation. *Harvard Law Review, 89*, 1281–1316.

Craig v. Boren, 429 U.S. 190 (1976).

Davis, K.C. (1942). An approach to problems of evidence in the administrative process. *Harvard Law Review, 55*, 364–393.

Ewing, C.P. (1985). *Schall v. Martin:* Preventive detention and dangerousness through the looking glass. *Buffalo Law Review, 34*, 173–226.

Fed. R. Evid. 201.

Gard, S.A. (1972). *Jones on evidence* (6th ed.). Rochester, NY: Lawyers Cooperative.

Globe Newspaper Co. v. Superior Court, 457 U.S. 596 (1982).

Grisso, T. (1981). *Juveniles' waiver of rights: Legal and psychological competence.* New York: Plenum.

H.L. v. Matheson, 450 U.S. 398 (1981).

Holmes, O.W. (1963). *The common law.* Boston: Little, Brown. (Original work published 1881)

Hyman, I.A., & D'Alessandro, J. (1984). Good, old-fashioned discipline: The politics of punitiveness. *Phi Delta Kappan, 65*, 39–45.

Ianni, F.A. (1980). A positive note on schools and discipline. *Educational Leadership, 37*, 457–458.

Leach v. Burr, 188 U.S. 510 (1903).

Lockhart v. McCree, 106 S. Ct. 1758 (1986).

Marvell, T.B. (1978). *Appellate courts and lawyers: Information gathering in the adversary system.* Westport, CT: Greenwood Press.

McCormick, C.T. (1951). Judicial notice. *Vanderbilt Law Review, 5,* 296–323.

Meador, D.J. (1983). The graduate degree program for judges at the University of Virginia. *Judges' Journal, 22*(2), 18–22, 54–56.

Melton, G.B. (1983). Minors and privacy: Are legal and psychological concepts compatible? *Nebraska Law Review, 62,* 455–493.

Melton, G.B. (1984a). Child witnesses and the First Amendment: A psycholegal dilemma. *Journal of Social Issues, 40*(2), 291–305.

Melton, G.B. (1984b). Developmental psychology and the law: The state of the art. *Journal of Family Law, 22,* 445–482.

Melton, G.B. (1984c). Family and mental hospital as myths: Civil commitment of minors. In N.D. Reppucci, L.A. Weithorn, E. Mulvey, & J. Monahan (Eds.), *Children, mental health, and the law* (pp. 151–167). Beverly Hills, CA: Sage.

Melton, G.B. (1987). The clashing of symbols: Prelude to child and family policy. *American Psychologist, 42,* 345–354.

Melton, G.B. (in press-a). Are adolescents people? Problems of liberty, entitlement, and responsibility. In J. Worell & F. Danner (Eds.), *Adolescent development: Issues for education.* New York: Academic Press.

Melton, G.B. (in press-b). The child in child welfare. In J. Gilgun, G.B. Melton, I.M. Schwartz, & Z. Eisikovits (Eds.), *Rethinking child welfare.* Lincoln: University of Nebraska Press.

Melton, G.B., & Pliner, A.J. (1986). Adolescent abortion: A psycholegal analysis. In G.B. Melton (Ed.), *Adolescent abortion: Psychological and legal issues* (pp. 1–39). Lincoln: University of Nebraska Press.

Melton, G.B., & Spaulding, W.J. (in press). *No place to go: Civil commitment of minors.* Lincoln: University of Nebraska Press.

Mnookin, R.H. (Ed.). (1985). *In the interest of children: Advocacy, law reform, and public policy.* New York: W.H. Freeman.

Monahan, J., & Walker, L. (1985). *Social science in law.* Mineola, NY: Foundation Press.

Monahan, J., & Walker L. (1986). Social authority: Obtaining, evaluating, and establishing social science in law. *University of Pennsylvania Law Review, 134,* 477–517.

Muller v. Oregon, 208 U.S. 412 (1908).

New Jersey v. T.L.O., 105 S. Ct. 733 (1985).

Ornstein, A.C. (1982). Student disruptions and student rights: An overview. *Urban Review, 14,* 83–91.

Parham v. J.R., 442 U.S. 584 (1979).

Perlin, M. (1981). An invitation to the dance: An empirical response to Chief Justice Warren Burger's "time-consuming procedural minuets" in *Parham v. J.R. Bulletin of the American Academy of Psychiatry and Law, 9,* 149–164.

Perry, G.S., & Melton, G.B. (1984). Precedential value of judicial notice of social facts: *Parham* as an example. *Journal of Family Law, 22,* 633–676.

Pound, R. (1908). Mechanical jurisprudence. *Columbia Law Review, 8,* 605–623.

Ricaud v. American Metal Co., 246 U.S. 304 (1918).

Rosen, P.L. (1972). *The Supreme Court and social science.* Urbana: University of Illinois Press.

Rosenberg, I.M. (1985). *New Jersey v. T.L.O.:* Of children and smokescreens. *Family Law Quarterly, 9,* 311–329.

Schall v. Martin, 104 S. Ct. 2403 (1984).

Schlesinger, S.R., & Nesse, J. (1980). Justice Harry Blackmun and empirical jurisprudence. *American University Law Review, 29,* 405–437.

Thayer, J.B. (1890). Judicial notice and the law of evidence. *Harvard Law Review, 3,* 285–312.

Thibaut, J., & Walker, L. (1978). A theory of procedure. *California Law Review, 66,* 541–566.

Triangle Publications v. Rohrlich, 167 F.2d 969 (2nd Cir. 1948).

United States v. Butler, 297 U.S. 1 (1935).

Wadlington, W.J. (1967). Portrait of the judge as popular author: An appeal for anonymity and restraint in domestic relations opinions. *Family Law Quarterly, 1*(4), 77–82.

Wadlington, W.J., Whitebread, C.H., & Davis, S.M. (1983). *Children in the legal system.* Mineola, NY: Foundation Press.

Wisconsin v. Yoder, 406 U.S. 205 (1972).

Zimring, F.E. (1982). *The changing legal world of adolescence.* New York: Free Press.

IV

Conclusions

Professional Responsibility in the Dissemination of Psychological Research in Legal Contexts

LOIS A. WEITHORN

This book and the study group that spawned it focus on the impact of child development research on legal policy. Contributors to this volume have examined some of the influences behavioral science has had on child and family policy, as well as the range of methods used by behavioral scientists to communicate psychological knowledge to legal policymakers, practitioners, and scholars. This chapter is an attempt to identify critical ethical issues and professional dilemmas raised by behavioral scientists' participation in the legal policy sphere through collection and dissemination of research data. Despite the special emphasis of this book on the impact of *child development* research on the law, the present chapter retains a somewhat broader focus on behavioral science research generically. Offering (or choosing not to offer) behavioral science findings for legal consumption raises similar general ethical and professional quandaries across the broad spectrum of subject matter and target populations. In that this chapter is an early attempt to highlight these special concerns, I feel that a generic approach is most appropriate.

Principles of ethics and professional responsibility rarely instruct us as to optimal behavior in the specific situations in

Lois A. Weithorn. School of Law, Stanford University, Stanford, California.

which we find ourselves. Rather, these principles provide us with a foundation from which to extract guidance, and tools with which we can recognize and resolve the inevitable dilemmas that face us in the pursuit of our professional activities. Although there are the occasional clear directives (e.g., "Thou shalt not fabricate data or plagiarize the work of another under *any* circumstances"), most ethical principles are not absolute. Rather, they comprise a set of relativistic guidelines that typically conflict with, and must be balanced against, each other. And resolution of any particular ethical dilemma demands a highly contextual and situation-specific application of the relevant guiding principles. Ultimately, not only must we analyze the costs and benefits to various persons or groups of particular courses of action, but we must inject our own personal values into the equation. For these reasons, this chapter refrains from offering ethical "advice," but focuses instead on those concerns that confront us all, and that we must balance when participating (or choosing not to participate) in the dissemination of child development research to legal contexts.

THE OBLIGATION TO BETTER SOCIETY THROUGH THE DISSEMINATION OF NEW KNOWLEDGE

The primary ethical justification for the conduct of most forms of behavioral science research lies in the principle of "beneficence"—that is, the duty to contribute to the welfare of others and to produce positive benefits for society (Beauchamp & Childress, 1983). The philosophical notion of beneficence incorporates an affirmative obligation to confer benefits on others, including the prevention and amelioration of harm, and the duty to balance possible good against possible harm that might result from one's actions (Beauchamp & Childress, 1983). Whereas ordinary citizens must confront their own personal moral standards when deciding what are the boundaries of their own beneficent obligations, most professions in the sciences, health services, and social services have assumed a higher, and nondisclaimable, beneficent obligation. Such professionals are viewed as having this higher obligation because they are in positions where, by virtue of their special skills, abilities, or circumstances, they have the opportunity to have a special positive impact on society. Furthermore, professionals such as behavioral scientists necessarily rely on societal resources for the conduct of their investigative activities. They may "use" human subjects, and expose those individuals to varying degrees of inconvenience, discomfort, or distress. They may be subsidized in their education or ventures directly or indirectly by public monies. The justification for the existence of an endeavor that relies so heavily on human and financial resources is the "payback" to society in the form of new knowledge, be it the product of basic or applied research. Although scholars have debated whether it is the new knowledge that is valued, or the applications that may follow from that knowledge (see Bermant, 1982), it will suffice for our purposes to recognize that both are deemed to be socially desirable. That we are contributing to the social good in some way through our research is the *raison d'être* of the scientific enterprise in most settings.

Reppucci (1984) suggests that psychologists have a responsibility "to disseminate and promote the use of the findings of psychological research. In other words, the traditional value of seeking knowledge for the sake of understanding is combined with the co-equal value of utilizing that knowledge for the sake of action" (p. 5). In support of his position, Reppucci cites Bandura: "As a science concerned about the social consequences of its applications, psychology must also fulfill a broader obligation to society by bringing influence to bear on public policies to ensure that its findings are used in service of human betterment" (Bandura, 1974, p. 859).

The American Psychological Association (APA) is among those professional organizations that has imposed upon its members an affirmative duty of beneficence—both to increase the knowledge base, and to apply that knowledge for the good of others. The Preamble to the Ethical Principles of Psychologists (American Psychological Association, 1981) underscores the responsibility to apply scientific findings to the public interest and states that psychologists "are committed to increasing knowledge of human behavior . . . and to the utilization of such

knowledge for the promotion of human welfare. . . .
[P]sychologists . . . strive for the preservation and protection of
fundamental human rights" (p. 633).

Thus, the scholars cited above and the Ethical Principles
of the APA suggest that behavioral scientists' duty of beneficence extends beyond conduct and publication of their findings.
Rather, these commentators and principles appear to impose
upon psychologists an affirmative duty to attempt to influence
public policies for the social good. They propose that behavioral
scientists have an obligation to disseminate their findings in
legal policy arenas in the public interest.

THE OBLIGATION NOT TO DISTORT TRUTH

Scientists are bound by a basic ethical obligation to tell the
truth—that is, the duty of "veracity" (Beauchamp & Childress,
1982). This duty includes derivative responsibilities not to distort the truth in any way, nor to engage in underdisclosure or
omission of information when to do so has the impact of affecting others' perceptions of the truth. Where the duty of
veracity is most relevant to behavioral scientists clearly is in the
dissemination of their research findings, in that this is the vehicle through which they communicate knowledge to others.
There are relatively standardized methods through which scientists disseminate their findings within their scholarly community. Peer-reviewed journals with standardized formats for
data presentation and interpretation and papers at professional
meetings provide primary outlets. Although there is unquestionably variation and at times miscommunication or distortion
in the use of these methods, the professional community believes that the peer review system, the custom of professional
discourse and debate, the sophistication of the audience, and
other procedures safeguard against unchecked flagrant or systematic distortion of truth. That is, if a researcher de-emphasizes the bias of his or her sample when making interpretations
from the data, one can be certain that a critique will soon appear
underscoring this point; the data dissemination enterprise within
the profession is generally viewed as self-correcting.

The APA elaborates upon our truthtelling responsibilities in Ethical Principles 1a and 4g, which bind psychologists:

> [to] plan their research in ways to minimize the possibility that their findings will be misleading . . . [to] provide thorough discussion of the limitations of their data, especially where their work touches on social policy . . . [*never* to] suppress disconfirming data . . . [and to] acknowledge the existence of alternate hypotheses and explanations of their findings[;] (Principle 1a, p. 633)

> [to] present the science of psychology . . . fairly and accurately, avoiding misrepresentation through sensationalism, exaggeration, or superficiality. Psychologists are guided by the primary obligation to aid the public in developing informed judgments, opinions, and choices. (Principle 4g, p. 635)

The Ethical Principles not only caution against suppression of disconfirming data and other forms of misrepresentation, but underscore the importance of identifying the limitations of one's data when the work touches on social policy. It is likely that the drafters of the Principles were concerned with two possible concomitants of a failure to do so. First, they may have realized that the consequences of premature or inappropriate utilization of research findings in a public policy context can be particularly damaging, because of the impact such dissemination can have on the lives of others. Second, the self-correcting safeguards that characterize dissemination in the scholarly community are typically absent in social policy contexts. There are few if any barriers to dissemination, such as peer reviewers who reject studies with serious methodological problems; there may be little opportunity for correction, such as a timely presentation of a critique or of conflicting data; and the audience is relatively unsophisticated as to the state of knowledge in the field and as to the methods and interpretive techniques of the behavioral sciences. The potential for unchecked or flagrant distortion is present to a much greater degree than when dissemination is confined to the professional community, and the consequences of such distortion may have far-reaching implications. For these reasons, the onus is heavy on individual scientists not to shortchange discussions of the limitations of their data, of conflicting findings, or of alternate hypotheses, and to guard against superficiality when presenting their own or their colleagues' data in a legal policy context. Ironically, however, as I discuss below, it is in such contexts where the responsibility to protect against distortion is the greatest that one may find it most difficult to abide by the Ethical Principles.

BALANCING THE DUTIES OF BENEFICENCE AND VERACITY

Behavioral scientists may find themselves facing an ethical dilemma when they attempt to influence legal policy and the public good through dissemination of research findings, and at the same time attempt to do so in a manner that is accurate and comprehensive, minimizes the likelihood of misuse of the data, and is in no way misleading or superficial. The primary difficulties they may encounter include (1) determining when and which scientific findings are "ready" or "appropriate" for dissemination in a public policy sphere, and (2) confronting the practical limitations imposed by various legal contexts on their ability to control the manner of presentation and subsequent use of their findings.

WHEN DO SCIENTIFIC FINDINGS CONSTITUTE THE "TRUTH?"

The process of scientific investigation is characterized by the conduct of multiple studies that build upon each other. Replications of findings permit us greater confidence, as do subsequent studies that vary methods or samples but obtain similar results. Yet each single study or methodological approach gives us but one piece of a puzzle, because advances in our knowledge base are necessarily incremental. This factor presents few problems in the dissemination of our findings in the scientific community. In fact, this form of dissemination permits other researchers to replicate, expand upon, vary, or otherwise build upon our investigations. Researchers will sometimes report "preliminary" results to encourage responses from the scientific community that will in turn facilitate the researchers' continued insights into the strengths and weaknesses of the work.

Quite a different scenario characterizes the circumstances of research disseminated in legal policy contexts. Here, data may be used to set into motion far-reaching policies and programs that, once in place, may be difficult or impossible to alter when and if new or contradictory research findings are revealed. Or data may be used in the disposition of a particular case on trial, the outcome of which will be long decided when and if new research findings come to light. And, if the case is an appellate decision, and the psychological data lead to a general legal precedent, the injection of contrary findings years later *may* permit the earlier principle to be overruled, but may do so at the expense of the court's perception of the reliability of behavioral science research. In sum, the dangers of premature dissemination of data in the policy sphere are great, in that we may harm those interests and concerns we aspire to promote (e.g., in supporting policies that we believe are in children's best interests but that we subsequently learn may be harmful); in that we may misrepresent what is eventually learned to be true; and in that we may lessen policymakers' willingness to incorporate research findings into their deliberations.

Because the dangers of premature dissemination are great, we must consider whether research findings are "ready" for dissemination in a particular legal context (McKenna, 1984). What standards should be applied in so deciding? How many confirming studies, and with what magnitude of findings and levels of statistical significance, are necessary before findings are presented in a forum where the impact on the lives of others is so great? Is a consensus in the field necessary, and how do we define a "consensus"? How much disagreement in the field is tolerable? And how do we balance these considerations against our ethical obligation to use our findings in the public interest? Given the unfortunate time lag in the planning and ultimate completion of research, lengthy delays in dissemination may render findings obsolete relative to a particular policy impact by the time we are "comfortable" with communicating our findings to a legal audience.

An example of the tensions presented by this conflict is

that of the McCloskey-Egeth and Loftus debate. McCloskey and Egeth (1983) raise several points about expert courtroom testimony on behavioral science findings regarding the limitations of eyewitness testimony. The authors criticize the research methodology and interpretations that characterize this body of investigation. They claim that even if the findings are valid, it is not clear that their presentation in the courtroom actually promotes the goals of the justice system. They argue that such expert testimony may have detrimental effects, such as increasing jurors' skepticism of eyewitnesses to a point where jurors are less, rather than more, able to discriminate between accurate and inaccurate eyewitnesses. The authors conclude that the state of knowledge in this area of research is not sufficiently supportive of "intervention into the workings of the justice system" at this time. In response, Loftus (1983) states that there is a critical need for the participation of behavioral scientists in this realm, demonstrated in part by the documented cases of convictions of innocent defendants with inaccurate eyewitness identifications. She states that although not "perfect," the body of research consists of carefully designed, conducted, and interpreted research, performed by many investigators in the past century.

In reaching their conclusions, the psychologists on both sides of this debate appear to have performed risk–benefit analyses. They appear to have evaluated the strengths and weaknesses of the relevant body of research, and to have determined whether the likelihood and magnitude of the benefits to be accrued by a specific type of dissemination (e.g., expert courtroom testimony) outweigh the likelihood and magnitude of the harms that might follow if either the data or their application in this particular context prove flawed. Clearly, McCloskey and Egeth have arrived at dramatically different conclusions from those of Loftus, most likely because they have perceived and weighed the possible benefits and harms differently.

In judging whether research findings are "ready" for dissemination in a legal forum, there are no hard and fast rules. The researcher must honestly evaluate the strength of a body of data and its applicability for the particular proposed use. How strong are the findings with a range of methods? How much disagreement exists in the field? How appropriate is generalization from the laboratory to the specific legal context in which the findings will be applied? Scientists must keep in mind that even if they are confident as to the validity of their findings, a particular application may be inappropriate because it requires them to speculate too far beyond those variables actually studied (or permits others to do so). An evaluation of the strength and relevance of the research findings, and the possible benefits to society from disseminating them, must be balanced against an analysis of the possible harm resulting from such dissemination. Thus, the ethical caveat here is not that researchers must reach a particular result in balancing the obligation to disseminate their work against the obligation not to distort the truth. Rather, the caveat is that they must recognize that the tension between these ethical principles always exists, and that they must perform a careful weighing operation on the likelihood of benefit versus harm, and then proceed to act in a manner consistent with their best professional and scientific judgment.

The subjectivity inherent in such decisions is clearly demonstrated by the continuing debate as to whether behavioral science testimony was appropriate in what is often regarded as the most significant and important use of psychological data in the courtroom: the case of *Brown v. Board of Education* (1954). In this famous and far-reaching school desegregation case, several psychologists, most notably Kenneth Clark, testified as to the psychological effects of segregated education on black children. Yet decades later, with a substantially richer data base available, scholars still disagree as to whether we knew then, or know now, enough about the psychological effects of segregated versus integrated schooling on black children to present these data in the legal policy context (Bersoff, 1986; Cook, 1979, 1984; Gerard, 1983; Goodman, 1972; Monahan & Walker, 1985). And irrespective of the state of the data base, one could argue that the injection of psychological data into certain cases is simply inappropriate.

For example, in *Brown,* the U.S. Supreme Court did not directly overrule the then-governing legal doctrine, as explicated in *Plessy v. Ferguson* (1896), that "separate but equal" public facilities are constitutional. Rather, it relied in part on the psychological findings to hold that "separate" as applied to segregated public school education simply was not "equal." Citing the psychological studies, the Court stated: "To separate [children in grade and high schools] . . . from others of similar age and qualifications solely because of their race generates a feeling of inferiority . . . that may affect their hearts and minds in a way unlikely ever to be undone. . . . Separate educational facilities are inherently unequal" (1954, pp. 494–495). Yet if the psychological data suggested that segregation had positive psychological effects on black children, or that there were no significant differences between segregated and integrated school settings relative to their effect upon psychological and educational development (i.e., that "separate" really was "equal" from the psychological standpoint), would this have justified the enforced maintenance of segregated public schools? Most of us would respond in the negative, because we believe that principles of fundamental civil rights should have predominated in this situation, and that the "separate but equal" doctrine blatantly violated such rights. Thus, might not the presentation of psychological data of the type presented by Clark and others merely have diverted attention to matters irrelevant to the central legal analysis? Although this question is open to debate, one might argue that the data in *Brown* perhaps permitted the Court to avoid formal repudiation of the *Plessy* doctrine. Although this analysis necessarily simplifies the complex historical and legal considerations in this case,[1] my point is to emphasize

1. The historical analysis of *Brown* provided by Kluger (1975) reveals that such indirect strategies were purposely chosen by the National Association for the Advancement of Colored People (NAACP) in its several-decade legal crusade against segregation that preceded *Brown*. Direct challenge of *Plessy* was not expected to succeed. Therefore, psychological data, although not relevant to what many viewed as the central legal analysis, provided the litigators and the Court with a way to achieve their end (i.e., a holding that public school segregation was unconstitutional) without explicit overruling of *Plessy*. Subsequent cases revealed that the failure of the Court explicitly to reject *Plessy* did not prevent additional holdings that segregation of other public facilities was also unconstitutional, although, interestingly, the Court chose *not* to issue opinions revealing the legal reasoning underlying these holdings. Whereas the use of the data in legal strategy may have facilitated the reaching of the legally correct result in *Brown* regarding desegregation, it is not clear that all use of data in such a fashion does so. The case study of *Brown* reveals the complexities of the choices faced by behavioral scientists relative to the use of their data in legal policy contexts.

that even when the data are felt to be "ready," their introduction may be distracting from or irrelevant to the fundamental legal analyses characterizing the matter to be resolved.

LIMITATIONS ON CONTROL OF DATA PRESENTATION IN PARTICULAR LEGAL CONTEXTS

In attempting to balance the obligation to disseminate research findings for the public good and the obligation to insure accuracy and comprehensiveness in presentation, researchers must consider the practical limitations that particular legal contexts or procedures may place upon their ability to control either the data presentation or the subsequent use or misuse of the data. The adversary process that is a cornerstone of our system of justice and the political and often adversarial nature of many legislative debates may deprive a behavioral scientist of the opportunity to present data fully and in an unbiased manner.

For example, behavioral scientists, like other expert witnesses, typically are hired by one "side" or another of a particular case before a court. Only in certain cases, such as some family cases, will an expert be invited to testify as *amicus curiae* (i.e., "a friend of the court"). As such, an expert may be given great control over his or her testimony, either through the open-ended examination by a neutral guardian *ad litem*, or through the intervention of the judge. And, despite proposals by some that a panel of scientific experts should be appointed by the court in an *amicus* format in other types of cases as well, this procedure is far from usual (Saks & Van Duizend, 1983). More frequently, expert testimony is limited by the questions asked by the attorney representing the side that has hired the expert (i.e., direct examination) and the questions asked by the attorney representing the opposing side (i.e., cross-examination). Whereas psychologists' ethics necessitate complete and unbiased disclosure of scientific information, lawyers are focused upon allowing into evidence only whatever information is beneficial to their clients' cases. Therefore, responsible attorneys may try to prevent any discussion of limitations of scientific data, if that discussion is unfavorable to their clients. When a researcher is negotiating with a lawyer and says, "I will testify only if you agree to ask me questions on direct examination about the methodological limitations of the research," it is very possible that the voice on the other end of the telephone will terminate the negotiations. Thus, one is presented with the opportunity to present one's findings, but only in the most positive light.

In the ideal, the adversary process promotes complete and full examination of the issues before the court, because each side uncovers the information that is favorable to it and unfavorable to the opponent; thus, the end product is thought to be a thorough investigation and revelation of the truth. Yet this presupposes equivalent resources and competency on each side of the case. As unsophisticated as attorneys unfortunately are about the strengths and limitations of social science data, it is unlikely that most will be knowledgeable enough to perform a cross-examination of a psychologist that permits or requires the psychologist to discuss the limitations in and alternate interpretations of the data. And it is not at all clear that the opposing side will be able to afford, find, or otherwise provide an adequate expert to counter the testimony of the first behavioral scientist. Even if another competent expert is found, this is no guarantee that the trier of fact (judge or jury) will be sufficiently sophisticated about the scientific findings to draw meaningful conclusions from the two rather extreme interpretations before him, her, or it. For example, can the trier really determine, without a more impartial expert to balance the overall strengths and weaknesses of the study, how damaging it is to the present application of the findings that the study involved used college students as subjects?

The adversarial process reserves for the parties in a dispute the right to guide the presentation of evidence, with each party controlling his or her side's contributions. Thibaut and Walker (1978) suggest that a legal system is best able to achieve distributive justice if the disputing parties are invested with such process control. On the basis of laboratory investigation, Lind and Walker (1979) report that this allocation of control appears to maximize perceptions of "fairness" and "justice" experienced by participants. These considerations underscore the ethical dilemmas facing social scientists in the courtroom. The very process that has been viewed as maximizing fairness may in some situations present serious conflicts for psychologists, who are ethically obligated to present research findings in a thorough and undistorted manner. This conflict is unavoidable. And, assuming no major changes in our legal system, psychologists must balance their sense of obligation to assist the parties and the factfinding process through dissemination of data against the particular constraints on thorough testimony presented by each context. Certain types of advance negotiation with the hiring parties or their attorneys probably provide the greatest opportunity for harmony between control by parties and by scientists over presentation of research findings. This is the case because it is through such negotiations that the scientists and attorneys can learn to what extent complete and unbiased testimony by the scientists is consistent with the needs of the hiring parties. Unfortunately, even if a scientist retains some decisional control over presentation of findings in the courtroom, it is also possible that in some instances the testimony may purposely be distorted, misinterpreted, or otherwise manipulated for the purpose of making the testimony appear more favorable to one side or another.

Another example of the lack of control behavioral scientists may have is in the provision of testimony before a legislature. Although a scientist may be permitted to submit written testimony, he or she may be given only a few minutes to present that testimony in a legislative hearing. Depending upon the context and circumstance, 5 minutes of oral testimony may present a great opportunity for influence. And yet it is unlikely that 5 minutes will allow anything other than a summary, and possibly superficial, rendering of scientific findings. Again, depending upon the data, this may not be problematic; it may be possible to summarize general findings, to indicate that limitations exist, and to note that all of the details are in the written testimony. However, in other cases, there is the possibility that legislators or their aides will not read the written testimony, and that they will draw quick conclusions from what the scientist says. Thus, if the data are too complex to be suitable for a 5-minute rendition, it may be impossible to avoid superficiality, and thus distortion, in such a presentation. Failure to qualify and clarify may lead to subsequent misapplication of the findings.

Finally, even if the initial dissemination of findings in a policy forum is complete, accurate, and appropriately qualified, this still does not guarantee that the findings will be interpreted correctly by policymakers. Misinterpretation can result from the lack of scientific sophistication of one in the chain of communication (e.g., a legislative staff member who communicates the findings to the legislator or other staff persons), or from intentional distortion to suit adversarial or political goals. The potential for exaggeration and sensationalism always exists when researchers are dealing in a political setting with hidden agendas and press participation.

There are no clear solutions here as well. Some might propose that behavioral scientists should refrain completely from providing testimony for parties in adversarial court cases because the possibilities for distortion of information are too great. Clearly, if a scientist has the opportunity to enter as an *amicus*, doing so will probably dramatically increase his or her control over data presentation. In fact, wherever possible, structuring one's role as that of an impartial consultant seems preferable. However, realistically, this opportunity is unlikely to be available often, with the exception of child custody and related cases. Therefore, the scientist must choose between the type of presentation offered in a particular case or no presentation at all. Clearly, the decision of whether to go forward under the circumstances will necessitate a risk–benefit analysis. The expected benefits of disseminating the findings in the particular context must be balanced against the likelihood that, given the specific data set and the questions and emphases of the attorneys, the data will be misconstrued or distorted. Obviously, the more complex the data set, the degree to which there are several alternate interpretations of the data, the more conflicting the findings of different studies, and/or the more limited the methods, the less appropriate the findings may be for presentation in the adversary context. By contrast, the greater the convergence of findings from disparate methods and studies, the fewer the alternate explanations for the findings, and/or the fewer the limitations of the data and problems of generalization, the more suitable the data set may be for such presentation. Again, each scientist must perform a balancing analysis of the possible benefits and harms accruing from the particular application of the findings. Is the likelihood or magnitude of distortion sufficiently minor to be outweighed by the likely benefits of dissemination in this forum? Are there ways to minimize the possible distortion or misinterpretation?

Presentation of scientific findings in the courtroom in a role other than *amicus*, or presentation before a legislative subcommittee, may at times be particularly challenging for those behavioral scientists who seriously try to abide by the Ethical Principles of the APA. There are other strategies for communicating findings that do not require such a loss of control in the manner and content of the presentation. For example, submission of *amicus curiae* briefs in appellate decisions provides scientists with an opportunity to structure their own treatises for presentation to the court. The APA, among other scientific groups, has submitted such briefs in cases involving issues such as civilly committed psychiatric patients' rights to refuse psychotropic medication, and state- or city-mandated provision of information to women considering abortion (see Tremper, Chapter 8, this volume).

Consultation with legislators and legislative aides provides another opportunity for dissemination of research findings in a context where scientists can control information presentation. In either an ad hoc or an ongoing consultative relationship, there is the possibility of interactive discussions that will serve to educate the policy community about the available knowledge base. Such discussions can serve to generate ideas for legislative initiatives, and can guide the policymakers as they respond to initiatives proposed by others. The potential for ongoing consultation is great. In a similar vein, participation by behavioral scientists on policy task forces or commissions provides another vehicle for communication of expertise in a manner that minimizes distortion of data.

THE OBLIGATION TO MAINTAIN OBJECTIVITY

Although there are arguably many factors that can limit the objectivity of a behavioral scientist, I focus on two considerations here: (1) the role of personal values and commitment to certain public and social goals, and (2) the role of relationships that may create a conflict of interest.

THE ROLE OF PERSONAL VALUES

Psychologists typically commence investigations with a commitment to particular hypotheses, based upon their analysis of existing scientific data. This type of commitment is *not* the focus here. Rather, beyond a commitment to particular scientific or scholarly interpretations of a data base, psychologists may maintain a commitment to certain social goals and values. For example, they may oppose racial segregation of schools or the death penalty; they may feel that the involuntary sterilization of the mentally retarded or the involuntary incarceration of children in psychiatric hospitals is inhumane; they may feel that more should be done in society to prevent child and spouse abuse. These personal views on controversial social issues may lead social scientists to hope that certain social goals will be achieved in our society, and may lead them to become active as private citizens in political volunteer work, communications to legislatures, or other vehicles to promote these goals.

However, when psychologists with strong commitments to certain social goals undertake scientific research relating to these goals, it is very likely that they will hope for particular outcomes in the data, over and above any intellectual satisfaction from confirmation of their hypotheses. It is in this type of situation that we, as ostensibly objective investigators, must be most reflective. We must be cognizant of the possibility that our social and political values will affect the way in which we design, conduct, analyze, and interpret our research. If we feel that we are unable to remain objective in each of these stages, we must reconsider whether this particular avenue of research is appropriate for us. If we believe we can be objective, but wish to double-check, consultation with colleagues who are known not to be as committed to the particular social goal as we are can serve to correct us if we begin to lose objectivity. Ideally, coinvestigators holding points of view different from our own can help us to maintain a balanced perspective.

Judge D.L. Bazelon (1982) recognizes that scientists are subject to particular value-laden perspectives. He recommends that scientists disclose these underlying values when they communicate their findings, and in so doing, indicate how they perceive these values to have influenced any choices they may have made during the research process. Bazelon's suggestion is a good one. Its utility is not only in permitting others to assess for themselves the role that the scientists' values may have played in the research process, but in requiring psychologists to be cognizant of how these predispositions may have influenced the process.

However, the ethical dilemmas multiply when a scientist is confronted with research findings that are not only contrary to his or her hypotheses, but that, if disseminated, could lead to certain damaging social consequences. Is it ever ethical to *suppress* data because its revelation may be more harmful than beneficial to society?

The APA Ethical Principles are silent on this question, noting only that it is unethical for psychologists to suppress disconfirming data, or for institutions employing psychologists to suppress data (the latter issue is dealt with below). Clearly, we can distinguish in theory between suppression of data for the purpose of enhancing a psychologist's professional reputation (i.e., failing to disclose that earlier findings were not confirmed in a later study) or for financial motives, and suppression of data for the purpose of protecting society or some of its citizens from harm. Beauchamp and Childress (1982) point out that complementing the obligations of beneficence (i.e., the affirmative duties to do good and to protect from harm) is an obligation to refrain from causing or inflicting harm—that is, a duty of "nonmaleficence." Under what circumstances does the duty of nonmaleficence predominate?

Once again, there are no easy answers. Some psychologists may believe that there are no circumstances that justify the suppression of research findings. Proponents of this position may point toward the inevitable subjectivity in decisions to what is socially harmful and what is not, and may prefer not to have individual scientists making such inherently biased decisions. Furthermore, suppression of information (for whatever reason) violates the duty of veracity, and will lead to a dangerous erosion of honesty and openness in the scientific enterprise. Whereas some instances of suppression may be sincere, others may be fraudulent attempts to abuse this "exception" to the obligation to tell the truth. In addition, unbeknownst to most of us, our bases of knowledge will become biased and inaccurate through systematic suppression of certain controversial sets of findings.

Ideally, the best way to avoid such dilemmas is for scientists to ask themselves the necessary questions *before* they commence a research endeavor. That is, if the findings are contrary to a researcher's hopes in a socially sensitive study, would he or she be willing to publish them? If a study suggests that there exist certain racial differences in intelligence, contrary to the researcher's hypotheses, and the researcher is concerned that revelation of such findings will foster prejudice and discrimination, would he or she be willing to publish the findings? If, counter to expectations, a researcher discovers a foolproof way *scientifically* to select jurors biased toward particular verdicts, and he or she is concerned about promoting a technique of this type that most likely can only be obtained by wealthy clients, would that researcher be willing to publish the findings? Any scientist who feels that he or she would be unwilling or hesitant to publish unfavorable results should probably not commence a research endeavor. Thus, if there is any single ethical imperative relevant to the issue of suppression, it is that psychologists should not get themselves into situations where they are likely to confront this dilemma. Prior to the commencement of any investigation of socially sensitive issues, or issues about which the investigator maintains a strong commitment to certain social goals, that investigator should carefully evaluate these ethical concerns and determine how they would lead him or her to resolve a dilemma raised by findings judged to be socially "dangerous." To enter into a project with the knowledge that the data will be published *only* if they confirm a certain image of the way things ought to be is irresponsible, in that scientists who do so consciously and willingly place themselves in a position where they may need to violate the duty of veracity.

Clearly, however, there are circumstances where even the most conscientious psychologists would not have anticipated certain findings. The focus of a large-scale study may be one set of variables, and yet some findings unrelated to the hypotheses may emerge from the data. Or an investigator may have commenced an investigation without careful prestudy deliberations, and now finds himself or herself with results he or she perceives to be socially dangerous, and is uncertain of what to do. The final decision as to dissemination versus suppression must result from a careful balancing of the detrimental consequences that will follow from violation of the principles of veracity or nonmaleficence. Are the data sufficiently harmful to society if published that the danger significantly outweighs the ethical imperative to disclose the truth? It is my personal judgment that the circumstances when the answer to this query is "yes" will be rare indeed, although they may occur. Clearly, the more "dangerous" the findings, the more "certain" one must be about them before dissemination. Therefore, one may choose to apply a stricter standard to publication in the scientific literature than would characterize one's dissemination typically.

RELATIONSHIPS CREATING A CONFLICT OF INTEREST

The APA Ethical Principles warn psychologists to "avoid relationships that may limit their objectivity or create a conflict of interest" (Principle 1b, p. 633). Is it possible that if even the most well-meaning behavioral scientist is requested to generate data by one "side" on a particular legal issue, that the zeal to obtain results favorable to that side will threaten objectivity? For example, if a psychologist is employed by a profitmaking organization, such as a television network, to conduct research that the network hopes will reveal that the current crop of violent television programs has no deleterious effects on children, might the knowledge of the financial stakes, or the identification with the employer and its goals, affect the psychologist's objectivity either consciously or unconsciously?

Obviously, as noted in the section immediately above, even the best attempts at objectivity may be compromised without our awareness by laudable motives such as a desire to contribute to the public good. There is no less of a possibility that devotion to an employer and internalization of that employer's goals will serve as any less biasing factors. Therefore, the recommendations are the same: Scientists should be deliberate and thoughtful about their ability to remain objective in advance of undertaking any such employment relationships. If they doubt their ability to retain the same objectivity they would have if the research were being conducted independently of the employer, then such employment situations probably should be avoided. Even more clear is the necessity to avoid employment relationships where there may exist either overt or covert pressure to obtain certain research findings, such that scientists may find themselves facing more conscious conflicts of interests between the employers' goals and the pursuit of truth.

Saks (1984; Saks & Van Duizend, 1983) notes that scientific experts may experience "role conflict" when confronted with the choice of acting as "neutral scientist" or "advocate" when testifying in the courtroom. Some have referred to a variant of this conflict as "objectivity versus advocacy" (Anderten, Stalcup, & Grisso, 1980). Within the context of the present analyses, this conflict appears to require the balancing of scientists' ethical obligation to present the complete and undistorted truth, and their perceived commitment to the attorneys or clients who have hired them to present expert testimony. Thus, beyond the question of control, psychologists must confront the conflict they experience if they feel ethically obliged to present information that may be detrimental to the "side" that is paying their salary and has made their appearance in court possible. Should their role in the courtroom be that of impartial scientists, or that of advocates for the position of a particular side in the dispute? Whereas the APA Ethical Principles are relatively clear in the abstract that objectivity may *not* be compromised, particularized applications are more difficult.

A corollary to these issues is the question of who should control the dissemination of the findings of research commissioned by an organization, agency, or employer. At one level, this question is answered straightforwardly by the contractual arrangements that characterize the relationship between the psychologist and the group "paying for" the study. From a legal standpoint, the psychologist's contract may clarify who "owns" the data. At another level, however, the psychologist must scrutinize the ethical concerns. Legal and ethical demands sometimes conflict, although, ideally, with foresight into the possibilities of these conflicts, psychologists will avoid the conflicts wherever feasible.

The APA invests its members with the "responsibility to attempt to prevent distortion, misuse, or suppression of psychological findings by the institution or agency of which they are employees" (Principle 1c, p. 633). It is difficult to identify circumstances where this prohibition against distortion and misuse of data is not appropriate. However, whereas the APA's caveat relative to suppression appears clearly relevant when there is a public interest in disclosure of findings (as is the case for most research that yields generalizable psychological knowledge of importance to the public), it may be less justified in certain exceptional situations. Perhaps here it is useful to distinguish between "protection" and "suppression" of data. There are two types of situations that come to mind in which there may be a countervailing justification for "protection" and nondisclosure of behavioral science data. The first such exception concerns data generated and applied by government agencies to achieve goals identified with the public good. For example, social scientists have assisted agencies of the federal government in developing certain "profiles" of persons likely to try to hijack airlines, smuggle drugs, or assassinate public leaders (Monahan & Walker, 1985). For obvious reasons, the specifics of many of these profiles remain "classified," and are published neither in the scientific literature nor for the general public's consumption. Whereas one could argue that use of the profiles violates constitutional rights (and such arguments have been the basis of legal battles), one cannot deny that many would perceive a countervailing public interest in the nondisclosure of these data. In short, despite the disagreements that such data uses are bound to generate, there is no question that some observers will conclude that the social benefits to be gained by maintaining the secrecy of the data are far greater than those that will accrue through dissemination of the data.

Another context in which the law has "protected" the secrecy of research data relates to "trade secrets." The policy
underlying trade secret law (as well as other areas of intellectual
property law) is the encouragement of research and development. The law expects that many businesses would not invest
financially in the development of new technologies if the law
did not assure protection against unauthorized disclosures regarding these efforts. The long-term social benefits accruing
from the fruits of these research endeavors are viewed as out-
weighing the short-term losses incurred from the delayed dissemination. An obvious nonpsychological example is the creation and application of new microelectronic technologies by
computer and software manufacturers, many of whom do not
disclose their research findings to other scientists or to the public. We could claim that the public has an interest in the dissemination of that information. Not only will disclosure enhance competition so that consumers can buy less expensive
computer equipment and software, but, arguably, disclosure
will promote the development of even more advanced technologies. The counterargument, however, is that, without trade
secret protection, these technologies may not be developed in
the first place. Further, the economic values of our capitalistic
society support the rights of businesses to benefit commercially
from their investments in research and development. From the
standpoint of ethics in psychology, one can argue that if nondisclosure of the research findings does not *interfere* with an
important public interest, there is no problem with a psychologist participating in such ventures. For example, a consumer
behavior psychologist may conduct research for a clothing man-
ufacturer on what are the social images of a particular target
group that may be tapped by a new line of designs, or how best
to reach that target group through advertising. Unless the psychologist has concerns about specifically deceptive business or
advertising techniques, there seems to be little in the way of a
public interest to warrant an ethical concern about disclosure.

Maintenance of "classified data" by the government for use
in protection of the public or guarding of trade secrets appear
to be dramatically different from purposeful suppression of

information when there is a strong public interest in such disclosure. Turning to another nonbehavioral example, A.H. Robins, the company that manufactured the Dalkon Shield intrauterine contraceptive device, has been accused of failing to alert the public to research findings revealing that the device was harmful to users. The company allegedly knew that the device was not as effective in preventing pregnancies as had been claimed, and that the device also caused miscarriages and severe infections sometimes leading to sterility or death (Kaplan & Weisberg, 1985). Yet, for financial reasons, the company reportedly chose to suppress this information. Few would deny that there was a strong public interest in the disclosure of that information, in that thousands of women were current users and others were future users. It also is difficult to find validity in the notion that there was any legitimate countervailing concern that justified the suppression. I would suggest that where suppression of data creates a clear public danger, as in the Dalkon Shield case, and it is suppressed solely because disclosure is not financially beneficial to the group that commissioned the research, suppression is unjustified. Therefore, participation and collusion by a behavioral scientist in such a process is unethical.

Returning to the initial hypothetical situation about the television network, we might conclude that suppression of data clearly demonstrating that watching violent television programs has a detrimental effect on children would not be justified. Suppression of such information would be directly contrary to the public interest, and the financial interests of the television network in continuing to draw profits at the expense of an unsuspecting and innocent audience would not seem to outweigh the public's right to that knowledge. The obligation to insure disclosure in this type of situation increases as the possibility of having an impact on legal policy emerges. Suppose, for example, that Congress or the Federal Communications Commission is considering measures to limit the proportion of certain types of violence in prime-time programming, and it is the existence of this movement which motivates the network to suppress the relevant data. A psychologist who has been engaged in the collection of such data and who evaluates the data as pertinent to the current legal debate must grapple with his or her ethical obligations to promote timely dissemination.

Obviously, scientists may differ in their analyses of these issues. However, in general, it appears that when a psychologist ventures to conduct research, the results of which will be important to the public, he or she should contract in advance with the employer to make sure that publication of the data in a scientific forum will materialize, regardless of whether the findings are favorable to the interests of the employer. Such contracting will allow the psychologist to avoid confronting an inevitable ethical quandary where commitment to the values of veracity and beneficence is inconsistent with loyalty to the employer or with legally contracted obligations to the employer.

Finally, there remains another dilemma that incorporates several conflicts discussed thus far. Should a psychologist or other scientific expert agree to conduct research specifically for use by one side of an adversarial legal dispute? For the sake of argument, let us assume that a psychologist does so agree, and that the data—contrary to the expectations of the psychologist and the party hiring the psychologist—not only are *not* supportive of the party's position, but are strongly supportive of the case of the adversaries. Obviously, if the other side does not learn about the data, it is unlikely that questions will be raised in pretrial discovery or in court eliciting their disclosure. As discussed above, however, a psychologist who testifies about a data base and purposely omits discussion of certain data because they are unfavorable to his or her side risks compromising the duty of veracity and violating the APA Ethical Principles. These ethical principles may conflict with the legal or moral obligation to the party hiring the psychologist, and with that party's right to pursue freely, and without fear of disclosure to the other side, investigative strategies in the preparation of the case. In resolving this inevitable conflict, the psychologist must balance these important values, and (let us hope) will have used foresight and good judgment in not entering into such a situation without adequate consideration of the possible ethical problems.

However, assuming that the hypothetical psychologist does not testify because the attorney feels that there are insufficient favorable data to warrant such testimony, what are the psychologist's ethical and legal obligations to the party and the public? From a legal standpoint, knowledge of the existence of the data probably will be protected from discovery by the other side if the psychologist does not testify (see, e.g., Fed. R. Civ. P. 26(b)(4)(B).). Furthermore, if the psychologist has entered into a contract with the hiring party not to disclose any such commissioned research findings during the course of the legal proceedings, he or she will be legally thus obliged. And, in addition, or in the absence of such a contract, he or she may feel morally obliged not to disclose the data because the hiring party probably would not have funded the research if the party thought it might be used against him or her. But should a psychologist enter into such a contract in the first place? Or, assuming that there is no contract with the hiring party as to the disposition of the data, is the psychologist bound ethically to (or not to) disclose the existence of the data to the other side? This is an exceptionally difficult dilemma. It seems unjust that one side in a legal dispute should benefit, and possibly win a dispute, as a result of the labors of an opponent who has made possible the creation of certain scientific data. However, if a psychologist is aware that the disposition of a particular case may be significantly influenced by the data (i.e., without the data, the court may not reach an accurate result), is the psychologist obligated to assist the court in ascertaining the truth? Assuming that there is not a more pervasive public interest to be served by public dissemination of the data more generally, is it not in the public interest that legal disputes reach scientifically accurate results?

We come full circle here, in that these queries return us to our starting place: What are psychologists' obligations to benefit society through dissemination of their data? Does that obligation outweigh the rights of parties in legal disputes to hire behavioral scientists to create empirical data with the security that the data will not be used against them? There remain no clear answers—only the recognition that participation in the legal system in this matter inevitably creates ethical dilemmas such as this one. Each scientist must decide how he or she will resolve these thorny issues if they manifest themselves, and make his or her decision known to those who request the collection of data.

CONCLUSIONS

In summary, I would like to re-emphasize that the most important aspects of responsible professional conduct in the situation described above and throughout this book are the careful analysis and balancing of competing ethical concerns inherent in the dissemination of behavioral science data in legal policy arenas. I have attempted to underscore that although there are guiding philosophical principles, these principles must be applied differentially in each unique situation in which one considers dissemination of a data set. The subjectivity inherent in these analyses is unavoidable. However, if each of us undergoes deliberate contemplation and "soul searching" regarding our ethical obligations, we will have taken a significant step toward insuring that our actions reflect the highest level of professional responsibility.

ACKNOWLEDGMENTS

I wish to thank Robyn M. Dawes, Robert Emery, N. Dickon Reppucci, and Elizabeth Scott for their reactions to an earlier draft of this manuscript. Appreciation is expressed to the other contributors to this volume, who provided useful commentary on these issues during the May 1985 study group.

REFERENCES

American Psychological Association. (1981). Ethical Principals of Psychologists. *American Psychologist, 36,* 633–638.
Anderten, P., Stalcup, V., & Grisso, T. (1980). On being ethical in legal places. *Professional Psychology: Research and Practice, 11,* 764–773.
Bandura, A. (1974). Behavior theory and the models of man. *American Psychologist, 29,* 859–869.

Bazelon, D.L. (1982). Veils, values, and social responsibility. *American Psychologist, 37,* 115–121.

Beauchamp, T.L., & Childress, J.F. (1983). *Principles of biomedical ethics* (2nd ed.). New York: Oxford University Press.

Bermant, G. (1982). Justifying social science research in terms of social benefit. In T.L. Beauchamp, R.R. Faden, R.J. Wallace, Jr., & L. Walters (Eds.), *Ethical issues in social science research* (pp. 125–143). Baltimore: Johns Hopkins University Press.

Bersoff, D.N. (1986). Psychologists and the judicial system: Broader perspectives. *Law and Human Behavior, 10,* 151–166.

Brown v. Board of Education, 347 U.S. 483 (1954).

Cook, S. (1979). Social science and school desegregation: Did we mislead the Supreme Court? *Personality and Social Psychology Bulletin, 5,* 420–437.

Cook, S. (1984). The 1954 social sciences statement and school desegregation: A reply to Gerard. *American Psychologist, 39,* 819–832.

Fed. R. Civ. P. 26(b)(4)(B).

Gerard, H. (1983). School desegregation: The social science role. *American Psychologist, 38,* 869–877.

Goodman, F.I. (1972). *De facto* school segregation: A constitutional and empirical analysis. *California Law Review, 60,* 275–437.

Kaplan, J., & Weisberg, R. (1985). *Criminal law.* Mineola, NY: Foundation Press.

Kluger, R. (1975). *Simple justice.* New York: Vintage Books.

Lind, E.A., & Walker, L. (1979). Theory testing, theory development, and laboratory research on legal issues. *Law and Human Behavior, 3,* 5–19.

Loftus, E.F. (1983). Silence is not golden. *American Psychologist, 38,* 564–572.

McCloskey, M., & Egeth, H.E. (1983). Eyewitness identification: What can a psychologist tell a jury? *American Psychologist, 38,* 550–563.

McKenna, J. (1984, August). *Ethical standards and presentation of scientific findings in the courtroom.* Paper presented at the meeting of the American Psychological Association, Toronto.

Monahan, J., & Walker, L. (1985). *Social science in law.* Mineola, NY: Foundation Press.

Plessy v. Ferguson, 163 U.S. 537 (1896).

Reppucci, N.D. (1984, August). *Psychology in the public interest.* G. Stanley Hall Lecture presented at the meeting of the American Psychological Association, Toronto.

Saks, M.J. (1984). *Role conflict and ethical dilemmas: Research psychologists as expert witnesses.* Paper presented at the meeting of the American Psychological Association, Toronto.

Saks, M.J., & Van Duizend, R. (1983). *The use of scientific evidence in litigation.* Williamsburg, VA: National Center for State Courts.

Thibaut, J., & Walker, L. (1978). A theory of procedure. *California Law Review, 66,* 541–566.

Guidelines for Effective Diffusion of Child Development Research into the Legal System

GARY B. MELTON

A clear underlying premise of this book (and a belief of the study group that wrote it) is that, when courts rely on empirical assumptions, justice will be best served by the application of scientific knowledge. Social science obviously cannot inform the law about the moral or legal legitimacy of a given decision or policy. In philosophical jargon, an "ought" cannot be derived from an "is." However, when the goals of law are established, social science can potentially provide information about the efficacy of various alternative means of achieving the goals. Furthermore, when application of a legal principle turns on an assumption about a social fact—for example, children's competence in making decisions (see Melton, Koocher, & Saks, 1983)—courts will come closer to finding the truth if they examine systematic empirical research than if they rely on intuition or the facts of a single case. We reject a positivistic approach to the normative ordering of child, family, and state, but we adhere to a belief in empiricism as the logical foundation for determination of fact.

The contributors to this book have diverse disciplinary

Gary B. Melton. Department of Psychology and College of Law, University of Nebraska–Lincoln, Lincoln, Nebraska.

backgrounds and research interests, but they share a commitment to the application of social science to promote human welfare (cf. American Psychological Association, 1981, Preamble). Their work is motivated by its potential benefit to the commonwealth (cf. Bermant, 1982), and its scholarly merit has earned the contributors the respect of peers. Nonetheless, the work's social utility is diminished substantially if it is not in a form that leads to its consideration and comprehension by users in the public arena. This book is designed to guide researchers toward diffusion of their work in a manner that insures that it is not conducted in vain, and particularly that it guides legal authorities in decisions about the lives of children and youths.

Two questions provide useful beginning points for consideration of optimal means of diffusion of child development research into the legal system. First, is there a need? Are there openings for introduction of child development research into legal decisionmaking about children and youths? Second, if so, is the need being met? Is child development research reaching legal decisionmakers?

DO THE COURTS USE CHILD DEVELOPMENT RESEARCH?

THE OPPORTUNITIES FOR INFUSION OF CHILD DEVELOPMENT RESEARCH

Perhaps more than any other area of law, juvenile and family law seems to invite the assistance of social scientists. At least five factors contribute to the apparently central importance of social science in children's law (Melton, 1984; Mnookin, 1985). These factors are sufficiently strong that courts may even expect, if not demand, that litigants introduce social science evidence in cases affecting child and family policy (Melton, 1986).

First, assumptions about the nature of childhood and family life have permeated children's law. Indeed, the juvenile court itself is based on assumptions about the moral reasoning and the treatability of youths. Consistent with this foundation, the juvenile court stimulated the development of child guidance centers (Levine & Levine, 1970). The juvenile court and the child mental health system grew up together, and the court exemplified the legal realists' goal of applying "science" (more accurately, social welfare principles) to the judicial process in order to enhance responsiveness to social realities.

Second, since the first recognition that children are "persons" within the meaning of the Bill of Rights and the Fourteenth Amendment (*In re Gault*, 1967), the U.S. Supreme Court has tended to treat minors as "half-persons." The Court has stacked the deck against minors' exercise of rights by using low levels of scrutiny of age-based discrimination. Although not rejecting the basic premise that children are entitled to the rights bestowed by the Constitution, the Court has tended to devote much more attention to why children should be treated differently from adults than to why their personhood should be respected (Melton, 1984; Melton & Pliner, 1986). The ironic result is greater reliance on social science evidence, or at least on social assumptions. Because of the ambivalent approach to children's personhood, balancing tests are commonly employed to determine whether their rights will be fulfilled. Such balancing tests commonly require consideration of the effects of recognizing children's rights, and thus invite empirical evidence.

Third, competency is the overriding issue in children's law (Melton, 1983b). Almost without exception, post-*Gault* considerations of issues related to children's rights by the Supreme Court have turned on assumptions about the competence of children and adolescents. The relevance of child development research is obvious.

Fourth, standards in juvenile and family law have typically been indeterminate (Mnookin, 1975). Consistent with the juvenile court's realist heritage, standards have been left ambiguous (e.g., "the best interests of the child") in order to promote the broad application of evidence about the welfare of youths.

Fifth, children's issues have an inherent indeterminancy. Children's policies hinge on predictions, and therefore are inevitably based on probabilistic judgments. Thus, the reliance on group probability data presents less vexing philosophical problems than it does in most legal decisions (Monahan & Walker,

1985). It is clearly unjust to rely on group probabilities to determine whether an individual committed a legally relevant act. In our legal system, courts distribute justice according to the merit of acts rather than character—what a defendant did, not what people like him or her are inclined to do. Nonetheless, consideration of statistical evidence is not very troubling when we are *forced* to rely on probabilities, as when we make judgments about the future (e.g., dangerousness, amenability to treatment). In deciding individual cases and making legal policy, such judgments are pervasive in children's law. For example, whether deciding the custody of a particular child or establishing standards for custody decisions, courts and legislatures must judge the probability that various custody alternatives will have various effects upon child development. With no choice but to consider probabilities, juvenile and family courts may be unusually open to the probabilistic evidence that social scientists bring.

In short, both the content and the philosophy of children's law appear to lead to extraordinary opportunities for social scientists to affect policy. As Koocher (Chapter 1, this volume) points out, the range of issues is remarkably broad. Courts are not simply concerned with historic questions of the welfare of individual children (e.g., child custody in divorce, disposition in delinquency and maltreatment cases). Even in these traditional areas of legal policy, the influence of the women's movement (see Derdeyn, 1978) and doubts about the efficacy of juvenile justice (see Morse & Whitebread, 1982) have opened the door to rethinking of the most settled doctrines of juvenile and family law.

Of even more consequence, though, the announcement that the Constitution protects children as well as adults brought with it a plethora of issues that were essentially moot previously. How much deference is to be given to children's newly recognized personal autonomy and privacy, and how much weight is to be placed on parental autonomy and family privacy (values historically protected in both constitutional and common law)? And in an era in which increasingly greater adaptive skills are necessary for the workplace and the voting booth, how is the state's interest in socialization of children to be weighed against the prerogatives of child and family? In this new three-way clash of values, a bewildering number of complex issues of child and family policy have reached the courts. The post-*Gault* deluge of cases has brought questions about such diverse problems as the effects of pinball parlors, the quality of pregnant adolescents' decisions, the ability of juvenile defendants to comprehend and apply *Miranda* warnings, the effects of open-court proceedings on child witnesses, the ability of children to distinguish religious prayer and secular meditation in school, and the effects of free political expression on school discipline.

This mushrooming of issues in children's law has coincided with postrealist jurisprudential developments that have made consideration of extralegal sources common, if not completely uncontroversial (see Hafemeister & Melton, Chapter 2, this volume; Melton, Chapter 9, this volume; Tremper, Chapter 8, this volume). In the proliferation of "law and . . ." movements, "law and child development research" is not a strange concept. Surely, then, with a combination of a plethora of hard questions that child development researchers might know something about, and a legal system more open than ever before to social science, the law would welcome the assistance of child development researchers.

THE LIMITS OF SOCIAL SCIENCE INFLUENCE

Conceptual Obstacles

Unfortunately, this rosy picture of interdisciplinary collaboration overlooks some significant qualifications and obstacles. Even if probability evidence is more easily applied to the predictive questions in children's law than to most legal issues, it does not follow that such application is without problems. A conceptual leap remains from the finding that 20% of children respond in a given way to joint custody to the conclusion about the probability that a particular child will respond that way. Also, univariate analyses may be of little help in understanding actual cases (cf. Clingempeel & Reppucci, 1982).

Even if the conceptual hurdle of moving from group to

individual can be crossed, courts may be reluctant to consider evidence based on social science research. The realist heritage of juvenile courts is not necessarily a heritage of scientific inquiry. Rather, the "science" in juvenile and family courts has generally consisted of clinical opinions about individual children and families that have had little if any scientific foundation. Indeed, we still know little about effective disposition in delinquency, divorce custody, and child maltreatment cases (Melton, 1984). The courts' tolerance—and encouragement— of experts' overreaching may have reflected a willingness to listen to the best evidence available amidst scarce information, or, less charitably, to duck hard cases. However, the strongest reason may have been that the courts had no reason to question the advice that they received or cajoled from social workers and mental health professionals. Unsurprisingly, given their common heritage, juvenile judges and child guidance workers generally have shared assumptions about the nature of children's and families' problems and the proper response to them. The courts may be substantially less pleased to hear the opinions of scholars who test these assumptions. Indeed, researchers' challenge is no less than to juvenile and family law itself, which starts from the premise that age-based distinctions in law are rationally related to empirically valid differences between legal "infants" (inclusive of adolescents) and adults.

As I argue in Chapter 9 of this volume, the appearance of reliance on empirical observation of social facts in children's law may be mere illusion. Rather, children's law may be driven by mythical perceptions of childhood, the family, and other institutions in authority over children. Judges' verbosity and eloquence in opinions in family law cases often may indicate the sociolegal significance of the relationships purportedly being described more than honest and thoughtful consideration of the reality. Symbols may be more important than facts in children's law; indeed, social "facts" often may be mere symbols. Although social science evidence may be expected in children's cases, it may be especially unlikely to be considered in such litigation.

Some evidence for this hypothesis comes from our (Melton, Weithorn, & Slobogin, 1985) survey of trial judges concerning the usefulness of mental health or social science consultation about various issues in which mental health expertise is commonly thought to be relevant. Despite the conventional wisdom that family conflicts are matters especially suited to mental health consultation, divorce custody and child maltreatment issues were the matters on which judges said that experts' assistance was least likely to be needed or useful. This unenthusiastic response apparently was not the product of an informed assessment of the strength of the foundation for experts' opinions in family law cases. Some of the issues on which judges were most impressed with experts' actual and potential contributions were one for which the scientific foundation is consensually regarded as weak (e.g., dangerousness; see Monahan, 1981; Slobogin, 1984).

The nature of legal disputes involving children and families thus may be such that courts resist a full development of the issues. The affective pull of the issues may be stronger than the need for fully rational decisionmaking. In the alternative, perhaps judges perceive little need for social science evidence in children's cases. Although issues such as dangerousness may seem sufficiently arcane to require the assistance of experts, issues involving childhood and family life may seem sufficiently familiar to require only common knowledge. Judges may believe that they know little about mental disorders, but being children and having children are matters about which they have experience and do not need the assistance of experts.

Use, Misuse, and Underuse

With such obstacles, the continuing minimal attention to child development research is perhaps unsurprising (see Hafemeister & Melton, Chapter 2, this volume). The lone dissent by Justice Douglas in *Wisconsin v. Yoder* (1972) remains the only U.S. Supreme Court opinion in which research related to children's competence was cited, despite the central importance of this issue. As I note in Chapter 9 of this volume, it also is not difficult to find examples of blatant misapplication of social science research when it is used in children's cases.

On the other hand, the nonuse of child development research is selective. Research *has* found its way occasionally into both judicial opinions and legal scholarship, especially when some care has been taken to disseminate work to legal audiences. For example, Grisso's work on juveniles' waiver of rights, especially as reported in the *California Law Review* (Grisso, 1980), has been considered by both trial and appellate courts with some frequency (see Grisso & Melton, Chapter 6, this volume). More generally, about one-third of the citations of secondary sources (i.e., sources other than cases, statutes, and regulations) in recent children's cases in the U.S. Supreme Court have been to nonlegal authorities (Hafemeister & Melton, Chapter 2, this volume).

Moreover, the underuse of child development research is not necessarily a product of lack of receptivity by the judiciary. As Tremper (Chapter 8, this volume) shows, neither the parties not the *amici* fully briefed the Supreme Court on information about adolescent decisionmaking in any of the minors' abortion cases that reached the Court prior to 1985.[1] The problem is as much (if not more) one of lack of effective dissemination as of decisions not to use social science research or to apply it inappositely or misleadingly.

It is possible that even the dissemination problem is being remediated through the development of structures for diffusion of child development research. Although we note that it is still nascent and fragile, Takanishi and I (Chapter 4, this volume) describe the issue network that has developed informally to communicate child development research to Congress and federal agencies. The development of interdisciplinary institutes in several law schools (see Melton, 1984) also ultimately may lead to greater ease of dissemination of information about child development to legal scholars and practitioners. Serious scholarship about the legal status of children and families requires attention to the psychological assumptions underlying

1. The American Psychological Association (APA) remediated this gap in the brief that it submitted to the Supreme Court in *Thornburgh v. American College of Obstetricians and Gynecologists* (1986), although the Court failed to decide the issues presented about minors and instead remanded that aspect of the case to the district court. The relevant portion of the APA brief is reprinted in Interdivisional Committee on Adolescent Abortion (1987).

the legal distribution of authority among child, family, and state. As a result, interdisciplinary programs on children's law are flourishing in several universities (e.g., Nebraska, Stanford, Virginia), and the most influential scholars in children's law are frequently active collaborators in empirical research (see Melton, 1986, discussing Mnookin, 1985).

WHAT CAN WE DO?

Some Caveats

Examination of those instances in which child development research has made it to the legal system gives some clues about ways in which to maximize the likelihood that the findings of the research reach their intended audience. However, some initial caveats are in order. First, researchers who are serious about the duty to disseminate their work should be prepared for a low hit rate. To use Weiss's (Chapter 3, this volume) felicitous phrase, knowledge "creeps." Although citations in judicial opinions give some basis for determining when information has reached legal decisionmakers and influenced their decisions (see Hafemeister & Melton, Chapter 2, this volume), the more common use may be when findings become so commonplace that their "notice" is automatic (see Melton, Chapter 9, this volume). Rosen (1984) found that U.S. Supreme Court decisions are highly correlated with prevailing views among affluent older Americans. Social science is apt to be most widely used when it enters the popular *Zeitgeist*. That process itself is apt to be incremental with many misses, even when researchers work actively to disseminate their findings. Weiss's (Chapter 3, this volume) discussion of the improbability that news releases will be used—and the even greater improbability that research will be discovered by the media without releases—is illustrative.

Second, whether research becomes known to legal authorities is to a certain extent uncontrollable, even if not random. For example, we (Melton et al., 1985) found that the variable that was by far the most powerful correlate of trial judges' frequency of reading behavioral science literature was the level of secretarial services available ($r = .72$). Judges, lawyers, court staff, and law enforcement and social service staff in nonmetropolitan jurisdictions are also commonly late to "hear the word," probably because of a combination of fewer court supports, less specialization, and less extensive networks for diffusion of information (Grisso & Melton, Chapter 6, this volume; Melton *et al.*, 1985; Wasby, 1976).

Third, researchers should be aware that their efforts to diffuse findings to the legal system are likely to be time-consuming and partial. Even if the researchers choose only to rely on the method of dissemination that they are apt to know best (i.e., publication), they will have to rely on different articles to reach different specific audiences. For example, to reach juvenile judges, one often has to reach probation officers first; and, as Grisso and I (Chapter 6, this volume) show, judges and probation officers rarely read the same journals. Moreover, substantial proportions of both groups rarely read any professional publications, even practitioner journals. Appellate judges, practicing lawyers, law professors, court-related mental health professionals, and child protection caseworkers are apt to have still different reading habits.

RECOMMENDATIONS

Lest the situation appear too bleak, though, some recommendations do follow from the findings and observations reported in this book.

Report Research Where It Is Accessible to Users

Although publication of an important, legally relevant study in *Child Development* or *Developmental Psychology* will advance a child psychologist's career, it will not inform legal authorities about the findings. For publication to serve such a purpose, multiple reports will be necessary (Grisso & Melton, Chapter 6, this volume). For discovery when lawyers and judges are actively seeking information about a given topic, findings should be published in a law review, preferably a "national" law review attached to a prestigious law school (see Hafemeister & Melton, Chapter 2, this volume). For lawyers and judges to find research, it must be locatable in the *Index to Legal Periodicals*. Publication in a recognized law review also gives the findings credibility, because law reviews have long been recognized as acceptable "secondary" authorities (Hafemeister & Melton, Chapter 2, this volume).

Publication so that findings will be uncovered in the course of legal professionals' general reading is more problematic, because reading habits are more discipline-specific and idiosyncratic, and because many professionals are apparently less than diligent in independent continuing education. As a general rule, however, passive discovery is much more likely to occur in practitioner journals (e.g., state bar journals) than in main-line scholarly journals. To reach juvenile court workers, the *Juvenile and Family Court Journal*, published by the National Council of Juvenile and Family Court Judges, is probably the best single outlet.

Besides relying on specialized publications, researchers also should provide their findings to the mass media. Although many researchers believe that their work will be distorted in such a process, the actual experiences that social scientists report with the mass media contradict this perception (Weiss, Chapter 3, this volume). As already noted, the media ultimately may be the most effective means of distributing work to professional audiences. As Grisso and I (Chapter 6, this volume) note, popular periodicals (e.g., *Psychology Today*) are probably more effective than even legal periodicals in diffusing social science findings to the legal community.

Use Informal Networks to Diffuse Information

The primary means of diffusing information is by word of mouth (see Grisso & Melton, Chapter 6, this volume; Weiss, Chapter 3, this volume). Probably the single most effective means of diffusing information, at least within limited geographic areas or highly specialized groups, is to "infiltrate" networks of legal professionals. Not only can one pass information informally over cocktails, but one is likely to be sought for information. If an "insider" adopts and transmits the knowledge, it has increased credibility (see Bermant & Wheeler, Chapter 5, this volume). Not only will diffusion be accelerated, but the acquaintance may help to facilitate future data collection and provide a "sponsor" among users to promote the research project with funding sources (e.g., private foundations).

Effective use of this strategy requires some savvy about organizations and relationships in the legal system. One needs to know who the key actors are, particularly those who are both influential and interested in new ideas. A political eye and knowledge of both legal processes and community psychology are helpful. However, identification of key potential users is often easy. Children's issues are usually heard in specialized courts, and there are only a handful of public interest law firms litigating children's cases (Mnookin, 1985). Small "issue networks" of legislative and agency staffs and representatives of professional organizations are commonly the principal route of information to legislative and executive policymakers (Takanishi & Melton, Chapter 4, this volume; Weiss, Chapter 3, this volume).

Through perusal of opinions and discussions with knowledgeable attorneys, one often can identify the jurists most likely to be interested in particular findings and willing to let colleagues know about them. The reasoning of judges, especially appellate judges, is a matter of public record. It is well known, for example, that Justice Blackmun is the primary user of scientific knowledge on the U.S. Supreme Court (Schlesinger & Nesse, 1980). Besides relying on an informal acquaintanceship, the researcher might invite the judge to be a discussant in study groups or colloquia, or might send him or her relevant reprints.

Use Professional Organizations

It is fashionable for scholars to regard activity in professional organizations as political bases for practitioners interested in narrow guild issues and essentially a waste of time for serious scholars. Whatever the merits of this perception as a general matter, it certainly is wrong for researchers who are interested in diffusing their work to policymakers. First, relevant professional organizations commonly have staff members who are a part of the children's issue network and whose job responsibilities include communication with policymakers. Second, as Saks (Chapter 7, this volume) notes, both the legal system's inherent conservatism and the law of evidence in many jurisdictions lead to greater weight being placed upon opinions that bear indicia of professional consensus. Similarly, professional standards and reports of official task forces (whether sponsored by government or professional organizations themselves) have been especially likely to be cited by the U.S. Supreme Court in children's cases (Hafemeister & Melton, Chapter 2, this volume). With the courts' increasing deference to professional judgments (see, e.g., *Woe v. Cuomo*, 1983; *Youngberg v. Romeo*, 1982), official statements of the state of scientific knowledge and professional practice are apt to become even more influential.

Thus, when research points toward particular conclusions about the effects of a policy or the validity of the assumption underlying it, researchers might seek to have a resolution adopted by a relevant scientific society or a task force appointed to develop a statement. Once a statement is adopted, of course efforts should be made to diffuse it systematically.

Look for Opportunities to Apply the Research

Several chapters of this volume suggest opportunities for applying research (see Grisso & Melton, Chapter 6; Saks, Chapter 7; Tremper, Chapter 8). Spending a few minutes each week reading the *United States Law Week* or a specialized law reporter (e.g., *Family Law Reporter*) is a wise investment of time for researchers interested in legal matters. Besides learning about questions that may be useful to study, one also will learn about any case that reaches the U.S. Supreme Court in which one's work might apply. Then the attorneys for either or both sides can be reached and offered assistance, or an *amicus* brief can be filed to inform the Court about the research.

Keeping in touch with relevant public interest groups, especially those that are frequently involved in litigation or legislation, is another good way of finding out about cases in which one's research might be helpful. For example, a researcher on adolescent abortion might become acquainted with the staff of Planned Parenthood or the Reproductive Freedom Project of the American Civil Liberties Union. Similarly, a researcher knowledgeable about children's involvement in the legal process might work with the National Legal Resource Center for Child Advocacy and Protection of the American Bar Association. Staff of policy offices in professional organizations, such as the APA or the Society for Research in Child Development, often can be helpful in identifying counterparts in other organizations who are useful resources.

Meet Legal Professionals on Their Own Terms

Injunctions to avoid the jargon of one's own discipline and to learn to speak the jargon of one's audience are common in discussions of interdisciplinary work. Although this recommendation is wise, it is not enough; in fact, it is not very important. To maximize diffusion of research into the legal community, one should be comfortable with legal methods and theories. The ability to apply legal reasoning and an understanding of legal culture are more important than knowledge of legal terms.

There are several reasons for such a focus on "thinking like a lawyer" and becoming a comfortable guest, if not an insider, in the legal community. First, the questions that one asks are far more likely to be legally relevant (see, e.g., Melton & Thompson, 1987; Monahan & Loftus, 1982). Second, the results are more likely to be framed in such a way that lawyers can easily see their relevance and apply them. Specifically, in that regard, publication in a law review requires presentation of the empirical evidence in legal style and within a legal argument. Although advocacy of a social position per se may be outside the role of neutral expert, advocacy of one's findings— presentation of the results so that their meaning and significance are clear and persuasive—is not (Hosticka, Hibbard, & Sundberg, 1983; Melton, 1985). Third, active involvement in the legal community and collaboration with legal scholars is useful, perhaps even crucial, in order to know how to reach legal audiences. For example, as Grisso and I (Chapter 6, this volume) note, procedures for law review publication are unique among scholarly disciplines and are likely to be difficult for social scientists to pursue, even with skill in legal writing, without tutelage by a law professor. Fourth, active involvement in the legal community, especially when the involvement is nonpartisan, is likely to increase one's credibility as an expert.

Academic psychologists interested in legal policy should become involved in the work of their law school colleagues (see Melton, Monahan, & Saks, in press). Ultimately, the infusion of child development research into children's law is probably most dependent upon influencing the professors who teach juvenile and family law and, for that matter, other legal subjects. When law students become more accustomed to application of social science research, it is likely that, over the long term, lawyers will also become more skilled in seeking and applying empirical evidence. The prerequisite to reaching law students, however, is reaching their professors. As already indicated, a growing number of scholars in children's law are expert in empirical analysis. There may be more ease of substantive collaboration than most developmental researchers would expect, even if the mores of law schools are mysterious to most professors in colleges of arts and sciences.

Know and Tell What You Don't Know

Social scientists interested in communicating what they do know about behavioral assumptions in legal issues also should be active in communicating what they *don't* know. The first reason is ethical. Exceeding expertise is a deceptive practice that shows disrespect for consumers of social science. Often failure to disclose the limits of expertise is a matter of not knowing what one doesn't know. In particular, in the legal arena, experts may confuse psychological questions with moral and legal judgments. Regardless of the reason, though, exceeding expertise may mislead legal decisionmakers. Moreover, whatever duty we have to disclose what we do know (a point considered in the following section) probably extends to what we don't know. Just as legal factfinders may be assisted by information outside common knowledge, their decisionmaking may be improved by knowing the level of uncertainty that they are facing.

For example, I requested that the APA enter *Palmore v. Sidoti* (1984) as an *amicus* when the case reached the U.S. Supreme Court. Relying on the ostensible psychological harm of a child in an interracial marriage, Florida state courts had forced a white mother to relinquish custody of her child from a previous marriage when she married a black man. I hoped that the APA would enter the case to inform the Court about the lack of scientific evidence on which to make such determination. The lack of research on point should have directed the Supreme Court to consider only the constitutional values at stake (the stance the Court in fact took).

The second reason for communicating what is unknown is strategic. Credibility in communicating what *is* known is likely to increase when the speaker has indicated points of uncertainty or ignorance. Unfortunately, there is a tendency to shrink away when issues arise about which knowledge is minimal. The APA declined to enter *Palmore* for just such a reason. Some staff and officers of the association feared that a brief about what is not known would put the profession into a bad light. Besides depriving the Court of useful information, such a strategy ultimately diminishes credibility. Research about lobbying indicates that complete honesty about the limits of one's knowledge increases one's influence over the long term (Melton, 1983a). I know of no reason to believe that the same principle does not apply in the legal system.

IS IT WORTH IT?

At the beginning of this chapter, I have noted the assumptions underlying this book: (1) that the law should attend to relevant social-scientific evidence, and (2) implicitly, that scholars in child development should learn how to disseminate their work in its most useful form and then do it. In conclusion, it is useful to ask whether the latter implicit assumption is valid.

The question of whether it is worthwhile to focus energy and expertise upon diffusion of information to the legal system raises two issues. First, active diffusion of research to potential users undeniably takes considerable time. The sorts of activities that I have suggested are also outside the conventional roles of scientists. Spending time getting to know key actors in the legal system or talking with reporters may not be enjoyable for most social scientists. Such activities certainly are not ones that academia rewards or that traditional graduate education prepares scientists to perform.

Second, the recommendation to "meet legal professionals on their own terms" raises difficult problems of professional responsibility. The scientific pursuit of truth may be infringed by entry into the legal arena, where adversary roles prevail and truth may be in conflict with and inferior to justice (Thibaut & Walker, 1978). The ethics of scientists' participation in the legal system was controversial in the meeting of the study group that prepared this book, as it is in the field of psycholegal studies as a whole (see, e.g., McCloskey, Egeth, & McKenna, 1986). Weithorn (Chapter 10, this volume) focuses on this set of problems, of course, but issues about scientists' loss of control over their findings and opinions and resulting potential distortions of the truth are raised throughout the book.

My own answer is "Yes, it is worth it." As Weithorn (Chapter 10, this volume) points out, social scientists have a duty of beneficence—the duty to create social benefit. Although this duty is shared by all persons (see Beauchamp & Childress, 1983), its significance is heightened for social scientists. This higher duty is derived in part from a norm of reciprocity and fair play. By accepting societal resources for their training and scholarship, scientists enter into an implicit social contract to promote human welfare. Moreover, as a general matter, respect for persons demands that their welfare be promoted. This principle applies especially to children. Without such attention, children are less likely to develop the skills ultimately necessary for the exercise of autonomy. Thus, when research may assist the legal system, a duty exists to diffuse it in order to promote human welfare, particularly child welfare.

This duty should be fulfilled even if it creates role conflicts for the scientist. I am not as troubled as some are when the adversary system requires subordinating the duty of veracity to the pursuit of justice. Although experts certainly should not lie or misrepresent, less than full disclosure (e.g., not volunteering answers to questions not asked) may be consistent with the goal of justice. All witnesses take an oath to tell the *whole* truth. Nonetheless, as a general matter, witnesses who attempt to do so—who, for example, spontaneously offer qualifications to their answers—are apt to find their answers striken from evidence as unresponsive to the question. The parties should control their cases. To have their "day in court," they should be able to put their best evidence forward. I see no reason why experts' testimony should differ from lay witnesses' evidence in that regard. The experts' duty is to make relevant information available, not to compel the legal system to change the rules of evidence and procedure about how it should be admitted and considered.

In fact, the major structural obstacles to consideration of relevant social science evidence may be more in the sciences themselves than in the legal system. Although research, teaching, and service all are classical purposes of academia, service certainly is the task given least attention. When attention is given to it, its meaning often is distorted to focus upon university administration. The only university faculty members who are apt to have a primary obligation for service are those in the extension services, and they certainly are not at the top of the academic hierarchy. Even if emphasis is not placed on spending time diffusing the research, just choosing applied topics may have a cost in academic standing.

A reconsideration of rewards in academia is needed. The duty to promote human welfare should include attention to diffusion of research as well as its generation. Even if each individual researcher does not diffuse the work directly, the integration of research with policy by others should be viewed as a valuable function. Also, when different audiences are involved, professional prohibitions of multiple publication should be lifted. Lawyers do not read the same journals as social scientists, and differing styles and content of presentation are appropriate.

There are signs of both increasing social responsibility of child development researchers and increasing receptivity of legal professionals. Bronfenbrenner's (1974) call to study socially significant topics in children's everyday lives has begun to be heeded, and child development research has begun to find its way into legal institutes and casebooks. Diffusion of child development research *is* worth it. We, the contributors to this volume, hope that researchers will learn more about how to make their work responsive to legal problems and accessible to lawyers, and that legal authorities will learn more about how to find and use child development research relevant to their work.

REFERENCES

American Psychological Association. (1981). Ethical Principles of Psychologists. *American Psychologist, 36,* 633–638.

Beauchamp, T.L., & Childress, J.F. (1983). *Principles of biomedical ethics* (2nd ed.). New York: Oxford University Press.

Bermant, G. (1982). Justifying social science research in terms of social benefit. In T.L. Beauchamp, R.R. Faden, R.J. Wallace, Jr., & L. Walters (Eds.), *Ethical issues in social science research* (pp. 125–143). Baltimore: Johns Hopkins University Press.

Bronfenbrenner, U. (1974). Developmental research, public policy, and the ecology of childhood. *Child Development, 45,* 1–5.

Clingempeel, W.G., & Reppucci, N.D. (1982). Joint custody after divorce: Major issues and goals for research. *Psychological Bulletin, 91,* 102–127.

Derdeyn, A.P. (1978). Child custody: A reflection of cultural change. *Journal of Clinical Child Psychology, 7,* 169–173.

Grisso, T. (1980). Juveniles' capacities to waive *Miranda* rights: An empirical analysis. *California Law Review, 68,* 1134–1166.

Hosticka, C.J., Hibbard, M., & Sundberg, N.D. (1983). Improving psychologists' contributions to the policymaking process. *Professional Psychology: Research and Practice, 14,* 374–385.

In re Gault, 387 U.S. 1 (1967).

Interdivisional Committee on Adolescent Abortion. (1987). Adolescent abortion: Psychological and legal issues. *American Psychologist, 42,* 73–78.

Levine, M., & Levine, A. (1970). *A social history of helping services: Court, clinic, school, and community.* New York: Appleton-Century-Crofts.

McCloskey, M., Egeth, H., & McKenna, J. (Eds.). (1986). The ethics of expert testimony [Special issue]. *Law and Human Behavior, 10*(1/2).

Melton, G.B. (1983a). *Child advocacy: Psychological issues and interventions.* New York: Plenum.

Melton, G.B. (1983b). Children's competence to consent: A problem in law and social science. In G.B. Melton, G.P. Koocher, & M.J. Saks (Eds.), *Children's competence to consent* (pp. 1–18). New York: Plenum.

Melton, G.B. (1984). Developmental psychology and the law: The state of the art. *Journal of Family Law, 22,* 445–482.

Melton, G.B. (1985). Organized psychology and legal policy-making: Involvement in the post-*Hinckley* debate. *Professional Psychology: Research and Practice, 16,* 810–822.

Melton, G.B. (1986). Litigation *In the interest of children:* Does anybody win? [Review]. *Law and Human Behavior, 10,* 337–353.

Melton, G.B., Koocher, G.P., & Saks, M.J. (Eds.). (1983). *Children's competence to consent.* New York: Plenum.

Melton, G.B., Monahan, J., & Saks, M.J. (in press). Psychologists as law professors. *American Psychologist.*

Melton, G.B., & Pliner, A.J. (1986). Adolescent abortion: A psycholegal analysis. In G.B. Melton (Ed.), *Adolescent abortion: Psychological and legal issues* (pp. 1–39). Lincoln: University of Nebraska Press.

Melton, G.B., & Thompson, R.A. (1987). Getting out of a rut: Detours to less traveled paths in child witness research. In S.J. Ceci, M.P. Toglia, & D.F. Ross (Eds.), *Children's eyewitness memory* (pp. 209–229). New York: Springer-Verlag.

Melton, G.B., Weithorn, L.A., & Slobogin, C. (1985). *Community mental health centers and the courts: An evaluation of community-based forensic services.* Lincoln: University of Nebraska Press.

Mnookin, R.H. (1975). Child-custody adjudication: Judicial functions in the face of indeterminancy. *Law and Contemporary Problems, 39,* 226–290.

Mnookin, R.H. (Ed.). (1985). *In the interest of children: Advocacy, law reform, and public policy.* New York: W.H. Freeman.

Monahan, J. (1981). *The clinical prediction of violent behavior.* Beverly Hills, CA: Sage.

Monahan, J., & Loftus, E.F. (1982). The psychology of law. *Annual Review of Psychology, 33,* 441–475.

Monahan, J., & Walker, L. (1985). *Social science in law.* Mineola, NY: Foundation Press.

Morse, S.J., & Whitebread, C.H., II. (1982). Mental health implications of the Juvenile Justice Standards. In G.B. Melton (Ed.). *Legal reforms affecting child and youth services* (pp. 5–27). New York: Haworth Press.

Palmore v. Sidoti, 104 U.S. 1879 (1984).

Rosen, D. (1984). Democracy and demographics: The inevitability of a class-based interpretation. *University of Dayton Law Review, 10,* 37–96.

Schlesinger, S.R., & Nesse, J. (1980). Justice Harry Blackmun and empirical jurisprudence. *American University Law Review, 29,* 405–437.

Slobogin, C. (1984). Dangerousness and expertise. *University of Pennsylvania Law Review, 133,* 97–174.

Thibaut, J., & Walker, L. (1978). A theory of procedure. *California Law Review, 66,* 541–566.

Thornburgh v. American College of Obstetricians and Gynecologists, 106 S.Ct. 2169 (1986).

Wasby, S. (1976). *Small town police and the Supreme Court: Hearing the word.* Lexington, MA: Lexington Books.

Wisconsin v. Yoder, 406 U.S. 205 (1972).

Woe v. Cuomo, 559 F. Supp. 1158 (E.D.N.Y. 1983).

Youngberg v. Romeo, 457 U.S. 307 (1982).

Index